EVALUATION OF STRAWS IN RUMINANT FEEDING

Proceedings of a workshop held in Perignat-les-Sarlièves, Aubière (France) from 2 to 4 June 1987 under the auspices of COST (European Cooperation in Scientific and Technological Research)—COST 84 bis, organised with the support of the Commission of the European Communities by INRA, Research Centre of Clermont-Ferrand, Theix.

EVALUATION OF STRAWS
IN RUMINANT FEEDING

Edited by

M. CHENOST

Laboratoire des Aliments, INRA—CRZV de Theix, Ceyrat, France

and

P. REINIGER

Commission of the European Communities, Brussels, Belgium

ELSEVIER APPLIED SCIENCE
LONDON and NEW YORK

ELSEVIER SCIENCE PUBLISHERS LTD
Crown House, Linton Road, Barking, Essex IG11 8JU, England

Sole Distributor in the USA and Canada
ELSEVIER SCIENCE PUBLISHING CO., INC.
655 Avenue of the Americas, New York, NY 10010, USA

WITH 54 TABLES AND 34 ILLUSTRATIONS

British Library Cataloguing in Publication Data
Evaluation of straws in ruminant feeding.
1. Feeding stuffs: Straw
I. Chenost, M.   II. Reiniger, P.   III.
Commission of the European Communities.
Directorate-General for Science, Research
and Development
IV. Institute national de la recherche
agronomique
636.08'6

ISBN 1-85166-337-1

Library of Congress CIP data applied for

Publication arrangements by Commission of the European Communities, Directorate-General
Telecommunications, Information Industries and Innovation, Scientific and Technical Communications
Service, Luxembourg

EUR 11471

Printed in Great Britain at the University Press, Cambridge

v

Contents

vi

Topic C: *In vitro* Methods for Predicting Straw Digestibility and Intake

INTRODUCTION

The Workshop reported in this volume is the third of a series sponsored by the Commission of the European Communities, Directorate-General for Science, Research and Development (DG XII), under the Concerted Action Project COST 84 bis, entitled "Use of lignocellulose containing by-products and other plant residues for animal feeding".

Three topics were treated:

- In-vivo methods for measuring intake and digestibility
- Feeding trials with producing animals - long term effects
- Advances in predicting straw digestibility and intake.

The papers were circulated among the participants in advance and were discussed in the eleven sessions of the workshop, a rapporteur summarizing the discussions in each session. Dr. E.R. ØRSKOV of the Rowett Research Institute, Aberdeen, UK, led the opening and concluding discussions and formulated the recommendations of the workshop.

There is a widening gap in staple food supplies between "South" and "North" in the present-day world. While lignocellulosic crop residues, such as cereal straw, are posing problems concerning their disposal and environmental pollution in developed countries, they are a badly needed source of animal feed in developing countries, as they represent a vast reservoir of nutrients. These nutrients can be either extracted within the rumen - a genuine natural fermentor - or a by using industrial processes.

As a "new" source of feed for ruminants, straw does not compete with richer feeds, such as cereal grains and oil cakes, suitable for the nutrition of monogastrics, which include man. Research in the field of ruminant digestion clearly demonstrated that straw could supply a major part of the diet of low-productivity animals at a given physiological life cycle or of animals lacking other sources of feed e.g. in developing countries, and that it could also provide a small part of the feed of high production animals.

While the potential nutritive value of straws is unquestioned, it can vary over a wide range according to variety, strain and growth conditions. The elaboration of satisfactory feeding systems requires, therefore, an accurate as possible measurement and prediction of the straw feeding value.

These measurements can help in choosing appropriate supplements to straw as the basic component of the diet, or in deciding whether or not one should resort to pretreatments to improve its feeding characteristics. But they can also lead to suggestions for the improvement of straw feed values through appropriate plant breeding programmes.

As straw is composed of very complex polysaccharides bound with lignin, the appraisal or prediction of its feed value requires the use of refined new techniques in this case. The traditional series of chemical analysis have been shown to be inappropriate, if not useless.

The aim of the present workshop which is to review the "state of the art" of the methodologies and techniques which are available now or foreseeable in the near future in order to assess and evaluate the actual feed value of a given straw, should be seen in this context.

CONDITIONS FOR OPTIMIZING CELLULOLYTIC ACTIVITY IN THE RUMEN

Michelle DURAND
Station de Recherches de Nutrition
INRA - Centre de Recherches de Jouy-en-Josas
78350 Jouy-en-Josas, France

Summary

In order to optimize rumen digestion of straw-based diets the following microbial-related factors are discussed : micro-or-ganisms involved and their interaction, effect of carbohydrate supplement and of pH, supply of microbial nutrients and absence of toxic substances. The required amounts of degradable nitrogen (N), sulphur (S), phosphorus (P) and magnesium should be expressed in terms of digestible organic matter (OMD). Total nitrogen requirement approximates 26 g N/kg OMD. Contribution of recycled N may reduce these figures by to 10 to 40% depending on straw treatments. 1.8 g S/kg OMD should be available. S availability in straw would not exceed 0.3. About 5 g soluble P/kg OMD are required in the rumen. They are supplied by salivary secretion when dietary P concentration and absorbability are adequate. Branched chain fatty acids and vitamin B may stimulate fibre digestion. Crossfeeding among microbes contributes to their supply. In addition to urea, a small proportion of protein may enhance the cellulolytic activity. The pH should be prevented from falling below 6.0 and all the required nutrients should be supplied along with cell-wall degradation which is a slow process. It is concluded that more research should be directed towards stimulation of ruminal implantation of fungi and quantification of endogenous N supply.

1. INTRODUCTION

Rumen fermentation of lignocellulosic feeds occurs in a complex system that is influenced by dynamic interactions among the animal, the diet and the microbial population. It is known that animal factors such as feed intake, rumination and chewing times and rate of passage of digesta affect the relative amount of ruminal digestion of plant cell-walls. Dietary factors such as intrinsic characteristics of the fibre including chemical and physical structure also affect the rate of digestion. The indigestible fraction of fibre is known to be closely related to the lignin content of forages. Delignification processes (chemical, biological or physical) improves the rate of fermentation. Grinding and alkali treatments can increase surface area for microbe attachment and/or accessible to enzymes. However, these animal and feed aspects have recently been discussed elsewhere (1,2) and will not be examined here.

The aim of the present paper is to review the conditions directly related to microbial activity which are required to optimize rumen digestion of straw-based diets. They concern the balance between microbial species and populations, physico-chemical characteristics of the environment such as pH, and dietary factors like the effect of carbohydrate supplement, the supply of nitrogen, minerals and growth factors and the absence of toxic substances.

2. MICROORGANISMS INVOLVED AND IMPORTANCE OF MICROBIAL INTERACTIONS

2.1. Fibrolytic microorganisms

Demeyer (3) reported that plant tissue particles entering the rumen are colonized within 5 min by bacteria, within 15 min by protozoa and within 2h by fungal sporangia and rhizoids. Up to now cellulolytic bacteria have been considered to carry out the major part of fibre digestion in the rumen. Bacteroides succinogenes a gram-negative rod, Ruminicoccus flavefaciens and Ruminicoccus albus gram-positive cocci are the most important cellulolytic species. The first two species synthesize the most active cellulases (4). They are attached to, or associated with, plant cell walls. They also degrade hemicellulose but do not always utilize the products of hydrolysis : xylan or pentose. Hemicellulases are also produced by non-cellulolytic species such as Bacteroides ruminicola and Butyrivibrio fibrisolvens. Most cellulolytic and hemicellulolytic bacteria can also degrade pectin but some do not use the uronic acids released.

Protozoa are also involved in rumen degradation of cellulose and they have frequently been reported to possess cellulases and hemicellulases and to engulf plant cell walls (5). Experiments with defaunated animals (removal of protozoa) generally indicate that overall fibre digestibility is decreased (3,6) although some contradictions are now apparent : defaunation may enhance plant cell-wall digestion of tropical forages supplemented with molasses (Jouany, personal communication). These discrepancies could be due to relative changes in bacterial and fungal populations : the removal of protozoa might be detrimental to some cellulolytic bacteria species but beneficial to cellulolytic fungi.

The phycomycete fungi are a recently discovered group of rumen microorganisms. At least 3 species are known and all ferment plant cell-wall polysaccharides as sole sources of carbon and energy. Their numbers are larger on a high fibre diet than on a high concentrate diet (7). They attach to lignified vascular tissues and degrade extensive amounts of sclerenchyma tissue. Recently Fonty et al. (8) isolated strains of Neocallimastix frontalis from the rumen of sheep. In vitro they colonize straw tissues, degrade cellulose and xylan and ferment several monoses with production of acetate, ethanol, lactate and H_2.

The presence of fungi in the rumen allows more tissues to be disrupted and increases the surface area exposed to bacterial enzymes (E. Grenet, personal communication). Therefore, factors which may stimulate fungi implantation may also improve the digestibility of straw-based diets.

2.2. Microbial interactions in the rumen

The many interactions between or within rumen populations have recently been reviewed (4,9,10,11). Of special importance is the synergism between fibrolytic species and non fibrolytic species. An efficient degradation of plant cell-wall can only be achieved by the activi-

ties of various populations : hydrolytic, fermentative and methanogenic.
The majority of non-fibrolytic bacteria in the rumen of animals fed high roughage diets are associated with plant material. They hydrolyze the non structural carbohydrates, starch and fructosans and protein and may ferment cellulose fragments, xylan, cellobiose and pentose (Butyrivibrio fibrisolvens, Selenomonas ruminantium...). They are in close association with fibrolytic species. They may increase fibre degradation by disposing of products such as pentose or succinate (ex : S. Ruminantium and B.succinogenes), thus alleviating catabolic repression and by providing the cellulolytic bacteria with amino acids and growth factors.

Interspecies transfer of hydrogen to methanogens in order to keep a low partial pressure of hydrogen in the medium is particularly important for many bacterial species. It allows more acetate and thus more energy production during fermentation through the production of ATP by substrate-level phosphorylation (SLP) with decreased amounts of propionate and lactate (3,12,13). Such hydrogen transfer also takes place between methanogens and populations of protozoa and fungi. Physical associations between entodiniomorphs and methanogens have been observed (3). The activity of fungal enzymes is enhanced by co-culture with methanogenic bacteria (5). Piromonas communis and Sphaeromonas communis degrade more cellulose and produce more acetic acid and less ethanol and lactate when co-cultured with a methanogenic bacteria (14).
Interspecies H_2 transfer allowing disposal of H_2 by the reduction of fumarate to succinate, sulphate to sulphide and nitrate to nitrite coupled to anaerobic electron transport phosphorylation (ETP) has been recently emphasized (15). Synthesis of ATP via ETP may play a vital role in some fibrolytic rumen bacteria such as B. succinogenes and B. fibrisolvens which may derive 50 and 26%, respectively, of their total substrate from ETP.
An optimized digestion of high straw diet relies on the right balance between microbial populations involved. Supplementation with other types of cabohydrates, inadequate nutrient supply and use of some additives can result in proliferation of organisms at the expense of fibrolytic species.

3. SUPPLY OF EASILY DEGRADABLE CARBOHYDRATES AND EFFECT OF pH

A stimulatory effect of low amounts of easily degradable carbohydrates (5-10% of the substrates) on cellulolysis has been reported in vitro (3). Only few in vivo experiments support these observations. Silva and Orskov (16) have recently shown that addition of 15% of sugar beet pulp in an untreated straw diet could increase straw dry matter disappearance from nylon bags by about 6-10%. Degradable β glucans present in pulp might be more effective than starch or molasses. However, degradation of ammonia-treated straw was not improved by beet pulp addition in Rusitec (17). Treated straws may contain sufficient amounts of available β glucans to allow for the synthesis of adhering glycocalyx fibres of G+ cellulolytic bacteria.
The inclusion of starchy concentrates in mixed diets has long been found to reduce fibre digestion (18). The reduction becomes significant when the diet contains about 30 to 40% grain (9) or even with lesser amounts. Henning et al. (19) observed that the digestibility of cellulose and hemicellulose declined linearly as the proportion of maize grain (in a diet based on maize straw) increased above 7.8%. The reduction of cellulolytic activity can be due to decreases 1) in number of cellulo-

lytic bacteria and/or their growth rates, 2) in rate of cellulases synthesis and 3) in enzyme activity. Both a decline of pH down to values below 6.2-6.0 often observed with grain supplementa-tion and the presence of easily degradable carbohydrates can exert at least one of these effects.

In vitro, in batch cultures, degradation of pure cellulose was much reduced by the presence of starch and cerelose which lowered the pH from 6.5 to below 5.5. This effect was not observed when the pH was maintained at the control level (20). When pure cultures of cellulolytic bacteria were grown in cellobiose-limited chemostats the cultures washed out at pH values ranging from 5.7-6.0, whereas non cellulolytic bacteria were resistant to lower pH (4). The sensitivity of cellulolytic bacteria to low pH might be related to a reduction in ATP synthesis from ETP (15). Proton motive force across the cell membrane can be dissipated at low pH (4).

In vivo, Mould et al. (21,22,23) clearly demonstrated that a decrease in pH below 6.0 was involved in the depression of cellulolysis. Offering roughage in a long form which stimulates the salivation, or inclusion of additional buffering material in the diet could help to maintain the pH above 6.0, thus reducing the negative associative effects of mixed feeds. The administration of dietary buffers such as sodium bicarbonate is largely utilized in that respect (24,25). However, buffers in some experiments only partially alleviate fibre depression (22) and a carbohydrate effect independent of pH appears to be involved.

Van Gylswyk and Schwartz (9) reported that the addition of starch increases the lag time in the degradation of grass fibre in vitro and that strains of B. succinogenes which can use both starch and cellulose preferentially digest starch. Production of cellulase by the latter bacteria can be decreased when grown on glucose instead of cellulose. This inhibitory effect of glucose on cellulase synthesis supports the fact that the number of cellulolytic bacteria does not change greatly when part of the forage is replaced by increasing amounts of readily fermentable carbohydrates (9). In vivo, there might be a selection for less pH sensitive strains or for strains which preferentially use starch or glucose.

It can be concluded, in conformity with Sutton (18), that in order to maintain cellulolytic activity when straw diets are supplemented 1) pH should be prevented from falling below 6.0 and 2) starchy concentra-tes with slow rates of degradability (such as whole grains rather than ground ones) or concentrates based on fibrous by-products should prefe-rentially be used.

4. SUPPLY OF NITROGEN

4.1. Amount of nitrogen required

Most cellulolytic bacteria require ammonia (NH_3) as N source for incorporation into cell protein. Ammonia is supplied by deamination of feed and endogenous protein amino acids or by degradation of dietary and endogenous non protein N (NPN) such as urea. The amount of N required can be related either to the concentration of NH_3 in the rumen medium or to the potentially degradable organic matter.

Ammonia concentration is only indicative as it reflects the balance between production, absorption and utilization. Levels of NH_3-N for maximum activities range from about 50 to 280 mg N/l although pure cul-tures generally require much lower ammonia concentration for growth (<1,4 mg N/l). These wide variations can be explained by different requirements for growth and fermentative activities and also by the different pathways of NH_3-incorporation, i.e. glutamine synthetase and glutamate dehydrogenase. These enzymes differ in their affinity for NH_3. The first pathway predominates at low NH_3 level in the environment, whereas the second acts at high NH_3 levels (26).

The type of substrates also influençes NH_3 requirement. It was recently shown that the minimum NH_3-N concentration required to maximize the degradation of barley (125 mg/l) was greater thant that for degradation of maize (61 mg/l) (27). Orskov (28) reported that only 20 mg/l of ammonia were required for maximal rate of digestion of alkali treated barley straw. Nevertheless, it seems reasonable to consider that values below 50 mg NH_3-N/l indicate N limitation.

Numerous determinations of the amount of N incorporated into microbes in relation to the organic matter apparently digested in the rumen (N/kg OMDR) or fermented (N/kg OMF), (efficiency of microbial protein synthesis or yield) have been carried out in vivo. Mean figures used in systems for feed protein evaluation (29,30,31) are around 30-34 g N/kg OMDR although wide variations between experimental conditions are shown. Values for high roughage diets and particularly for alkali-treated straws reported in (32) and recently by Vérité et al. (personal communica-tion) are within 28-36 g N/kg OMDR. Therefore, it seems correct to adopt a mean requirement of about 32 g available N/kg OMDR or of about 21 g available N/kg of organic matter digestible in the total digestive tract (OMD) assuming that 0.65 OMD is digested in the rumen (29,31).

The efficiency of capture of degradable N is not known precisely but should be around 0.8 for non protein N (31). Therefore total requirement for available N approximates 40 g/kg OMF or 26 g/kg OMD. In in vitro experiments, using continuous culture systems (ex : Rusitec) these values represent the minimum amounts required to optimize straw degradability.

In vivo, the amount of N being recycled into the rumen may contribute significantly to fulfil microbial requirements. The processes of nitrogen recycling have been reviewed recently (33). It is suggested that 4-12 g of protein N/d enter the forestomach of sheeps coming from muco-proteins in saliva and keratinized protein in cells sloughed from the rumen wall. However, the extent of fermentation of these forms of N is not known.

Urea enters the rumen via saliva and diffusion through the rumen wall. The recycling of urea in saliva is function of saliva flow rate and urea concentration which is positively related to plasma urea concentration. The overall amount depends on factors which affect flow rate such as ruminating and chewing time. The rate of passage of urea through the rumen wall is inversely related to rumen NH_3 concentrations and is positively influenced by feeding readily fermented carbohydra-tes. Increased permeability of rumen wall may be due to butyrate production which may act either on the wall-attached microbial activity or on epithelial cell division.

In sheep, saliva contributes to 0.5-2 g urea-N/d and passage across rumen wall to 1-2 g up to 13 g N/d under diverse dietary circumstances. With sheep fed on dried grass (34) the total daily recycled urea amounted to 3.5 g N/d, representing 11.2 g N/kg OMDR as 0.39 kg OM were digested in the rumen. In this case 28% of the requirement could be provided by recycled N. Some of the systems account for N recycling directly. For instance it has been proposed to relate recycled N (RN) to ingested N

(IN), with RN=0.15 IN for lactating cows (35). Such a relationship might underestimate RN when IN is low. In the PDI system (36) it is considered that the entry of endogenous N balances a true efficiency of capture of 1. N recycling may also be underestimated by this way. However, certain small apparent deficits of ruminal degradable N are allowed.

With straw-based diet, supply of salivary urea might be maximal, but transfer through the wall rather limited by the absence of readily fermented carbohydrates, especially when straw is untreated. In sheep fed this type of diet, it can be assumed that about 4 g of available N are recycled daily. It is clear that the contribution of recycled N to microbial requirement will be more significant with untreated straw than with treated straw, especially when diet is fed ad libitum. A rapid calculation indicates that for untreated or alkali-treated straws recycled N could represent 37 or 10% respectively of the microbial requirements.

It should be noted that with high straw diets, goats appear to be more efficient than sheep in nitrogen recycling to the rumen : in the absence of N supplementation, ruminal NH_3 concentration, VFA concentration and fibre degradation in nylon bags in situ are much larger for goats than for sheep (37).

4.2. Source of nitrogen

Recent evidence indicates that the proportion of rumen microbial N which is derived from NH_3-N may be as low as 20% and varies with dietary protein content (3). Bacterial population attached to solid particles were recently shown to incorporate a larger proportion of N derived from amino acids or/and peptides than bacteria associated with the liquid phase of a Rusitec (46% vs 19%) (38).

Although direct amino acid or peptide incorporation does not decrease the energy cost of cell formation it may decrease transport energy expenditure (32). Furthermore some strains of cellulolytic bacteria require small amounts of amino acids and peptides. Amino acids can serve as precursors for branched chain fatty acids (BCFA) which are growth factors for a number of bacterial species including cellulolytic organisms (39).

In most practical diets, sufficient degradable protein is normally present together with an extensive turnover of microbial protein and supply of endogenous protein to meet any specific needs for preformed peptides, amino acids and BCFA (31). This is particularly true when the provision for sulphur is adequate. However, with straw diets with a low degradable protein content it would be important to determine whether preformed amino acids are required or not to optimize cell wall degradation.

Positive responses to protein supplementation have been observed and will be reported in detail in a subsequent paper by Hvelplund (40). Several trials indicate that fishmeal addition stimulates fibre digestion. Some recent results, showing that rates of digestion of ammonia-treated straw in nylon bag in situ were significantly increased when fishmeal was added to the basal diet of sheep (41) corroborate previous observations. Therefore it can be suggested that, adding together with urea a small proportion of slowly degraded protein, providing a steady supply of peptides and/or amino acids would favour cellulolytic activity in straw-based diets.

Replacing urea by a slow release NPN source may help to adjust the rate of release of NH_3 to that of cell-wall degradation which is a rather slow process. However, these late release compounds (biuret-IBDU-gluco-syl-urea...) are often swept out of the rumen before they are fully metabolized but this nitrogen may be partly recycled to the rumen after absorption. When urea can be mixed thoroughly with straw, use of such compounds does not seem to be necessary. If this cannot be achieved, the use of slow release NPN sources might be advantageous.

5. MINERAL SUPPLY

The essentiality and role of mineral elements in rumen microbe metabolism have recently been emphasized in reviews dealing with sulphur (42,43) or with other minerals and trace elements (24,44). With straw-based diet, an adequate supply of the required elements is of particular significance as mineral content or/and availability in straw can be very low.

In this report we shall consider the requirements for sulphur (S), phosphorus (P) and magnesium (Mg) in terms of digestible organic matter rather than in terms of in total dry matter content or as optimal concentrations in the environment as already suggested (25). This approach is particularly advisable for straw based diets, their digestibility differing within treatments.

The direct effect of sodium (Na), potassium (K) and calcium (Ca) as "nutrients" is difficult to distinguish from their indirect effect on the physicol-chemical characteristics of the environment : buffering capacity, dilution rate and osmolality. These characteristics are important for optimizing cell-wall degradation. The effect of pH was already discussed. An excess of Na intake may increase dilution rate and thus reduce the time allowed for cellulose fermenta-tation. It may also increase the osmolality in such a manner that rumination, salivation and fermentation may be depressed. However, these aspects have been dealt with elsewhere (24,44) and will not be discussed further here.

Trace elements which may have a direct effect on microbes will be briefly considered.

5.1. Sulphur

The main function of S is to support the synthesis of sulphur-amino acids, methionine and cystine needed for the elaboration of microbial protein. Some microorganisms are capable of reducing sulphate into sulphide which is also produced from protein degradation. Sulphide (S^{2-}) is then incorporated into amino acids. However, sulphide which is not used for protein synthesis is absorbed very rapidly through the rumen wall and some is lost with the flow. Sulphide absorption is much faster than for ammonia and is a function of sulphide concentration.

Smith (43) calculated the amount of available S required in the rumen taking into account losses and recycling. The latter author considered a mean S:N ratio of 0.06 in rumen microbes and from the average efficiency of microbial protein (around 32 g N/kg OMF), sulphur microbial uptake was assumed to be around 2.0 g/kg OMDR or 1.3 g/kg OMD. However, even in vitro the efficiency of uptake is not total. In order to optimize protein synthesis in batch cultures, the optimal amount was above 1.6 g S/kg OMD (25).

In vivo, sulphide losses and the amount of recycled S would represent about 0.5-0.8 and 0.1-0.2 respectively of the true requirement. Therefore, total requirements for available S (Sa) should range around 2.8 g/kg OMDR or 1.8 g/kg OMD.

In vitro, when using the Rusitec technique the supply can be somewhat lower : 2.5 g S/kg OMF or 1.6 g S/kg OMD.

S-availability in some forages is rather low and particularly in straws. This was recently demonstrated using the Rusitec technique (Stevani et al., unpublished results). The same batch of straw (1.3 g S/kg DM), either alkali-treated or untreated, was either supplemented or not with sulphate. The addition of sulphate to the medium increased all the fermentative parameters with treated straw. With the non-treated one only volatile fatty acids were slightly increased (table I). Therefore, a supply of 3.6 g S/kg OMF or 2.3 g/kg OMD in treated straws is well below microbial needs, whereas 5.7 g/kg OMF or 3.7 g/kg OMD in untreated straw, is only slightly deficient. This trial shows that alkali treatment apparently does not increase the availability of straw S which may be strongly associated with cell walls. The same trend was observed in vivo in sheep for protein synthesis (45). Sulphate supplementation of alkali-treated straw plus urea increased bacterial total amino N from 10.6 to 16.7 g/d.

With natural diets, the dietary S levels for which positive responses in fibre digestibility to S addition are obtained, may vary considerably between less than 2.5 to 5.7 g/kg OMD (25). The optimal dietary supply depends on the amount and rate of S release in the rumen in order to match microbial activity. With natural feeds it is likely that the S fraction associated to protein follows protein degradability which varies widely with feedstuffs.

However, with some particular forages such as tall fescue, S availability (Sa) appears to be very low. This might apply to straws in which Sa would not exceed 0.3. Therefore, if the S content of untreated straw is assumed to be around 1.2 g/kg DM, it can be calculated that it should be supplemented with 0.4 g Sa/kg DM. With the same straw but alkali-treated the supply should be about 0.6 g Sa/kg DM.

With discontinuous feeding, slow-release S compounds, such as elemental sulphur or methionine, which minimize sulphide loss from the rumen ought to be used preferentially to fast release compounds such as sulphate.

However, the supply should not exceed the requirements as excessive S intake upsets animal zinc absorption and copper availability.

5.2. Phosphorus

Phosphorus (P) is a constituent of primary cell metabolites such as nucleotides, coenzymes, teichoid acids of the cell walls of Gram-positive (G+) bacteria and phospholipids. Bacterial P:N ratios vary from one author to another. The assumed P:N ratios in rumen microbes (0.188 (24) and 0.145 (43)) result in P incorporation estimates of 5.7 and 4.3 g P/kg OMF respectively.

A series of assays using either semi-continuous (Rusitec) (46,47,48) or entirely continuous (49) culture systems were undertaken to examine the effect of P on the principal parameters associated with degradative and synthetic processes and to ascertain more precisely the minimal phosphorus requirements for each of these processes. The mean results are summarized in table II. Compared to a P-supplemented medium,- levels of P lower than 3.0 g/kg OMF drastically reduced degradative activities. In every assay, cellulose was much more affected than hemicellulose degradation and volatile fatty acid (VFA) production.

It has been shown that cellulases isolated from mixed rumen bacteria have specific P requirements (50). Phosphorus is probably an important factor of cellulolytic activity. Results reported above show a different requirement for optimal protein synthesis and for cellulose digestion : 4.3 and 6.9 g P/kg OMF, respectively for the former and latter parameters. Therefore available P requirements for cellulose digestion are around 4.5 g P/kg OMD.

It should be noted that in the ammonia-treated straw trial quoted in table II (46) urea addition which improved cellulose degradation in P-supplemented fermentors, had no effect in P depleted ones. This indicates that P in that particular straw was the first limiting factor.

In vivo it is well recognized that when adult animals are fed diets containing the amount of P recommended for the host, salivary P secretion is greater than dietary P supply. However, the situation is different with low-P diets, especially when they are high in calcium (Ca). A decrease in plasma P level can dramatically reduce ruminal inorganic P levels (51) which, in turn, may affect synthetic and degradative ruminal processes. Some trials reported in (25) show a positive effect of P supplementation of low P diets on OM or cell-wall digestibilities. They confirm the in vitro observation that cell-wall digestion is highly sensitive to P deficiency.

However, the dietary P concentrations needed to obtain a positive response to supplementation vary widely, probably as a result of differences in endogenous P return. P requirement for lactation obviously reduces the amount of salivary P relative to digestible energy intake (25).

Only a few data allow the estimation of ruminal endogenous P in relation to dietary energy in low P diets. For digestion of acid detergent fibre with a natural diet, P returns of 4.8 g/kg OMD were not sufficient compared to 10.9 g. The values of cellulose digestibility were 63.2±4.1 and 70.1±2.3% respectively. Moreover, some dietary P might also be available to microbes ; therefore, it is clear from these data that the supply of available P to the rumen should be higher in vivo than in continuous cultures.

It can be stated that in vivo, in the rumen in situ, the available P supply should be at least 5 g/kg OMD in order to optimize cell- wall degradation. Assessment of the optimal dietary levels should involve factors influencing the secretion of salivary P, i.e. dietary P content, its absorbability, the composition of the diet (roughage vs concentrate) and the physiological state of the animal.

In conclusion, the absorbability of P contained in straws is still unknown but may be considered to be very low. As for S, P supplementation is a prerequisite for optimizing straw digestibility.

5.3. Magnesium

Magnesium (Mg) is essential to all microorganisms. It activates many bacterial enzymes, including phosphohydrolases, phosphotransfe-rases and pathways involving ATP and thiamin pyrophosphate reactions. Cellulases from Ruminococcus flavefaciens in the rumen was shown to be actived by Mg^{2+} (52). As already reported (24), several in vitro studies have shown that the addition of Mg improves cellulolytic activity in batch cultures.

Using the Rusitec technique no effect of Mg supplementation of alkali-treated straw could be observed even in the absence of manganese (Durand, unpublished data).

In vivo, a few experiments using semi-purified diets have studied the consequences of Mg deficiency on rumen metabolism (25). In all of them a reduction of cellulose digestion was seen ; the same effect was recently mentioned with rye-grass hay (53) but it cannot be ascertained whether the response was entirely due to Mg or to the S moiety since Mg was supplied in the form of sulphate.

It can be assumed that in order to satisfy rumen microbial requirements, dietary Mg concentration should be in the range of 1.5-2.0 g/kg OMD, depending on in situ Mg solubility in the rumen. Untreated and alkali-treated straw may supply around 1.2 and 0.9 g of Mg/kg OMD respectively. Therefore they should be supplemented with Mg, although more experimental data need to be obtained to accurately assess the amount of Mg required.

5.4. Trace elements

Trace elements play an important role in the metabolism of the rumen microbial population. Many enzymatic activities require iron (Fe), manganese (Mn), zinc (Zn), copper (cu), cobalt (Co), selenium (Se) and other ultratrace elements such as nickel and molybdenum (24). However the lack of one element can be compensated by the presence of another one. Examples of changes in the metal component of metallo-enzymes have been given recently : Co can replace Zn in several enzymes (54).

The microbial requirements for Fe, Mn and Zn assessed in animals consuming natural diets (24) were in conformity with the dietary concentration suggested by Lamand (55) for the host. However, the Co level (0.1 mg/kg DM) recommended by the latter for optimizing vitamin B_{12} synthesis in the host, seemed rather too low to support adequate microbial activity.

Cobalt and/or vitamin B^{12} formed by bacteria are required for the growth of rumen ciliates (56). Several works have shown an activation of overall rumen digestion by Co supplementation. This was confirmed recently with sheeps (57) and cows (58). In sheep (57) 1 mg Co/day had greater effect than 50 mg. The latter level was probably at the limit of toxicity (24).

It is most likely that in straws the availability of some trace elements is particularly low. With a same plant fed as grass or as hay, Cu and Zn digestibilities were lower with the latter forage, whereas that of Mn was not affected by hay-making (59). Responses to Co and Cu supplementation of straw based diets have been clearly demonstrated in terms of crude fibre digestibility in calves (60) or of cellulose digestibility in nylon bags (61). The highest effects were observed with a mixture of these two elements.

It is concluded that with straw diets the estimation of the additional supply of Fe, Mn, Se and I can follow Lamand's recommendations (55). But, as Co, Cu and Zn contained in straws are not likely to be available, they should be entirely supplied in the mineral mixture. A dietary Co concentration of 0.5-1 mg/kg DM is recommended. However, it should be stressed that the boundary separating a stimula-tory from a toxic concentration is narrow and especially with Cu (24), therefore, these minerals must be added with care.

6. GROWTH FACTORS

Branched chain volatile fatty acids (BFA) can stimulate fibre digestion as they are required by cellulolytic strains (4). The conversion of leucine, isoleucine and valine to isovalerate, 2-methyl-butyrate and isobutyrate can be carried out in substantial amounts by B. ruminicola and M. elsdenii. But the formation of these VFA is influenced by cultural conditions such as the availability of energy source (62). In vitro, addition of isobutyric, isovaleric and 2-methylbutyric increased isolated plant cell-wall digestion (63), and digestibility of dry matter regardless of crude protein content of the incubated substrate (64).

3-phenylpropanoic acid was also shown recently to dramatically stimulate the rate of cellulose digestion by strains of R. albus (65).

The effect of vitamin B supplementation on microbial protein synthesis has been observed both in vitro and in vivo as reported in (66). Recently using the Rusitec technique, vitamin B addition improved the degradation rate of straw (67). Whether all the B vitamins added or only one of them are required for straw degradation was not demonstrated.

It must be stressed that the availability of growth factors can have considerable influence on growth rate of bacteria as shown for B. ruminicola when grown with BFA (4). The right supply of these factors is often dependent on crossfeeding among bacteria or on the recycling of microbial matter in the rumen. Should these compounds be added or not to straw diets has not yet been fully elucidated.

7. ABSENCE OF TOXIC SUBSTANCES

Although the addition of fat to straw-based diets is not common, it should be stressed that lipids, depending on their nature and the amount fed, can depress cellulolytic activity. This depression can be partially alleviated by the addition of metal cations especially Ca (25).

Manipulation of rumen fermentation with chemicals such as methane inhibitors, ionophores or other antibiotics can affect cellulolytic activity. Compounds which shift hydrogen transfer from methane to propionate (propionate enhancers) were expected to lower lignocellulose fermentation (68). As mentioned above methanogenesis would allow maximum ATP yield via SLP during fibre degradation. Its inhibition generally decreases efficiency of microbial protein synthesis. Furthermore, with such products as monensin or avoparcin which decrease protein degradation, there might be a deficiency in available nitrogen.

However, it is well known that feeding of monensin (12) or of other antibiotic such as avoparcin (10) inhibits gram positive bacteria i.e. R. albus or R. flavefaciens but gives gram negative i.e. B. succinogenes a selective survival advantage. Bergen (69) considers that all of the observable ionophore effects are consequences of disruption of normal membrane physiology. Gram positive bacteria which depend on SLP are inhibited while the gram negative organisms which are capable of some ETP will adapt and survive. This partly explains, the inconsistent effect of monensin on rumen crude fibre degradation in vivo. This antibiotic can decrease digestibility which can or cannot recover after a long adaptation time or have no influence. Any negative effect may also be counteracted by a longer ruminal retention time of particles often observed with monensin.

Though additives can increase the supply of glucogenic precursors (propionate) to the host which may be low with straw-based diet, their use with low quality forage is not be presently advised.

Other substances such as phenolic monomers which can be solubilized during chemical treatments of straw might be detrimental to cellulolytic activity. These compounds have been reported to inhibit attachment of fibrolytic bacteria to cellulose and xylan, thus reducing their digestion (2). Further information is required to know whether some microbial species may adapt and degrade these compounds, thus detoxifying the environment for other species.

8. CONCLUDING REMARKS

The discussion clearly shows that optimizing rumen digestion of plant cell-walls in straw-based diets depends on the interaction of the following factors : 1) the right balance between microbial populations, 2) the adequate and permanent supply of required nutrients from the diet or/and from recycling and 3) the absence of disturbance of the rumen environment. Some of these factors are reasonably known or can be deduced from results obtained with other forage diets. Others, such as microbial interaction, amounts of recycled nitrogen, requirements for dietary protein, cobalt and growth factors and role of additives, deserve further studies. In particular, more research should be directed towards conditions of rapid microbial attachment and ruminal implantation of fungi.

ACKNOWLEDGEMENTS

Dr F. Meschy for comments on the manuscript, Geneviève Hannequart for help with the bibliography,Kirsten Rérat for English corrections and Colette Balinoff for excellent secretarial assistance are gratefully acknowledged.

REFERENCES

(1) OWENS, F.N. and GOETSCH, A.L. (1986). Digesta passage and microbial protein synthesis. In : MILLIGAN, L.P., GROVUM, W.L., DOBSON, A. Control of digestion and metabolism in ruminants. Proc. 6th Int. Symp. Ruminant Physiol., Banff Canada, 10th-14th sept. 1984. Prentice-Hall. Englewood Cliffs, pp 196-223.

(2) ALLEN, M.S. and MERTENS, D.R. (1987). Evaluating constraints on fibre digestion by rumen microbes. Proc. 28th Ann. Rum. Conf. at Ann. Meet. Fed. Am. Soc. Exp. Biol. Washington, D.C.

(3) DEMEYER, D.I. (1981). Rumen microbes and digestion of plant cell walls. Agric. Environ. 6, 295-337.

(4) RUSSEL, J.B. (1984). Factors influencing competition and composition of the rumen bacterial flora. In : GILCHRIST F.M.C., MACKIE, R.I. Herbivore nutrition in the subtropics and tropics. The Science Press, Craighall, South Africa, pp 313-345.

(5) AKIN, D.E. (1986). Chemical and biological structure in plants as related to microbial degradation of forage cell walls. In : MILLIGAN, L.P., GROVUM, W.L., DOBSON, A. Control of digestion and metabolism in ruminants. Proc. 6th Int. Symp. Ruminant Physiol., Banff Canada, 10th-14th sept. 1984. Prentice-Hall. Englewood Cliffs, pp 139-157.

(6) JOUANY, J.P. and SENAUD, J. (1982). Influence des ciliés du rumen sur la digestion de différents glucides chez le mouton. I. Utilisation des glucides pariétaux (cellulose, hémicelluloses) et de l'amidon. Reprod. Nutr. Dévelop., 22, 735-752.

(7) ORPIN, C.G. and LETCHER, A.J. (1983/84). Effect of absence of ciliate protozoa on rumen fluid volume, flow rate and bacterial populations in sheep. Anim. Feed Sci. Technol., 10, 145-153.

(8) FONTY, G., BRETON, A., FEVRE, M., CITRON, A., HEBRAUD, M. and GOUET, Ph. (1987). Isolement et purification des champignons anaérobies stricts du rumen de moutons. Premiers résultats. Reprod. Nutr. Dévelop., 27 (1B), 107-108.

(9)   VAN GYLSWYK, N.O. and SCHWARTZ, H.M. (1984). Microbial ecology of the rumen of animals fed high-fibre diets. In : GILSCHRIST, F.M.C.., MACKIE, R.I. Herbivore nutrition in the subtropics and tropics. The Science Press, Craighall, South Africa, pp 359-377.

(10) STEWART, C.S., GILMOUR, J and Mc CONVILLE, M.L. (1986). Microbial interactions, manipulation and genetic engineering. In : New developments and future perspectives in research on rumen function. Ed. NEIMANN-SORENSEN, A. Comm. Eur. Comm., Luxembourg, pp 243-257.

(11) GOUET, Ph., GRAIN, J., DUBOURGUIER, H.C. and ALBAGNAC, G. (1986). Interactions entre espèces microbiennes anaérobies dans le rumen. Reprod. Nutr. Dévelop., 26 (1B) 147-159.

(12) DURAND, M. (1982). Orientation du métabolisme du rumen au moyen des additifs. Ann. Zootech., 31, 47-75.

(13) DEMEYER, D.I. and VERVAEKE, I. (1985). Rumen digestion and microbial processes for increasing the feed value of poor quality materials. In : Improved utilization of lignocellulosic materials in animal feed, O.E.C.D., Paris, pp. 31-61.

(14) FONTY, G., GOUET, Ph. and SANTE, V. (1987). Influence d'une bactérie méthanogène sur l'activité cellulolytique et le métabolisme de deux espèces de champignons cellulolytiques du rumen in vitro. Resultats preliminaires. Reprod. Nutr. Dévelop. (in press).

(15) ERFLE, J.D., SAUER, F.D. and MAHADEVAN, S. (1986). Energy metabolism in rumen microbes.In : MILLIGAN, L.P., GROVUM, W.L., DOBSON, A. Control of digestion and metabolism in ruminants. Proc. 6th Int. Symp. Ruminant. Physiol. Banff Canada, 10th-14th sept., 1984. Prentice-Hall. Englewood Cliffs, pp 81-99.

(16) SILVA, A.T. and ORSKOV, E.R. (1985). Effect of unmolassed sugar beet pulp on the rate of straw degradation in the rumens of sheep given barley straw. Proc. Nutr. Soc., 44, 50A.

(17) RAMIHONE, B., JOUANY, J.P. and CHENOST, M. (1987). Part de l'azote apporté par le traitement à l'ammoniac dans la digestion microbienne d'une paille de blé en fermenteur semi-continu (Rusitec). Reprod. Nutr. Dévelop. (in press).

(18) SUTTON, J.D. (1986). Rumen fermentation and gastro-intestinal absorption : carbohydrates. In : New developments and future perspectives in research on rumen function. Ed. NEIMANN-SORENSEN A, Comm. Eur. Comm. Luxembourg, pp 21-38.

(19) HENNING, P.A. VAN DER LINDEN, Y., MATTHEYSE, M.E., NAUHAUS, W.K. and SCHWARTZ, H.M. (1980). Factors affecting the intake and digestion of roughage by sheep fed maize straw supplemented with maize grain. J. agric. Sci. Camb., 94, 565-573.

(20) DURAND, M. (1978). Effet des autres constituants de la ration sur la digestion des matières cellulosiques au niveau du rumen. In : Cycle approfondi d'alimentation animale. I.N.A. Paris, pp 105-113.

(21) MOULD, F.L. and ORSKOV, E.R. (1983/84). Manipulation of rumen fluid pH and its influence on cellulolysis in sacco, dry matter degradation and the rumen microflora of sheep offered either hay or concentrate. Anim. Feed Sci. Technol., 10, 1-14.

(22) MOULD, F.L., ORSKOV, E.R. and MANN, S.O. (1983/84). Associative effects of mixed feeds. I. Effects of type and level of supplementation and the influence of the rumen fluid pH on cellulolysis in vivo and dry matter digestion of various roughages. Anim. Feed Sci. Technol., 10, 15-30.

(23) MOULD, F.L., ORSKOV, E.R. and GAULD, S.A. (1983/84). Associative effects of mixed feeds. II. The effect of dietary addition of

bicarbonate salts on the voluntary intake and digestibility of diets containing various proportions of hay and barley. Anim. Feed. Sci. Technol., 10, 31-47.

(24) DURAND, M. and KAWASHIMA, R. (1980). Influence of minerals in rumen microbial digestion. In : RUCKEBUSCH, Y., THIVEND, P. Proc. 5th Int. Symp. Ruminant Physiol. Clermont-Ferrand, 3rd-7th sept. 1979. MTP Press Ltd. Lancaster, pp 375-408.

(25) DURAND, M. and KOMISARCZUK, S. (1987). Influence of major minerals on rumen microbiota. J. Nutr., in press.

(26) HESPELL, R.B. (1984); Influence of ammonia assimilation pathways and survival strategy on ruminal microbial growth. In : GILCHRIST, F.M.C., MACKIE, R.I. Herbivore nutrition in the subtropics and tropics. The Science Press, Craighall, South Africa, pp 346-358;

(27) ODLE, J. and SCHAEFER, D.M. (1987). Influence of rumen ammonia concentration on the rumen degradation rates of barley and maize. Br. J. Nutr., 57, 127-138.

(28) ORSKOV, O.R. (1982). Protein nutrition in ruminants. Academic Press INC. (London) LTD.

(29) INSTITUT NATIONAL DE LA RECHERCHE AGRONOMIQUE (1978). Alimentation des Ruminants. INRA Publ., Versailles.

(30) AGRICULTURAL RESEARCH COUNCIL (1980). The nutrient requirements of ruminant livestock, Commonwealth Agricultural Bureau, London.

(31) AGRICULTURAL RESEARCH COUNCIL (1984). The nutrient requirements of ruminant livestock, Suppl. n°1 Commonwealth Agricultural Bureau, London.

(32) DEMEYER, D. and VAN NEVEL, C. (1986). Influence of substrate and microbial interaction on efficiency of rumen microbial growth. Reprod. Nutr. Dévelop., 26 (1B) 161-179.

(33) EGAN, A.R., BODA, K. and VARADY, J. (1986); Regulation of nitrogen metabolism and recycling. In : MILLIGAN, L.P., GROVUN, W.L., DOBSON, A. Control of digestion and metabolism in ruminants. Proc. 6th Int. Symp. Ruminant Physiol. Banff Canada, 10th-14th sept. 1984. Prentice-Hall. Englewood Cliffs. pp 386-402.

(34) SIDDONS, R.C., NOLAN, J.V., BEEVER, D.E. and MACRAE, J.C. (1985). Nitrogen digestion and metabolism in sheep consuming diets containing contrasting forms and levels of N. Br. J. Nutr., 54, 175-187.

(35) RUMINANT NITROGEN USAGE (1985). National Academy Press, Washington, D.C.

(36) VERITE, R., JOURNET, M. and JARRIGE, R. (1979). A new system for the protein feeding of ruminants : the PDI system. Livestock Prod. Sci., 6, 349-367.

(37) ALRAHMOUN, W., MASSON, C. and TISSERAND, J.L. (1986). Etude comparée de l'activité microbienne dans le rumen chez les caprins et les ovins. II. Effet du niveau azoté et de la nature de la source azotée. Ann. Zootech., 35, 109-120.

(38) KOMISARCZUK, S., DURAND, M., BEAUMATIN, Ph., HANNEQUART, G. (1987). Utilisation de l'azote 15 pour la mesure de la protéosynthèse microbienne dans les phases solide et liquide d'un fermenteur semi-continu (Rusitec). Reprod. Nutr. Dévelop., 27 (1B) 261-262.

(39) OWENS, F.N., WEAKLEY, D.C. and GOETSCH, A.L. (1984). Modification of rumen fermentation to increase efficiency of fermentation and digestion in the rumen. In : GILSCHRIST, F.M.C., MACKIE, R.I. Herbivore nutrition in the subtropics and tropics. The Science Press, Craighall, South Africa, pp 435-454.

(40) HVELPLUND, T (1987). Protein evaluation of treated straw. Work-shop : "Methods of evaluation of straw in ruminant feeding". Comm. Eur. Comm. Cost. 84 bis, 2-4 june Theix, France.

(41) RAMIHONE, B. and CHESNOT, M. (1987). Effet de la nature du complément protéique sur la digestion dans le rumen d'une paille de blé traitée ou non à l'ammoniac. Reprod. Nutr. Dévelop. (in press).

(42) KANDYLIS, K. (1984). The role of sulphur in ruminant nutrition. A review. Livestock Prod. Sci., 11, 611-624.

(43) SMITH, R.H. (1984). Minerals and rumen function. In : Nuclear Techniques in Tropical Animal Diseases and Nutritional Disorders. International Atomic Energy Agency, Vienna, Austria, pp 79-96.

(44) MACKIE, R.I. and THERION, J.J. (1984). Influence of mineral interactions on growth efficiency of rumen bacteria. In : GILCHRIST, F.M.C., MACKIE, R.I. Herbivore nutrition in the subtropics and tropics. The Science Press, Craighall, South Africa, pp 455-477.

(45) ELLIOTT, R. and ARMSTRONG, D.G. (1982). The effect of urea and urea plus sodium sulphate on microbial protein production in the rumens of sheep given diets high in alkali-treated barley straw. J. agric. Sci. Camb., 99, 51-60.

(46) DURAND, M., BEAUMATIN, Ph., DUMAY, C., MESCHY, F. and KOMISARCZUK, S. (1986). Influence de l'addition de phosphore sur la digestion d'une paille traitée à l'ammoniac par les microorganismes du rumen en fermenteur semi-continu (Rusitec). Reprod. Nutr. Dévelop., 26, 297-298.

(47) KOMISARCZUK, S., DURAND, M., DUMAY, C. and MOREL, M.T. (1986). Use of a semi-continuous culture system (Rusitec) to study the effects of phosphorus deficiency on microbial digestion. In : Biology of Anaerobic Bacteria (H.C. DUBOURGUIER et al. eds.), pp 47-53. Elsevier Science Publishers B.V., Amsterdam.

(48) KOMISARCZUK, S., DURAND, M., BEAUMATIN, Ph. and HANNEQUART, G. (1987). Effects of phosphorus deficiency on rumen microbial activity associated with the solid and liquid phase of a fermentor (Rusitec). Reprod. Nutr. Dévelop. (in press).

(49) KOMISARCZUK, S., MERRY, R.J. and McALLAN, A.B. (1987). Effect of different levels of phosphorus on rumen microbial fermentation and synthesis determined using a continuous culture technique. Br. J. Nutr. 57, 279-290.

(50) FRANCIS, G.L., GAWTHORNE, J.M. and STORER, G.B. (1978). Factors affecting the activity of cellulases isolated from the rumen digesta of sheep. Appl. Environ. Microbiol., 36, 643-649.

(51) DURAND, M., BERTIER, B., HANNEQUART, G. and GUEGUEN, L. (1982). Influence d'une subcarence en phosphore et d'un excès de calcium alimentaire sur la phosphatémie et les teneurs en phosphore et calcium des contenus de rumen du mouton. Reprod. Nutr. Dévelop., 22, 865-879.

(52) PETTIPHER, G.L. and LATHAM, M.J; (1979). Characteristics of enzymes produced bu Ruminococcus flavefaciens which degrade plant cell walls. J. Gen. Microbiol., 110, 21-27.

(53) WILSON, G.F. (1980). Effects of magnesium supplements on the digestion of forages and milk production of cows with hypomagnesaemia. Anim. Prod., 31, 153-157.

(54) MATHUR, G.N., GELMAN, A.L., SCAIFE, J.R. and TOPPS, J.H. (1985). Influence of the concentration of trace elements on the composition and growth of rumen bacteria. In : Trace element metabolism in

man and animals-5- Ed. MILLS, C.F., BREMNER, I., CHESTERS, J.K. Rowett Research Institute, Aberdeen.

(55) LAMAND, M. (1978). In : Alimentation des ruminants I.N.R.A. Publ. Versailles, pp 143-159.

(56) BONHOMME, A., DURAND, M., QUINTANA, C. and HALPERN, S. (1982). Influence du cobalt et de la vitamine B_{12} sur la croissance et la survie des ciliés du rumen in vitro, en fonction de la population bactérienne. Reprod. Nutr. Dévelop., 22, 107-122;

(57) KRASNODEBSKA, I. (1982). The effect of cobalt on protein synthesis from urea in the rumen of sheep. Roczniki Naukowe Zootechniki, Monografie i Rozprawy (n°20) 127-148.

(58) LODOCHKINA, A.V. (1983). Utilization of cobalt and manganese by lactating cows. Zhivotnovodstvo (N°3) 53.

(59) LAMAND, M., AMBOULOU, D. and RAYSSIGUIER, Y. (1977). Effect of quality and forage on availability of trace elements and some major elements. Ann. Rech. Vét., 8, 303-306.

(60) SAXENA, K.K. and RANJHAN, S.K. (1978). Effect of cobalt and copper supplementation, separately and in combination, on the digestibility of organic nutrients and mineral balances in Hariana calves. Indian J. Anim. Sci., 48, 566-571.

(61) SAXENA, K.K. and RANJHAN, S.K. (1978). A note on the effect of cobalt and copper supplementation on in vivo cellulose digestion by nylon-bag technique in Hariana calves. Indian J. Anim. Sci., 48, 833-835.

(62) COTTA, M.A. and HESPELL, R.B. (1984). Protein and amino acid metabolism of rumen bacteria. In : MILLIGAN, L.P., GROVUM, W.L., DOBSON, A. Control of digestion and metabolism in ruminants. Proc. 6th Int. Symp. Ruminant Physiol., Banff Canada, 10th-14th sept. 1984. Prentice-Hall. Englewood Cliffs, pp 122-136.

(63) GOROSITO, A.R., RUSSELL, J.B. and VAN SOEST, P.J. (1985). Effect of carbon-4 and carbon-5 volatile fatty acids on digestion of plant cell wall in vitro. J. Dairy Sci., 68, 840-847.

(64) CUMMINS, K.A. and PAPAS, A.H. (1985). Effect of isocarbon-4 and isocarbon-5 volatile fatty acids on microbial protein synthesis and dry matter digestibility in vitro. J. Dairy Sci. 68, 2588-2595.

(65) STACK, R.J. and COTTA, M.A. (1986). Effect of 3-phenylpropanoic acid on growth of and cellulose utilization by cellulolytic ruminal bacteria. Appl. Environ. Microbiol., 52, 209-210.

(66) VERITE, R., DURAND, M. and JOUANY, J.P. (1986). Influence des facteurs alimentaires sur la protéosynthèse microbienne dans le rumen. Reprod. Nutr. Dévelop., 26, 181-201.

(67) BOUILLE-OUDOT, M., BELFADLA, A. and CANDAU, M. (1987). Influence de l'addition de vitamines du groupe B sur la dégradation des constituants pariétaux (paille-foin-pulpe) par les microorganismes du rumen en fermenteur semi-continu. Reprod. Nutr. Dévelop. (in press).

(68) DEMEYER, D.I. and VAN NEVEL, C.J. (1985). Chemical manipulation of rumen metabolism. Vol. 1 The ruminant stomach. Proc. intern. Workshop Antwerp 17-20 march, Belgium Vet. Res. Comm. Ed. OOMS, L.A.A., DEGRYSE, A.D., MARSBOOM, R., pp 228-250.

(69) BERGEN, W.G. and BATES, D.B. (1984). Ionophores : their effect on production efficiency and mode of action. J. Anim. Sci., 58, 1465-1483.

DISCUSSION

Conditions for optimizing cellulolytic activity in the rumen (Rapporteur: Mrs. M. DURAND, Chairman: E.R. ØRSKOV)

After the introductory paper by Mrs. Durand which underlined the main factors influencing cellulolytic activity in the rumen during a straw-based diet, the discussion centred on the main issues which should be seen as relevant for the aim of the workshop.

It was understood that out of the two main uses of straw by ruminants, either as a small part of the diet for high-production animals, or as a major part of the diet for low production animals, the latter was of major interest and should be given preference.

Evaluating straw as a feed for ruminants is both a fascinating and extremely complex exercise. It involves not only a characterization of the physical properties of straw and a measurement of digestibility but, also, a knowledge of the dynamics of the degradation of straw in the rumen.

Therefore, the conventional approach for the evaluation of feedstuffs was found to be inadequate for straw. The characterization of the degradation process should comprise the actual rate of degradation which will provide information on straw intake, related to the physical regulation of intake by ruminants, and also the potential degradation, which will provide information on the potential digestibility.

Biological measurements of digestibility and feed intake trials have recently identified a great variability in the nutritive value of straws which is due to genetic, agronomic, and other environmental factors.

Likewise, research still in progress has already provided evidence that the various morphological components of straw, such as leaves, nodes and internodes, show large differences in their nutritive value. Therefore, to make the best use of straw for ruminants it becomes more and more important to consider the post-harvest separation of these components.

The meeting should therefore aim at improving

- the characterization of the intrinsic parameters of straws affecting their nutritive value,
- the identification of the various factors that influence these parameters,
- the knowledge of the physiological processes in the plant which govern the expression of these factors.

Topic A:

IN VIVO METHODS FOR MEASURING THE FEED VALUE OF STRAWS

INTAKE   MEASUREMENT

J.M.C.Ramalho Ribeiro
Estação Zootécnica Nacional
PORTUGAL

Summary

The main problem in terms of straw voluntary intake measurements   is   the way it is measured and expressed which   makes
difficult the comparison of the results. To reach a common
methodological procedure it is necessary at first to discuss
completely how intake is controlled,and what are the   main
factors affecting intake. Knowing that it is important to
discuss how straw intake can be manipulated as well as the
different ways of presentation or feeding the straw.
So the various techniques for the evaluation of voluntary
feed intake either in general terms or in terms of straw
feeding are briefly described. At last, procedures and conditions already accepted by some research teams are shown in
order to reach an European Common Methodological procedure
for the evaluation of voluntary intake of straw diets.

1. INTRODUCTION

To evaluate the nutritive potential of a feedstuff it is
essential to know its nutritive value with digestible trials,
being also necessary for pratical aplications,   to know its voluntary feed intake.
If the standardization of methodological procedures for
nutritive value determinations are relativelly simple,   the same
cannot be said for voluntary intake. In the past, it has been
difficult to compare and understand some results found in the
literature because conditions were not always completely described and the ways of expressing intake had not been uniform.
To help the discussion of this subject, in order to reach a
final agreement on a framework among research groups and laboratories studying intake, it was decided to present and discuss the
following points:

- Physiological mechanisms for the control of feed
intake
- Factors affecting intake
- Straw intake
- Methods of feeding straw
- Methods of measuring intake of straw
- Methodological conditions used by some research
groups exaustively.
It was not our aim to describe or discuss every subjects
presented, but highligh the main factors affecting the definition
of methodological procedure.

2. PHYSIOLOGICAL MECHANISMS

Feeding is controlled by centres in the hypothalamus, si-
tuated beneath the cerebrum in the brain (1),(2),(3),(4). It was
originally proposed that there are two centres of activity. The
first of these is the feeding centre (lateral hypothalamus),
which causes the animal to eat food unless inhibited by the
second, the satiety centre (ventromedial hypothalamus), wich
receives signals from the body as a result from consumption of
food.
The actual neurochemical events subserving this function are
not well understood, although specific roles for each of the
neurotransmitter systems have been proposed (5). More recently

certain neuropeptids have been shown to affect feeding behavior in sheep namely the opioid peptides (which include enkephalins, endophirns and dynorphirns) and the cholecystokinin peptides (6). It seems that peptides are likely to be involved in the interface beetween the energy balance regulator and contoller of feed intake. In fact, the observation that the long-term preservation of a relatively constant body weight, combined with an animals desire to return to that body weight, if it is altered by starvation or forced feeding, implies that some agent associated with the energy storage acts as a signal for the long-term regulation of food intake.

However, it seems that in Ruminants short-term control of feed intake is primarly restricted by rumen capacity (7). Evidence for the physical limitation of intake comes from observations of a relationship between voluntary intake and digestibility (8) (7) or digestible energy concentration (9).

Even during this meeting, Aerts expressed the opinion that, for diets with small amounts of straw, digestibility is the most important factor but, with high straw diets the intake measurement becomes more important.

It was commonly assumed that animals shared the same attitudes to food, as far as senses were concerned, as ourselves but it is now generally accepted that the senses play a less important role in food intake in farm animals than they do in man.

Although it is clear today that the control of feed intake is highly complex, involving many peripheral and central nervous systems factors, the knowledge of the work of all these mechanisms is far to be fully understood.

Nevertheless it has been shown that several factors may affect intake.

2.1 Summary

Feeding is controlled by centres in the central nervous system receiving information from peripheral receptors.

There is a long and short-term control of feed intake and with ruminants fed low quality roughages the rumen capacity seems to be the main restricting factor.

3. FACTORS AFFECTING INTAKE

These factors are related either with the food or with the animals and with the environment.

The composition and availability of the diet are the major factors influencing voluntary intake and a positive correlation between intake of roughages and their digestibility was proposed since the early 1960s (7).

It has been suggested (10) that the bulk of the food and the time it stays in the gut are important in determining the level of intake and there is a great deal of evidence that cell wall constituints, as measured by the acid detergent fibre method gave the best prediction (10) (11).

Recently (12) an exponential mathematical model was proposed as adequately describing the intake-digestibility relationship. However, and using the dracon bag technique, a research team at Theix (13) suggests that potential degradability was better related to voluntary intake than "in vivo" digestibility did.

In adition, factors as feed structure and particle size will also affect intake, because rumination activity tends to be greater with loose than with pelleted mixtures and with chopped rather than ground straw in loose feed (14), leading to a higher intake with the chopped form of straw (15). So, reducing the lenght of wheaten straw particles from 30 to 10 mm increased intake rates from 5.5 to 12.4 g/min and resulted in an absolute preference for the short material (16).

Related to the factors of food intake, stimulant substances such as monosodium glutamate have been shown to promote quadrupled intakes of chopped straw (15).

When the diet is low in fibre concentration, species differences in intake are relatively unimportant, but on low quality, high fibre diets, sheep tend to digest DM (and fiber) more completely than goats, but with lower levels of intake (17). In a

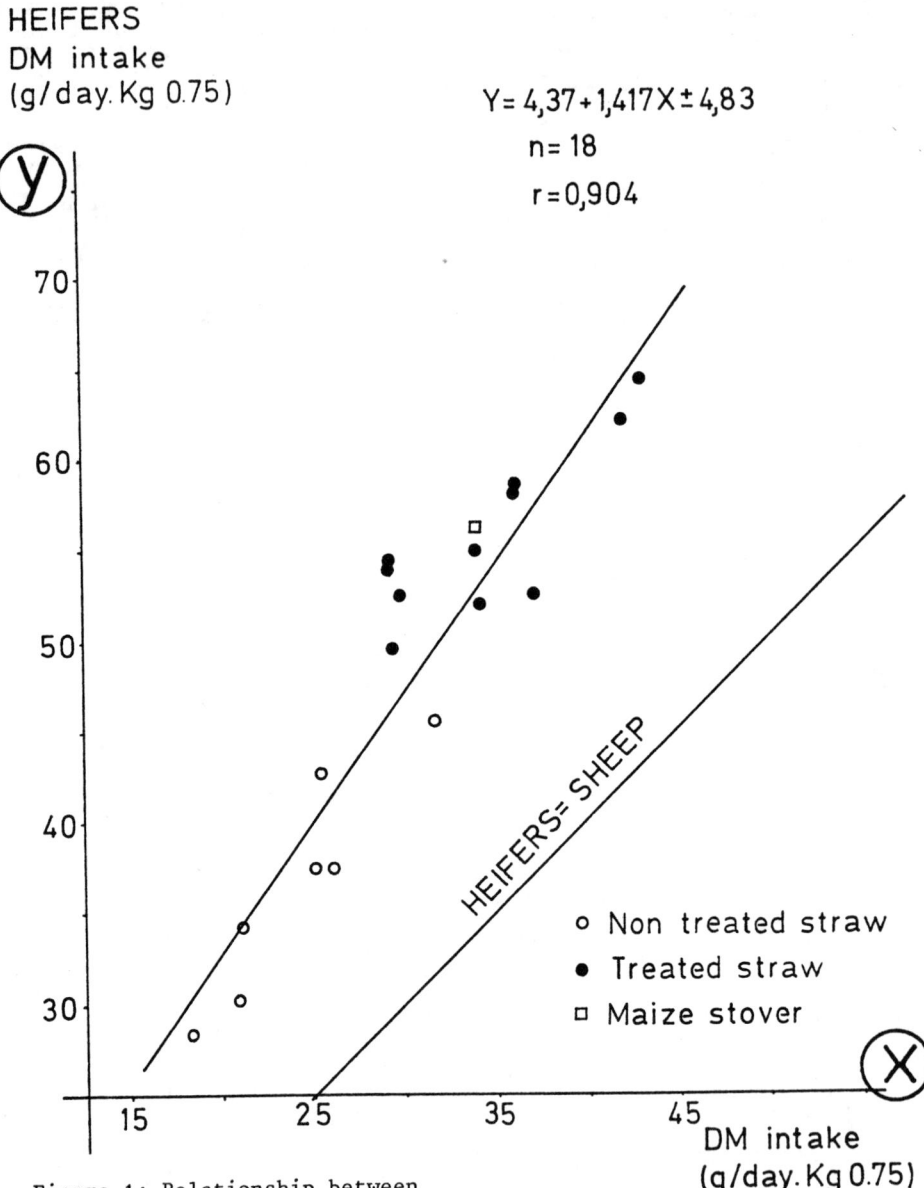

Figure 1: Relationship between sheep Dairy heifers and adult male sheep feed straw diets "ad libitum" (CHENOST, personal communication)

non published experiment Chenost (personal communication) have
shown an important difference in intake between heifers and sheep
when fed straw.(Fig.l). Comparing (18) males and females from
weaning to maturity it was observed that rams had both a higher
asymptote and a slower rate of decline in feed intake than ewes,
and also, that age differences has been demonstrated for example
in Australia (19) where heifers 16 weeks old fed wheat straw to
apetite had an intake of 40% of that one of lucerne, which increased to 64% in 50 weeks old animals.
    A comprehensive study made in Britain (20) involving 306
females from 25 British cattle breeds indicated that genetically
larger breeds consumed relatively more feed at early ages, compared with later ages.
    An important animal factor affecting intake is its physiolo-
gical stage and differences has been shown with lactating animals
compared with non lactating animals and even along the lactation
period. Pregnancy reduces rumen capacity and therefore the daily
intake but another important feed fack information controlling
intake relates to the fatness of the growing or fattening animal.
    Besides animal factors, one must also consider the envi-
ronmental factors affecting intake. Within the zone of thermal
neutrality there is little change in voluntary intake.

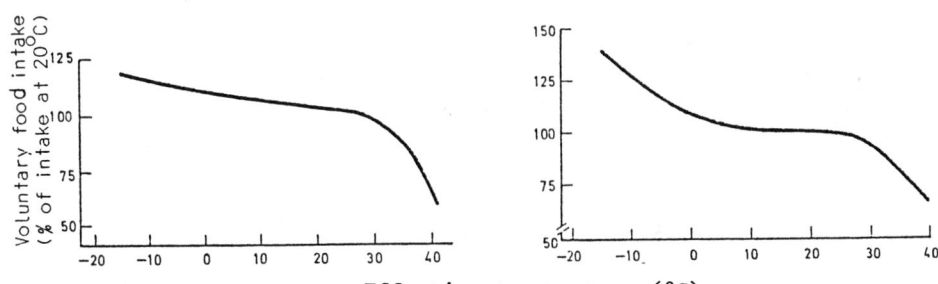

Effective temperature (°C)
Figure 2: Food intake responses of cattle to different ambient
temperatures: (a) growing cattle; (b) dairy cows (after NRC. 1981)

    Figure 2 summarises the effects of environmental tempe-
rature on the voluntary intake of cattle (21).
    Below the critical temperature the animal must increase
its rate of heat production in order to maintain its deep body
temperature within the narrow range compatible with normal
function. This increase in energy requirements would be espected
to result in increase food intake and this is indeed so (22).
    Shearing increases heat production in sheep which is
matched by increased food intake. At a fixed level of feeding,
sheep eat faster on a colder environment and there is an increase
in rumen motility, a reduction in the volume of rumen contents
and an extent of digestion of cell wall constituents (23).
    As it is easier to shelter farm livestock from cold than
from heat, more research has been done on the latter. Above the
thermonentral zone, body temperature rises and so food intake
decreases in order to reduce the heat production associated with
feeding, digestion, absorption and metabolism and to prevent an
excessive increase in body temperature.
    Rapid change of climate conditions affects intake and
productivity but slowly the animal tends to adapt to the new
environmental situation up to a stable response which will be
below the optimum but above of what has been observed during the
response to the climate variation.
    The overall feeding pattern is related to photoperiode,
with larger, and more frequent meals during the day what can be
modified if the middle of the day is very hot or when cattle eat
more at night, especially if the noon is bright (24).
    The effects of photoperiod on food intake in domesticated
ruminants have been reviewed recently (25).

Social factors may also influence the animal's eating behaviour and so the voluntary intake. In fact, the common observation that sheep intend to feed at the same time as each other was corroborated by an experiment (26) which showed that isolated lambs ate less than those in groups and particularly if they were kept in individual metabolic cages (27) (28). However it must be said that intake variation between animal groups exists and even between animals which is sometimes difficult to explain and turns the evaluations into a problem and the observations not easy to understand.

Infestation with helminths causes a primarly depression of food intake in sheep (29) possibly by the continuous stimulation by the parasites of receptors in the gut wall.

A relatively low level of dosing with Fasciola hepatica (liver fluke) for 25 weeks caused a 0.15 descrease in intake in sheep (30) but larger doses severely depressed intake (31).

3.1 Summary

The nutritive value of the diet directly or indirectly affects intake in ruminants.

Animals show differences in feeding behaviour related to species, age, physiological state and structure or particle size of the diet. This differences are even great for low quality roughages.

Climate conditions such as cold or heat stress, in adition to photoperiod variations also affect intake.

Social factors and in special the case of isolated animals in metabolic cages was discussed.

Finaly disease has a direct influence in the animals voluntary intake, in particular the parasities infestation.

4. STRAW INTAKE

Although species differences in chemical composition are frequent among cereal straw, there are always two common characteristics:

a)   Low nitrogen content
b)   High structural carbohydrates content (fibre) – representing 70 to 80% of its DM.

High fibre means that straw digestive utilization must occur predominantly by microbial fermemtation. However the extent of the process is reduce and its rate is slow, due to the structure and composition of the fibre, and deficiencies in growing factors required for the rumen microbial population, specially nitrogen.

In adition, being low the rate of particle reduction, to an adequate size able to cross the orifice reticulo-omasum, and being limited the rumen capacity, the intake of cereal straws is always reduced and unable "per si" to guarantee the energy maintenance requirements of the ruminants.

Among the cereal grains it is generally accepted that oat straw is more digestible than barley straw, being the last one more digestible than wheat straw.

It is also frequent to find references in the literature (32) showing that differences in digestibility among crop cultivars within a specie, were greater than those between species of cereals.

Several factors have been pointed (33) as influencing crop residues feed value but the most importants of them (34) seems to be:

- Maturity
- Irrigation, climate
- Fertilization and
- Weathering

These are sometimes uncontrolled or difficult to control aspects which may shift completely the intake of straws.

In order to provide enough net energy and absorbable protein for maintenance and production, the animals have to consume larger quantities of straw. This enphasizes the importance of rumen capacity on straw intake and explains the attention that the French energy system put on the inclusion of a factor to take this effect into consideration. It is the known UE (unités d' encombrement) which comes as an improvement on the nutritive value prediction of a feedstuff and becomes crucial when dealing with very low quality roughages like straw.

But the low voluntary feed intake of the straws is also due to a low degradability and rate of passage through the intestinal tract.

To overcome this limitation, a lot of work has been done to improve the nutritive value of straw and consequently its voluntary feed intake.

4.1 Improvement of straw feeding value

Feeding value is an altribute involving nutritive value and voluntary intake. In terms of straw on can follow two way of improving the feeding value. First by supplementing the straw with its limiting nutrients and secondly by treating or processing the straw with a roughage type of feed. Not all feedstuffs can be used as supplements as some of them due to its nature and/or quantity would reduce the intake of the basal diet, and act as substitutes instead of supplements.

4.1.1 Supplementation

Looking at the straw chemical composition it seems that its first limiting nutrient would be the nitrogen as it is seldom obtained, with straw, a level of 2.0 mM ammonia Nitrogen per litre of rumem liquor. Reports suggesting rumen ammonia nitrogen levels required of 5 mg/100ml has been presented (35) or 1% nitrogen in the diet as adequate for cellulose digestion of feeds up to 50% digestibility of the energy (36).

The N supplementation would be more efficient when given by a low degradability supplement and this is more evident in terms of LWG rather than in terms of intake (36). Regarding the utilization of N by low quality feeds it must be remembered the role of endogen recycled Nitrogen which can act as a buffer, helping the rumen micro-flora in getting levels of N near its requirements. This sometimes delays the effect of a low N diet specially on a short term esperiment and when the animals come from an adequate protein "status".

Today it is commonly accepted that low quality feeds would be improved if supplemented with protein nitrogen (34). Casein infused into the duodenum of sheep feed low nitrogen forages increases the voluntary intake (37). A possible explanation could be the fate of this extra protein into gluconeogenesis (38) which in these cases would also be a limiting metabolic nutrient and glucose production is possible responsible for the increased intake that has been observed.

There are also some indication that rumen microbes has a specific requirements for Amino-Acids or small peptides and 1/3 of N supplementation as protein N is frequently mentioned (39).

The energy is also a limiting nutrient for straw utilization and the maximum intakes of cereal residues ocurred when small amounts of starch type of carbohydrats are fed in adition to protein supplementation but high levels of starchy supplements would reduce crude fiber digestibility (40).

Both adequate nitrogen and limited amounts of ready available carbohydrtats are needed for optimum fibre digesting activity by rumen microorganisms. It is likely that adequate mineral supplementation is also necessary, but there does not seem to be any reports demonstrating responses in intake of straws due to mineral supplementation. However, specific demands for sulphur on microbial growth (41) and cobalt on vitamin B12 synthesis (42) would suggest its inclusion as supplements of straw based diets.

Also no information is available concerning ruminant animal response to vitamin supplementation when straw is fed. Because of the very low levels of fat soluble vitamins. In most straws it would (34) only be prudent to supplement animals with vitamins A and D.

It was our intention just briefly mention the main supplementing points because a comprehensive paper from M. Duran (43) was presented before where the factors and the levels of required supplementation were adequately described.

4.1.2 Chemical processing

Many papers published in recent years (44), (45), (46) indicated that chemical treatment of low quality feeds, particularly with alkalis such as sodium hydroxide, could substantially enhance the degradation of cell wall polysacharides by rumen - microorganisms. This improvement of nutritive value is well known and chemicals have been applied, to cereal straws and other low-quality crop residues with varying degrees of success.

Several attempts have been made but the most successful were the use of sodium hydroxide, ammonia and urea treatment of straw. In a recent review (47) of digestibility measurements with sheep and cattle, it was concluded that the improvement of OM digestibility with sodium hydroxide treatment, was as much important as low digestibility presented the untreated initial straw.

Most of the trials involving "in vivo" evaluations, have used levels of 3-6% NaOH considered as optimum (44), varying the most effective level with the material being treated, the type of animal consumer, the levels of feeding, the degree of dilution with other feeds, and the conditions under which the processing occurs (34). Above 6% level "in vivo" digestibility and voluntary daily intake all intend to level off or even decrese while the IVDMD continues to increse.

The use of NH_4 as the anhydrous gas or as aqueous NH_4OH has improved digestibility and voluntary intake similar to those achieved with NaOH when conditions for treatment were appropriate (34). If this is so the increase in OM digestibility and nitrogen content is normally 10-12 and 0.8 - 1.0 percentage units respectively (46).

Increasing dosage of ammonia up to 3-4% of the straw, temperature, moisture content of the straw and the time of treatment all seem to have positive effects on the treatment response. The combination of treatment involving grinding and ammoniation seem to be specially effective in increasing DM intake (48).

The utilization of urea added to straw in stack covered with polyethylene sheet is based on the demonstration that there is extensive breakdown of urea to ammonia (49).

The increase in intake of 47% (49) has been shown together with values as high as 60% (50). Perhaps the effect of N supplementation on straw and an increase rate of passage of digesta could explain such figures.

4.1.3 Physical processing

Straw is a bulky low density feed, weighing 100-150 Kg per cubic-metre, and processing is adopted partly to facilitate its inclusion in mixed diets, as well as to improve its nutritive value. The latter is achieved through rupture of the outher lignin layer, what makes the cellulose fibres more accessibles for breakdown by rumen microorganisms. In adition, it is known that one of the major factors limiting intake of low quality forages by ruminants is the rate of passage of the undigestible residues through digestive tract. It is thought that the main control is made at the reticulo-omasal orifice which works to restrict passage of particles above a certain size (51). The increase of intake is therefore due to an increase in density of ground material – which is even greater if it is followed by pelleting procedure, – and to a reduction in rumination time per unit of intake food. The grinding process decreases straw digestibility, but the increase in intake will compensate resulting an overall positive effect, which is greater with the lowest quality forage (52). This benefit can be lost if the proportion of the straw in the diet falls to values around 20% (45).

Fine grinding alone without pelleting has given variable responses. This may be related to dustiness of the unpelleted ground feed.

The application of water vapor pressure to straw, seem to

increase digestibility up to a certain level depending on the treatment conditions but the intake can be depressed if the pressure is too high (53).

In 1974 a new treatment process has been proposed, which is a mixture of a chemical and physical method (54) claimed to promote an 100% improvement on straw intake.

4.2 Summary

The straw intake depends on straw quality, which varies with the different species and therefore in chemical composition. However, two commom characteristics affect straw nutritive value: low nitrogen and high fibre content. This will be responsible by a low rate of digestion and so a low level of intake. To improve straw digestibility, the supplementation with nitrogen ready available carbohydrates or even minerals has been used. The chemical breakdonw of structural carbohydrates with NaOH and NH_4 has also been tested with a great degree of success.

The physical processing in particular grinding followed by pelleting has been another approach. Leading all these processes to an adequate satisfaction of rumen microbes requirements (N, energy and minerals), together with a breakdown or an increase in surface area for enzyme activity, will improve straw digestibility, reduce retention time and increase level of voluntary intake.

5. METHODS OF FEEDING STRAW

Liveweight losses resulting from feeding of all straw diets have been reported in all ruminant species and appropriate supplementation shall be done otherwise it will be difficult to understand and compare intake results from experiments with straw. With the alkali treated straw, a further limitation is imposed related with the levels of treated straw in the diet to the 35% (55).

The overall effect of supplementing diets with moderate levels of concentrate, is to increase not only straw, but also, total dry and organic matter intake, however, when increased quantities of concentrate are fed, roughage digestibility is depressed. The most affected nutrient is the crude fibre: its digestibility decreases (56) with little donward change in the other constituents.

In addition, when using straw as a dilution component of the diet, there is some indication that above 30% straw inclusion, feed intake is reduced (57). With up to about 20-30% straw in mixed diets, therefore, the higher total feed intake compensates aproximatly for the lower digestibility, to give similar dry and organic matters, as well as energy intake. In excess of 20-30% straw, digestible energy intake is depressed (58).

There is an optimum inclusion rate for straw in mixed rations which seems to be some what between 20 and 30% (59).

This is probably based on the associated advantages of a high DM intake and a satisfactory utilization of the ration's nutrients. A recent review of literature values (60) strongly supports a positive relationships between roughage quality and substitution rate, which means the decrease in roughage DM intake for an unit increase in concentrate allowance. Negative substitution rates can occur when the roughage is low in protein (as in straw) and the supplement alleviates this deficiency, which leads to an increase in forage intake.

5.1 Summary

Straw treated or untreated must be properly supplemented if included in complete diets. The inclusion rate above which a depression in intake has been observed seems to be somewhat between 20 and 30%.

6. METHODS OF MEASURING FOOD INTAKE

In order to study voluntary food intake and to develop

methods of prediction, we need to be able to measure intake in a variety of experimental and farm situations.

Regarding the diets with straw, the methods to apply are those measuring intake in group fed and individual penned animals.

In view of the variability between individuals, it is necessary to use a sufficient number of animals, in order to get a reliable estimate of intake. Variability between animals in a group does not differ greatly between different feeds, and it is smaller when they are penned individually than when they are penned together (61).

Group fed animals are more defficult to control specially if the straw is supplemented with concentrates and a certain degree of selection is possible. There are the callan type doors, allowing an individual recording of intake, with animals mantained in a group, or, more sophisticated proposals with video tape, being even now possible for a feed-dispensing system to recognise an animal identity (62). Recently, a new system has been proposed for dairy cows (63) where a bunker containing the roughage can be weighed automatically and the animals identified as they ate, then, full details of meal patterns of individuals in a group would be observed.

If this type of equipment is not available, then the alternative for the individual control of a group fed would be the use of a marker dilution technique, in which each animal is dosed by mouth with a known amount of an inert material. After several days to allow equilibrium to be reached, faeces are collected from each animal, either by grab sampling from the rectum, or by collection of faeces identified by observation or coloured plastic particles, which can be given by mouth at the same time as the marker. From the content of the marker in the faeces, total faecal output can be calculated. It is then necessary to know the digestibility of the feed in order to calculate the food intake.

This method has the disadvantage of the dilution approach, the sampling difficulties and the lack of a good solid phase marker.

With the individually penned animals, several proposals have been made (64) (65) (66) either recording feeding behaviour, or even the weight of eaten food.

Unless it is for a specific objective, those systems are expensive and not advisable to use in most experimental stations. For straw feeding experiments group fed animals would always have a pratical feeding intake measurement which will not be easy to standardize. It will be recommended that full description of the experiment shall be done, in order to be possible comparisons between experiments.

For the individual controlled animals, experimental conditions can be discussed and a common proposal accepted.

Care must be taken to avoid diet selection (67) particularly when the data are obtained from sheep trials, since sheep intakes are often exaggerated owing to their alibity to select (68). At this meeting,in a previous communication (69), it was shown that the extent of selection is a function of the total straw available. Owen observed that intakes of barley straw in the long form can be increased by a third or more if refusal rates of 50% of straw offered rather than the conventional 15 to 20% are tolerated.

Moreover, the use of wether sheep as the standard animal may not predict relative intakes for dairy cows (70) because large ruminants have more spacious fermentation chambers, relative to their body weights, than smaller animals. Bigger ruminants seem to achieve a longer retention time of the feed in the rumen what would facilitate more extensive fibre digestion (71). It seems that some of the medium size ruminants are able to adapt to fibrous, low quality roughages by increasing their forestomach capacity.

Another form of adaptation is that shown by sheep on long term fed low protein intake. This very common situation under drought conditions is always what happens to animals on a long term intake of a straw based diet. These sheep seem to adapt (72) by reducing urinary N excretion and recycling the conserved N to the rumen.

It was shown (72) that after 50-60 days on low protein diets, sheep achieved a positive N balance while receiving only

60% of maintenance requirements.
     The relationship between straw intake and the adaptation
period was presented long ago (73) when Xandé showed that the
intake of straw alone was 20 g DM/kg0.75 going to about 38 g
after a period of 45 days adaptation. It seems that the
adaptation is progressive and increases with the N
supplementation and in the short term is perhaps due to an
increase in Rumen capacity and an increase rate of passage.
     Generally, NaOH treatment of straw increases ash content.
This makes analysis on a DM basis somewhat nebulous,since NaOH −
treated materials were not washed after the treatment, and the
inorganic salts contributed to an increased ash content (74),
consequently, all comparisons must be done on an organic matter
basis.
     Voluntary intake shall also be expressed in terms of
animals LW or, better, in terms of metabolic body wheight.

6.1 Summary

     The methods for measuring intake of straw are those used
for group or individually fed animals.
     Group fed animals may be controlled by a sophisticated
equipment or by a marker dilution technique, depending the option
of the experimental conditions which are difficult to standardize.
     Individually fed animals may also be controlled by auto-
matic equipment recording feeding behaviour and/or weight of
eaten food. Here, standardized conditions are advisable and shall
be adopted.
     In both cases it must be taken account the diet selection
and the animal species under study.
     It must be said that selection and adaptation period can
play an important role on the total amount of straw intake.
     When alkali treated straw is used, OM rather than DM shall
be used as unit of reference.
     Intake shall be expressed as g/day;kg/100 kg L.W.;g/kg0.75
g DOM/day or g DOM/kg0.75   .

7. METHODOLOGICAL CONDITIONS USED BY SOME RESEARCH TEAMS

     Having mentioned the main factors affecting intake, and
the principal methods used for measuring voluntary feed intake it
is important to present some methodological conditions, followed
by several researck groups, in order to serve as a basis for
discussion and an attempt to reach a common methodological proposal to study and measure the voluntary feed intake of straw.

Minimal Nº of animals	Nº of meals	Adaptation period (days)	Pré-period (days)	Control period (days)	Laboratoire
6	2	24	−	10	EZN−Portugal
6	−	20	−	10	SARAG−Spain
6	2	−	15	10	THEIX−France
−	−	−−	45	−−	ART−Cyrus
4−8	−	−	15−24	10	UTAD−Portugal

     The ingestibility of poor quality forages such as straw
depends more on their nitrogen content than any other characteristics. Nitrogen and sometimes minerals, are the factors limiting their digestion in the rumen. Therefore, they must be
correctly supplemented to obtain measurements of its potential
ingestibility.
     Providing this nutrient supplementation is done then there
are two main points where standardization shall be looked at:

     1 − Feeding methods and
     2 − Number and choice of animals
     This subject has been recently reviewed (75) and the main
conclusion applying to straw will be presented here:

                "Feeding methods"
     − Straw shall be fed in excess

- Refusals maintained at a 10% level
- Meals at 08 00 and 16 30 h
- Preliminary period of at least 15 days
- Measurement period of at least 10 days
- If labour is a problem - 6 days (from Sunday morning to saturday morning).

"Number and choice of animals"
- Intake expressed in g/kg
- Animals with a variability of more than 1.5 standard deviation from mean, shall be eliminated
- Animals between 1.5 and 4 years old
- When possible, values shall be corrected to data on a common control feed.

7.1 Summary

Providing straw is adequatly supplemented,experimental conditions with group fed animals shall be fully described. For individually penned animals a common methodological proposal shall be reached on feeding methods; number and choice of animals.

REFERENCES

(1) LARSSON, S., (1954). On the hypothalamic organization of food intake. Acta Physiol.Scand. 32 (Suppl.): 115.
(2) WYRWICKA, W. and C. DOBRZECKA, (1960). Relationship between feeding and satiation centers of the hypothalamus. Science 132: 805.
(3) BAILE, C.A., MAHONEY and J. MAYER, (1968). Induction of hypothalamic aphagia and adipsia in goats. J. Dairy Sci. 51:1474.
(4) BAILE, C.A. and J.M.FORBES, (1974). Control of feed intake and regulation of energy balance in ruminants. Physiol. Rev. 54:160.
(5) DRIVER, P.M., J.M. FORBES and C.G. SCANES, (1979). Hormones, feeding and temperature in sheep following cerebro - ventricular injection of neurotransmitters and carbachol. J. Physiol. 290:390.
(6) DELLA-FERA, M.A. and C.A. BAILE, (1984). Control of feed intake in sheep J. of Animal Sci., vol. 59. Nº 5.
(7) BALCH, C.C. and R.C. CAMPLING, (1962). Regulation of voluntary food intake in ruminants. Nutr. Abs. and Rev., 32, 669-686.
(8) CRAMPTON, E.W., E. DONEFER and L.E. LLOYD, (1960). A nutritive value index for forages. J. of Ani. Sci., 19, 538-544.
(9) BLAXTER, K.L., F.W. WAINMAN and R.S. WILSON, (1961). The regulation of food intake by sheep. Ani. Prod., 3, 51-61.
(10) VAN SOEST, P.J., (1965). Symposium on factors influencing the voluntary intake of herbage by ruminants - voluntary intake in relation to chemical composition and digestibility. J. of Ani. Sci. 24, 834-843.
(11) OSBOURN, D.J., R.A. TERRY, G.E. OUTEN and S.B. CAMMELLES, (1974). The significance of a determination of cell walls as the rational basis for the nutritive evaluation of forages. Proceedings of the XII Inter. Grassland Congress, 3, 374.
(12) MENCHACA, M.A. and R.RUIZ, (1984). Mathematical modelling of the voluntary intake in ruminants. I. Influence of digestibility in rams fed pelleted rations. Cuban J. of Agr. Sci. 18 (3) 291-300.
(13) CHENOST, M., E. GRENET, C. DEMARQUILLY and R. JARRIGE (1970). The use of the nylon bag technique for the study of forage digestion in the rumen and for predicting feed value. Proc. 11 th Int. Grassl, Congr. Surfers Paradise, pp 697-701. Univ. Queensland Press, St. Lucia, Australia.
(14) LENK, R., M. HOFFMANN, H. DABERITZ, D. PREDIGER and A. DITTRICH,(1985). Intake and rumination behaviour in sheep. I. the effect of feed structure on rumination behaviour in wethers. Archiv. fur Tierernahrung 35 (1) 53-59.

(15) GROVUM, W.L., (1984). Controls over the intake of straw by sheep: effects of form of diet and intake stimulants on sham feeding. Can. J. of Ani. Sci. 64, 150-151.

(16) KENNEY, P.A. and J.L. BLACK, (1984). Factors affecting diet selection by sheep. I. Potential rate and acceptability of feed. Aust. J. of Agri. Res. 35 (4) 551-563.

(17) BROWN, L.E. and W.L. JOHNSON, (1984). Comparative intake and digestibility of forages and by-products by goats and sheep: a raview. Inter. Goat and Sheep Res. 2 (3) 212-226.

(18) THOMPSON, J.M., J.R. PARKS and D. PERRY, (1985). Food intake, growth and body composition in Australian Merino sheep selected for high and low weaning weight.I. Food intake, food efficiency and growth. Ani. Prod.40 (1) 55-70.

(19) LEIBHOLZ, J., (1984). Roughage intake comparisons between calves and adult cattle. Canadian J. of Ani. Sci. 64, 154-155.

(20) TAYLOR, ST. C.S., A.J. MOORE and R.D. THIESSEN, (1986). Voluntary food intake in relation to body weight among British breeds of cattle. Ani. Prod. 42 (1) 11-18.

(21) NRC., (1981). Effect of environment on nutrient requirements of domestic animals. Washington; National Academy Press, 152.

(22) CHAI, K.,P.M. KENNEDY, L.P. MILLIGAN and G.W. MATHISON, (1985). Effects of cold exposure and plant species on forage intake, chewing behaviour and digesta particle size in sheep. Canadian J. of Ani. Sci. 65 (1) 69-76.

(23) KENNEDY, P.M., R.J. CHRISTOPHERSON and L.P. MILLIGAN, (1985). Digestive responses to cold. Proc. VI Inter. Symp. on Rum. Phy. Banff, Canada.

(24) DULPHY, J.P., B. REMOND and M. THERIEZ, (1980). Ingestive behaviour and related activities in ruminants. In Digest. Phy. and Met. in Ruminants, Lancaster, MTP Press., 103-122.

(25) FORBES, J.M., (1982). Effects of lighting pattern on growth, lactation and food intake of sheep, cattle and deer. Livestock Prod. Sci. 9, 361-374.

(26) WEBSTER, A.J.F., J.S. SMITH and J.M. BROCKWAY, (1972). Effects of isolation, confinment and competition for feed on the energy exchanges of growing Lambs. Ani. Prod. 15, 189-201.

(27) HOLDER, J.M. (1963). Chemostatic regulation of appetite in sheep. Nature, 200, 1074-1075.

(28) FOOT, J.Z. and A.J.F. RUSSEL, (1978). Pattern of intake on three roughage diets by non-pregnant, non-lactating Scottish Blackface ewes over a long period and the effects of previous nutritional history on current intake. Ani. Prod., 26, 203-215.

(29) DARGIE, J.D., (1980). The pathophysiological effects of gastrointestinal and liver parasites in sheep. In Dig. Phy. and Met. in Ruminants. Lancasted MTP Press 349-371.

(30) SYKES, A.R., R.L. COOP and B. RUCHTON, (1980). Chronic subclinical fascioliasis in sheep: effects on food intake, food utilisation and blood constituents. Res. in Vet. Sci. 28, 63-70.

(31) HAWKINS, S.D. and R.S. MORRIS, (1978). Depression of productivity in sheep infected with Fasciola hepatica Vet. Parasi. 4, 341-351.

(32) WHITE, L.M., G.P., HARTMAN and J.W. BERGMAN, (1981). In vitro digestibility, crude protein and phosphorus content of straw of winter wheat, spring wheat, barley and oat cultivars in eastern Montana. Agron. J. 73: 117-121.

(33) COXWORTH, E., J. KERNAN, J. KNIPFEL, O. THORLACIUS and L. CROWLE, (1981). Review: crop residues and forages in western Canada; potential for feed use either with or without chemical or physical processing. Agri. Environm. 6: 245-256.

(34) NICHOLSON, J.W.G., (1984). Digestibility, nutritive value and feed intake. In Sundstol, F. and E. Owen (ed), Straw and other fibrous by-products as feed, Elsevier Sci. Publ. 346-372.

(35) SATTER, L.D. and R.E. ROFFLER, (1975). Nitrogen requirements and utilization in dairy cattle. J. Dairy Sci. 58: 1219-1237.

(36) PIGDEN, W.J. and F. BENDER, (1972). Utilization of lignocellulose by ruminants. Wld. Ani. Rev. 4: 7-10.

(37) EGAN, A.R., (1965). Nutritional status and intake regulation in sheep. III. The relationship between improvement of nitrogen status and increase in voluntary intake of low-protein roughages by sheep. Aust. J. Agric. Res. 16: 463-472.

(38) KEMPTON, T.J., J.V. NOLAN and R.A. LENG, (1979). Protein nutrition of growing Lambs. II. Effects on nitrogen digestion of supplementing a low-protein cellulosic diet with either urea, casein of formaldehyde-treated casein. Br. J. Nutr. 42: 303-315.

(39) TISSERAND, J.L., (1987). Les fourrages pauvres. École Nat. Sup. des Sci. Agron. Appliquées chaire de Zoot. et des Prod. Animals. Dijon-France.

(40) SMITH, T., V.J. BROSTER and R.E. HILL, (1980). A comparison of sources of supplementary nitrogen for young cattle receiving fibre-rich diets J. Agr. Sci. 95: 687-695.

(41) ELLIOT, R. and D.G., ARMSTRONG, (1982). The effect of urea and urea plus sodium sulphate on microbial protein production in the rumen of sheep given diets high in alkali-treated barley straw. J. Agri. Sci. Camb. 99: 51-60.

(42) TRESSOL, J.C. and M. LAMAND, (1979). Cinétique d'apparition et du traitement de la carence en cobalt chez le mouton. Ann. Rech. Vét. 10: 71-75.

(43) DURAND, M. (1987). Conditions for optimizing cellulolytic activity in the rumen. Cost 84 workshop. Methods of evaluating straw in ruminant feeding. Theix – 1987 (in press).

(44) JACKSON, M.G., (1977). Review article: the alkali treatment of straws. Ani. Feed Sci. Techonol., 2: 105-130

(45) OWEN, E., (1978). Processing of roughages. In: W. Haresign and D. Lewis (eds.): Recent Advances in Animal Nutrition. Butterworths, London, 127-148.

(46) SUNDSTOL, F. and E.M. COXWORTH, (1984). Ammonia treatment. In Sundstol, F. and E. Owen (ed), Straw and other fibrous by-products as feed, Elsevier Sci. Publ. 196-247.

(47) CHENOST, M. and C. DEMARQUILLY, (1985). Utilization par les ruminants des fourrages et de sous-produits à très faible valeur nutritive. Symp. on optimizing Ani. Prod. from rou-ghages rations. FAO, Geneva, January 21-25.

(48) MORRIS, P.J. and D.N. MOWAT, (1980). Nutritive value of ground and/or ammoniated corn stover. Can. J. Ani. Sci. 60:327-336.

(49) HADJIPANAYIOTOU, M., (1982). The effect of ammoniation using urea on the intake and nutritive value of chopped barley straw. Grass Forage. Sci., 37:89-93.

(50) DIAS-DA-SILVA, A.A. and SUNDSTOL, (1986). Urea as a source of ammonia for improving the nutritive value of wheat straw. Ani. Feed Sci. and Tech., 14:67-79.

(51) BALCH, C.C. and R.C. CAMPLING, (1965). Rate of passage of digesta through the ruminant digestive tract. In R.W. Dougherty (ed): Physiol. of Dig. in the ruminant, 108-123.

(52) MINSON, D.J., (1982). Effects of chemical and physical composition of herbage eaten upon intake. In Nutr. Limits to Ani. Prod. from pastures: 167-182.

(53) WALKER, H.G., (1984). Physical treatment. In Sundstol, F. and E. Owen (ed), Straw and other fibrous by-products as feed, Elsevier Sci. Publi. 79-105.

(54) BERGNER, H. and R. GORSCH, (1974). Compuestos nitrogenados no proteicos en la fabricación de gránulos de paja. Acribia, Zaragoza.

(55) DIAS-DA-SILVA, A.A., (1985). Valorizaçao alimentar das palhas de cereais usando a ureia como fonte de amoniaco. Univ. Téc. de Lisboa. Inst. Sup. de Agronomia.

(56) CHURCH, D.C. and A. SANTOS, (1981). Effect of graded levels of soybean meal and of a non protein nitrogen-molasses supplement on consumption and digestibility of wheat straw. J. of Ani. Sci. 53, 1609-1615.

(57) O'DONOVAN, P.B. and M.D. GHADAKI, (1973). Effect of diets containing different levels of wheat straw on lamb performance feed intake and digestibility. Ani. Prod. 16, 77-85.

(58) O'DONOVAN, P.B. (1983). Untreated straw as a livestock feed. Nutr. Abs. and Rev. 53: 7.

(59) DEVENDRA, C., (1982). Perspectives in the utilization of untreated rice straw by ruminants in Asia. Paper presented at the Second Annual meeting of the Australian-Asian Fibrous Agr. Res. Research Network, May 3-7: 34.

(60) BINES, J.A., (1985). Feeding systems and food intake by housed dairy cows. Proceeding of the Nut. Soc. 44:355-362.

(61) HEANEY, D.P., G.I. PRITCHARD and W.J. PIGDEN, (1968). Variability in ad libitum forage intakes by sheep. J. of Ani. Sci. 27:159-164.

(62) STREET, M.J., (1979). A pulse-code modulation system for automatic animal identification. J. of Agric. Eng. Res. 24, 248-258.

(63) JACKSON, D.A., J.M. FORBES and C.L. JOHNSON, (1985). A method for the automatic recording of the meals of individual cows offered silage ad libitum and housed in a group. Ani. Prod. 40, 146.

(64) WANGSNESS, P.J., L.E. CHASE, A.B. PETERSON, D.J. KELLMEL and B.R. BAUMGARDT, (1976). System for monitoring feeding behaviour of sheep. J. of Ani. Sci. 42, 1544-154.

(65) CHASE, L.E., P.J. WANGSNESS and B.R. BAUMGARDT, (1976). Feeding behaviours of steers fed a complete mixed ration. J. of Dairy Sci. 59, 1923-1928.

(66) SUZUKI, S., H. FUJITA and Y. SHINDE, (1969). Change in the rate of eating during a meal and the effect of the interval between meals on the rate at which cows eat roughages. Ani. Prod. 11, 29-41.

(67) KENNEY, P.A. and J.L. BLACK, (1984). Factors affecting diet selection by sheep. 4. Levels of feeding. Aus. J. of Agric. Res. 35 (6) 839-843.

(68) OWEN, E. and J.A. KATEGIL, (1984). Straw etc. in practical rations for sheep and goats. In: Sundstol, F. and E. Owen, (ed), Straw and Other Fibrous by-products as Feed, Elsevier Sci. Publ. 454-486.

(69) OWEN, E. (1987). Increasing the intake of straw by goats and sheep by allowing selective feeding - Cost 84 workshop - Methods of evaluating straw in ruminant feeding - Theix - 1987. (in press).

(70) INRA, (1979). Alimentation des ruminants. Versailles; Inst. Nat. de la Rech. Agronomique, 597.

(71) ENGELHARDT, W. von, (1981). Some physiological aspects on the digestion of poor quality, fibrous diets in ruminants. Agric. Environm. 6:145-152.

(72) FARID, M.F.A., (1985). Long-term adaptation of sheep to low protein intake under simulated drought conditions. J. of Arid Environment, 8 (1) 79-83.

(73) XANDÉ, A. (1978). Valeur alimentaire des pailles de céréales chez le mounton. I - Influence de la complémentation azotée et énergétique sur l'ingestion et l'utilization digestive d'une paille d'orge. Ann. Zootech. 27(4) 583-599.

(74) McBURNEY, M.I., (1985). Physical-Chemical and Nutr. Evaluation of Chemical treated feeds for ruminants. Ph. D. Thesis Cornell University.

(75) DULPHY, J.P. and C. DEMARQUILLY, (1983). Voluntary feed consumption as an attribute of feeds-In Feed Information and Ani. Prod. - Ed. G.E. Roboads and R.G. Packham-Com. Agric. Bureau U.K.

IN VIVO DIGESTIBILITY MEASUREMENT of STRAWS

B.G. COTTYN, J.L. DE BOEVER and J.M. VANACKER
National Institute for Animal Nutrition, Scheldeweg 68,
9231 Melle-Gontrode, Belgium

Summary

Sheep are normally used to determine digestibility of straws. Due to a lack of N, digestibility trials with straws must be carried out by difference trials. Straw is generally fed together with a protein rich feedstuff as soybean oil meal to reach 11 % CP in the dry matter of the ration. The reliability of a digestibility trial is lower according as the digestibility of the investigated feedstuff is lower. Digestibility trials with straws conducted by difference trials are therefore less reliable than comparable trials with other feedstuffs in which the feedstuff can be fed alone. Using 5 experimental animals, the standard error on the average organic matter digestibility for digestibility trials with straws amounts to 3.0 comparing with 1.5 for most other feedstuffs. If there is a change in the ration of the experimental animals, an adaptation period of 14 days likes necessary in order to allow an optimal adaptation of the microbial flora in the rumen to the straw ration. To reach a reasonable accuracy in straw digestibility trials a collection period of 10 days is necessary. From literature data, we can assume that for long or coarsely chopped roughages as straws, an increase in feeding level has little or no effect on digestibility. Digestibility trials at maintenance level are easier to standardize and seem therefore also obvious for straws.

1. TYPE OF ANIMALS

Digestibility of feeds for ruminants is commonly determined with sheep in the assumption that cattle and sheep have equal digestive capacity. For the purpose of dairy cattle nutrition, it seems more logical to use cows rather than sheep as experimental animals in digestion trials. Since digestion trials with cows are expensive (animals, feed, equipment) and difficult in execution (separation of faeces and urine), they are usually replaced by the cheaper and simpler digestion trials with sheep, assuming an equal digestion capacity for cattle and sheep.

82 comparative digestion trials, involving 26 maize silages, 24 grass silages, 18 grass hays and 14 other feedstuffs were carried out at our Institute to investigate whether cows and sheep differed in their digestive capacity (1).

From these trials and other literature data (2,3,4,5,6) evidence was presented for some differences in digestive capacity between cows and sheep.

Organic matter of maize silage is somewhat better digested by cows than by sheep, but the difference is small (1-2 %) so that the practical significance of this difference can be questioned. For grass hay, grass silages and mixed ration differences in digestive capacity between cows and sheep depend on quality. Organic matter is better digested by cows in rations of low quality and better by sheep in rations of very high quality. For rations of moderate and good quality, which constitute the major part of the rations in temperate zones, differences are so small that corrections can be neglected. Beyond which quality a correction is needed is not well defined, but until more experimental data are available, positive corrections can be proposed for sheep organic matter digestiblilties lower than 65 % and negative corrections for sheep digestibilities higher than 80 %.

The size of the required corrections for sheep organic matter digestibility (Y) can be estimated with the equation (7)

Y in (%) = 34.8 - 0.48 sheep organic matter digestibility

Lack of data precludes the calculation of corrections for most individual nutrients. Protein is usually better digested by sheep than by cows. For grass hay, grass silage and many mixed rations, a mean difference of 7 % between sheep and cows, as proposed by van Es (8) may be used. However, the difference is rather variable within and between feeds, and for most individual feedstuffs its size is still unknown. In contrast to grassland products and many mixed rations, there appears to be no difference in protein digestibility of maize silage between cows and sheep.

In literature, almost no data are available concerning the digestibility of straws determined simultaneously by sheep and cows. We carried out 2 digestion trials with untreated barley straw with respectively wethers and cows and 2 digestion trials with the same barley straw but treated with 3 % NH$_3$.

The in vivo digestibility was determined by total faeces collection during 10 days with respectively 5 wethers or 5 dry cows. It was strived for feeding animals at maintenance level. Such was not always possible for sheep because straw intake was often too low to reach maintenance level.

The control straws were supplemented with soybean oil meal to reach 11 % CP in the DM of the ration.

Table 1. Digestibility of barley straw fed to wethers or cows

| | Untreated | | + 3 % NH$_3$ | |
	wethers (W)	cows (C)	wethers (W)	cows (C)
Digestibility (%)				
Dry matter	46.5 + 2.1	45.8 + 1.7	60.9 + 1.3	58.4 + 0.9
Organ. matter	48.3 + 2.3	46.4 + 1.8	62.3 + 1.3	59.4 + 1.0
Crude protein	neg.	neg.	30.8 + 7.8	33.5 + 4.1
Crude fibre	55.8 + 2.4	54.6 + 2.2	74.1 + 1.8	69.1 + 1.5
Ether extract	50.0 + 4.1	51.1 + 8.5	49.7 + 6.8	49.5 + 4.8
N-free extract	45.2 + 1.6	43.0 + 2.2	53.0 + 0.8	52.0 + 1.5
Cell walls	53.3 + 2.5	51.6 + 1.9	71.3 + 1.6	66.8 + 1.4

underlined figures are significantly different at P = 0.01

As well the untreated as the treated barley straw was somewhat better digested by wethers than by dairy cows (table 1). For untreated straw the difference was negligible. The dry matter, the organic matter, the crude fibre and the cell walls of the treated straw however were significantly better digested by wethers than by cows. Such is in contradiction with the tendency as above stated that cows digest roughages of low quality better than sheep.

In experiments of Amaning-Kwarteng et al. (9) coarsely-milled NaOH-treated wheat straw was ad libitum fed to 6 wethers or 6 heifers. In accordance with our results for NH_3-treated straw, organic matter digestibility by sheep was 6 % higher than by cattle. N digestion of treated NaOH-straw was 14.6 % higher in sheep than in cattle and amounted to respectively 74.5 and 65.0 %. In our experiments protein digestibility of NH_3-treated straw was however lower in sheep than in cattle and amounted to only 30.8 and 33.5 % (table 1). Such corresponds with an average sheep crude protein digestibility for NH_3-treated straw of 38.8 % reported by Steg and den Boer (10). Due to the low N-content of untreated straw, calculated crude protein digestibility was in our experiments even negative. Negative crude protein digestibility of straw was also found by Steg and den Boer (10) and De Boever et al. (11).

From the above mentioned experiments Amaning-Kwarteng et al. (9) conclude that the assessment of the nutritive value of straw diets should be made with the animal species for which the feeds are intended.

Looking forward to more similar digestion trials with straws carried out simultaneously by sheep and cows, we mean to propose that sheep can be used to determine digestibility of straws. In order to facilitate separation of faeces and urine, castrated male sheep of the local breed are normally used in digestion trials. Extended research on the possible influences of sex, breed or kind of production on digestibility is lacking, but existing data do not suggest any important differences in the digestive capacity of different breeds or sexes or any significant influence of the kind of production of the animal. Digestion coefficients with all kinds of feedstuffs obtained in different places with sheep of different breeds may probably still be used for the different breeds of dairy cows, dry as well as lactating, if these data are obtained in a comparable manner.

2. Required number of animals

Variation in digestive capacity between individuals has been less studied and is usually assumed to be small. Wöhlbier et al. (12), Charlet-Lery (13), Schiemann et al. (14) and Daccord and Schneeberger (15) concluded that the number of experimental animals per digestion trial must amount to a minimum of 3 or 4. Following Forbes et al. (16), Raymond et al. (17) and Balch (18) the required number of animals depends on the desired accuracy : for most purposes 4 animals per treatment are suffi- cient ; to demonstrate small differences in digestibility more animals are required. Daccord and Schneeberger (15) demonstrated that for all rations, it was possible with 4 animals per treatment to discriminate a difference corresponding to 6 % of the digestibility of the organic matter. Schiemann (19) stated that the number of required animals to obtain reliable diges- tion coefficients ($s_{\bar{x}} \leqslant 2.0$ units if the digestibility of the organic mat- ter is lower than 50 % ans $s_{\bar{x}} \leqslant 1.5$ for other cases) depends on the manner upon which digestibility is determined. If the feedstuff to investigate is fed as only feedstuff to the animals, 3 animals are sufficient ; by diffe- rence trials as it is the case for digestion trials with straws 4, 6 or 8 experimental animals are needed depending on the percentage of the feed- stuff to investigate amounts to 50 %, 25 % or less than 25 % of the total ration.

175 digestion trials from which 117 with sheep and 58 with dry cows were carried out at our Institute with respectively maize silage, grass silage, grass hay and concentrates. All these digestion trials were conducted with 5, sometimes 4 experimental animals per digestion trial. For each of these digestion trials, the standard error of the digestibility of each of the nutrients was calculated. The arithmetical average of these standard errors are shown in table 2.

Table 2. Individual variation in digestibility : average standard error (s) on the digestibility of the different nutrients

Feedstuffs	Number of digestion trials	OM	CF	CP	NFE	EE
a. sheep						
Maize silage	46	1.6	3.4	3.5	1.3	1.6
Grass silage	20	1.4	2.1	1.8	1.7	1.7
Grass hay	19	1.4	2.0	2.3	1.4	2.7
Concentrate	32	1.5	5.1	2.3	1.2	1.6
b. Cows						
Maize silage	28	1.5	2.6	1.9	1.3	1.5
Grass silage	15	0.8	1.2	1.4	1.2	1.2
Grass hay	15	0.8	1.1	1.7	1.2	2.0

Animals were fed at about maintenance level (23 g DOM/kg $W^{0.73}$ (20) for sheep and 42.4 VEM $W^{0.75}$ for cows (21) and the feedstuffs were given as sole feedstuffs excepted for digestibility trials with concentrates where a ration of 80 % concentrate and 20 % grass hay was fed. Total faeces collection was always carried out during 10 days.
Table 2 shows that digestion trials carried out as described higher give reliable figures for the digestibility of a feedstuff. The average standard error of organic matter digestibility for trials carried out with sheep varied from 1.4 to 1.6 units and for trials with dry cows only from 0.8 to 1.5. Digestion coefficients obtained with cows are thus on an average more reliable than these obtained with sheep. Such was also demonstrated in trials carried out by Jordan and Staples (22) and Alexander et al. (23). Table 2 shows that little differences between the different feedstuffs seem to exist.
Standard deviation of crude fibre digestibility is highest for maize silage rations and concentrate mixtures. For maize silage rations it amounts to 3.4 and 2.6 for digestibility trials carried out with respectively sheep and cows. Daccord and Schneeberger (15) reported also large standard deviations of the digestibility of crude fibre for maize rations (3.8). Following the authors, maize rations often have a physical structure too fine for optimal fermentation conditions and a normal rate of passage.
Standard deviation of crude protein digestibility for maize silage and of ether extract for grass hay rations in sheep trials are also higher than for other feedstuffs.

18 digestion trials from which 14 were carried out with sheep and 4 with dry cows were carried out with straws. 8 lots of wheat straw and 10 lots of barley straw all or not treated with 3 % NH_3 or urea were involved in the experiments.

The in vivo digestibility was always determined by total faeces collection during 10 days with respectively 5 wethers or 5 dry cows. It was strived for feeding animals at maintenance level. Such was not always possible, as entioned higher, especially for sheep due to the low free intake of straw. The straw was always supplemented with soybean oil meal to reach 11 % crude protein in the dry matter of the ration. Because the value of the added NH_3 by the treated straw for the protein supply of the ruminant remains questionable, about the same ration was fed to determine digestibility of the treated straw.

The digestibility of the soybean meal was determined in a separate digestion trial in which it was fed together with hay with known digestibility so that digestion coefficients of the soybean meal were calculated by difference.

Finally the digestibility of the different nutrients of the straws were calculated by difference from the digestion coefficients of the rations and the digestion coefficients of the soybean meal.

Table 3 shows the individual variation in digestibility of the different nutrients of straw.

Table 3. Individual variation in digestibility average standard error (s) on the digestibility of the different nutrients

	Number of digestion trials	OM	CF	CP	NFE	EE
a. sheep	14	3.0	2.8	7.3	2.4	4.8
b. cows	4	1.6	1.7	4.3	1.9	6.1
c. sheep + cows	18	2.7	2.5	6.8	2.3	5.1
Richter et al. (24)	19	2.6				
Richter et al. (25) sheep	11	2.4	2.5	11.2	2.9	5.7
Steg and den Boer (10) sheep	16	2.5		5.5		

The average standard error obtained by sheep digestion trials carried out by difference, for organic matter, amounts to 3.0 and is considerably higher than the standard error calculated for other feed- stuffs (table 2). For the four digestion trials carried out with dry cows, the average standard error for organic matter digestibility amounts how- ever to only 1.6. Such is in accordance with the data for other feed- stuffs shown in table 2 and confirms that digestion coefficients obtained with cows are more reliable than those obtained with sheep.

Richter et al. (24, 25) and Steg and den Boer (10) obtained standard errors for sheep organic matter digestibility of straw of respectively 2.6 , 2.4 and 2.5 units (table 3). Due to the low crude protein and ether extract content of straw, standard errors of their digestibility coefficients are high.

From a ring test in which 4 centres participated to determine the in vivo digestibility of one lot of wheat- and one lot of barley straw Barber et al. (26) concluded that the repeatability standard deviation between sheep at one centre was $\pm$ 3.1. The reproducibility standard deviation between centres was $\pm$ 4.4.

From these 193 digestion trials from which 18 were carried out with straws, we can conclude that the reliability of a digestion trial decreases according as the digestibility of the investigated feedstuff is lower. Digestion trials with straws carried out by difference trials are therefore less reliable than comparing trials with other feedstuffs in which the feedstuff can be fed alone. We can further conclude that the used experimental technique, with 5 experimental sheep is sufficiently accurate for digestibility research in general. For most feedstuffs the standard error on the average organic matter digestibility remains lower than 1.5. For straw trials carried out with sheep, this value amounts to the double (average st. error of 3.0). Straw digestion trials carried out with dry cows seem to be more accurate (average st. error of organic matt. digest. of 1.6). More data are however desirable to confirm this appointment.

3. Adaptation period

Each change in ration composition causes a change in the microbial rumen composition. Such means that the microbial activity in the rumen is temporary not optimal adapted to the ration from which the digestibility must be determined resulting in a less good utilization. That animal production was indeed pressed during the adaptation period was shown by the results obtained by Chandler et al. (27) with dairy cows and Cook et al. (28) with growing heifers.
It's therefore important to know to what extent digestibility can be influenced during the adaptation period of a digestibility trial. Sasaki et al. (29) demonstrated that the number of protozoa after modification of the ration decreased to reach a minimum value after 3 to 5 days. After that, the number increased gradually to reach its typical value for the new ration after 30 to 35 days. Moseley et al. (30) found however that the microbial population was already adapted to the new ration after 15 days.
Since the microbial population in the rumen varies with the feed, a sufficient long adaptation period for stabilization of the rumen microbes is necessary. In digestion trials with a short preliminary period, risks for diminished digestibility are real, but opinions on the necessary length of this preliminary period are conflicting.
Authors mention a variable duration of their adaptation period by conducting digestion trials with straw rations varying from 7 to 21 days.
Most of them use however an adaptation period of 14 days. In our digestion trials with all kinds of feedstuffs we used an adaptation period of 14 days on the understanding that, before conducting each digestion trial, the animals had passed through a rest period of several weeks, during they were fed grass hay supplemented with concentrate. Xandé (1978) (31) studied the influence of the length of the adaptation period on digestibility of straw rations. For animals which did not receive straw as sole forage before, it seems necessary to insert an adaptation period of minimum 4 to 6 weeks during they receive straw and a supplement.
The necessary duration of the adaptation period remains therefore questionable. Taking into account the possible influence on the digestibility and also the practical and financial influence (time and costs) of a long adaptation period we agree with a variable adaptation

period as proposed by Schiemann (19) :
- 20 days by a radical change in the ration
- 10 days by a normal change in the ration
- 7 days for a similar ration type

4. Duration of measurement

Even with a fixed feeding scheme where the experimental animals are fed on a constant feeding level, daily faeces production of each animal fluctuates (17, 32). Following Schneider and Flatt (33) these fluctuations are more important according as the digestibility of the ration is lower and according as feed intake of the experimental animals is lower.
The necessary collection period to reach a determined accuracy in digestibility will therefore vary in function of feeding level and quality of the ration.
The inaccuracy caused by the daily fluctuations in faeces excretion can be reduced by the prolongation of the collection period (17, 34, 35, 36).
The length of the faeces collection period used by different authors is variable. Specific for digestion trials with straw rations, we noted in the literature collection periods varying from minimum 5 to maximum 10 days, the last period eventually spread over 2 weeks. Schiemann (19) prescribes for feedstuffs a collection period of minimum 6 days with a recommendation of 10 days. Following van Es and van der Meer (37) the length of the collection period should be two weeks following a preliminary period of 10–20 days or longer (the longer the greater the change in the diet). Taking into account that fluctuations in faeces production are more important according as the digestibility of the ration is lower, a collection period for straw digestibility trials of minimum 10 days seems us necessary.

5. Feeding level

Aerts (7) showed from a comprehensive review of existing literature data that the influence of feeding level on digestibility is a very complicated and conflicting subject. Although some authors report a significant decrease in digestibility according to higher feeding level, most agree actually that for long or coarsely chopped roughages, as straws an increase in feeding level has little or no effect on digestibility. Possible reasons are that the aperture between the reticulo-rumen and omassun constitutes a physical barrier against increase in rate of passage of the roughage, or that the possible increase in feeding level with roughages is too small to cause a clear and significant effect. Both reasons do not hold for ground and pelleted roughages so that it is not surprising that with such feeds a distinct decrease in digestibility with increasing feeding level is usually observed. However its magnitude per unit increase in feeding level is very variable.
In experiments with maize silage and concentrates Aerts (7) reported indeed a decrease in digestibility of 4 % per increase of the feeding level with one unit as accepted in the VEM system of van Es. For mixed diets published data mainly indicate a negative but variable influence of feeding level on digestibility, but the effect may also be absent or even positive.
Van Es and van der Meer (37) stated that the effect of feeding level is small (in most cases less than 3 units of digestibility per multiple of maintenance). The authors stated further that deviations ranging from 10 to 25 % from maintenance level are permitted for digestibility trials. Taking all data together, there seems to be no simple relation between the magnitude of the feeding level effect and the percentage of concentrates in the diet.

This leads to 2 main conclusions :
1. The effect of feeding level on digestibility seems to be variable and complex, possibly with interactions between feeding level and other factors such as physiological status of the animal, diet composition (ingredients and/or chemical components), animal species, duration of adaptation to the diet, etc. Until now, little is known on these interactions ; the subject needs further investigation.
2. Since the effect of feeding level is variable and as far unpredictable, conversion of digestibility coefficients determined at higher feeding levels to maintenance level and vice versa is problematical.
    Digestibility trials at maintenance level are easier to standardize and have the advantages that the results are more reproducible (no refusals) and also that most digestibility coefficients in the world determined sofar at maintenance level can be used as they are reasonably comparable. A disadvantage is the insufficiently known correction needed for conversion of the maintenance data to higher feeding levels. Determination at higher feeding levels or ad libitum intake, as is done in France, partly obviates the feeding level effect, but in practical dairy cattle feeding, feeding levels may vary between 1 and 5 times maintenance level, and furthermore it is not known whether the feeding level effect of a given feed will be the same in other diet combinations.
Following norms are recommended in the literature to calculate maintenance level of sheep for digestibility trials :
    23 g DOM/kg $W^{0.75}$ (Osbourn et al. 1975, 20)
    26 g DOM/kg $W^{0.75}$ (INRA, 1978, 38)
    13 $\pm$ 2 g DM/kg L.W. average ash content 100 g/kg DM
        (Schiemann, 1981, 19)
    40 g DM/kg $W^{0.75}$ (Van Es and van der Meer, 1980, 37)

6. Level and nature of supplementation - Rationing
    Schiemann (19) prescribes that a feedstuff can be fed alone in digestibility trials, if the digestibility of the organic matter remains between 55 and 75 %, and if the physical structure guarantees a normal rumen fermentation. If difference trials are necessary (digest. OM < 55 or > 75 %), it's important to replace a large part of the basic ration by the feedstuff from which the digestibility must be determined.
Inclusion of at least 20 % long forage in the ration prevents abnormal fermentation ; the diets should also not contain more than 5 % unsaturated, 10 % saturated fat or 10 % di- and monosaccharides (37).
Following ration norms are recommended by Schiemann (19) : crude fibre content $\geqslant$ 180 g/kg DM ; crude protein content (incl. NPN) $\geqslant$ 120 g/kg DM and maximum 200 g/kg DM ; starch content $\leqslant$ 400 g/kg DM and sugar content $\leqslant$ 200 g/kg DM.
Feedstuffs as straw with a strong divergent composition cannot therefore be fed alone in a digestibility trial. Lack of nitrogen disturbs a normal microbial growth and digestibility in the rumen. Following van Es and van der Meer (37) rumen microbes need for optimal growth and fermentation both ammonia-N and small amounts of protein- or peptide-N and at least 1.6 % total N in the dry matter. Because some peptides are required by the cellulolytic bacteria, rations or feed with less than 1.6 % N should be fortified with soybean meal-N up to that level. Lower N-contents should lead to lower digestibility of the cell walls. High crude protein contents (> 13 %) are also poorly suited, as they result in higher ammonia levels in the forestomachs. Most of this ammonia is absorbed into the blood, so that the analysis of feed and faeces suggests a higher digestibility of N x 6.25 than is actually the case.

44

Following Xandé (31) the addition of N on the one side stimulates appetite in straw rations by re-establishing N equilibrium of the animal and on the other side, it allows an increase of the rumen microflora and the cellulolytic activity resulting in a decrease of the rate of passage of the straw in the rumen.

As well soybean meal, urea-N or an other protein rich feedstuff can be used to increase N-content of straw rations.

A comparison of ME measurements in straw using either the difference technique (straw + hay) or feeding ad libitum with urea and minerals (direct method) has been reported by den Braver (39) in Sweden and indicated little difference between the two methods. If urea is added it's assumed that the urea-N is digested to 100 % ; this is not fully correct as some urea is utilized by microorganisms that does not become entirely digested. If soya bean meal is added its digestibility must be determined in a separate difference trial in which it's fed together with a long forage.

In work carried out in the UK (40) three evaluation methods were used to determine digestibility of straw : straw fed ad libitum supplemented with 25 g urea per 100 kg liveweight for untreated straw only ; straw fed with dried grass and the digestibility values calculated by difference and straw fed at 2 levels with maize germ meal and the results calculated by regression. The smallest within centre variability was observed using the ad libitum method and the largest variability was observed using the difference method.

REFERENCES

(1) AERTS, J.V., DE BOEVER, J.L., COTTYN, B.G., DE BRABANDER, D.L. and BUYSSE, F.X. 1984. Comparative digestibility of feedstuffs by sheep and cows. Anim. Feed Sci. Technol. 12 : 47.

(2) WAINMAN, F.W. 1977. Digestibility and balance in ruminants. Proc. Nutr. Soc. 36 : 195.

(3) PLAYNE, M.J. 1978. Differences between cattle and sheep in their digestion and relative intake of mature tropical grass hay. Animal Feed Sci. Technol. 3 : 41.

(4) VAN SOEST, P.J. 1980. The limitations of ruminants. Proc. Cornell Nutr. Conf. p. 78.

(5) POPPI, D.P., MINSON, D.J. and TERNOUTH, J.H. 1981. Studies of cattle and sheep eating leaf and stem fractions of grasses. 1. The voluntary intake, digestibility and retention time in the reticulo-rumen. Aust. J. Agric. Res. 32 : 99.

(6) POPPI, D.P., MINSON, D.J. and TERNOUTH, J.H. 1981. Studies of cattle and sheep eating leaf and stem fractions of grasses. 3. The retention time in the rumen of large feed particles. Aust. J. Agric. Res. 32 : 123.

(7) AERTS, J.V. 1984. Studie van de VEM-waarde van voedermiddelen voor melkvee. Doctorale tesis, Louvain-la-Neuve, Belgique, 1984, 382 p.

(8) VAN ES, A.J.H. 1978. Feed evaluation for ruminants. 1. The systems in use from May 1977 onwards in the Netherlands. Livestock Prod. Sci. 5 : 331.

(9) AMANING-KWARTENG, K. KELLAWAY, R.C., SPRAGG, J.C. and KIRBY, ADRIENNE C. 1986. Relative intakes, digestibility and bacterial protein synthesis by sheep and cattle fed high-roughage diets. Anim. Feed Sci. Technol. 16 : 75.

(10) STEG, A. en den BOER, D.J. 1982. Voederwaardeschatting van ontsloten ruwvoer. Bedrijfsontwikkeling 13 : 607.

(11) DE BOEVER, J.L., COTTYN, B.G., DE BRABANDER, D.L. et BUYSSE, F.X. 1987. Traitement de la paille. 1. Effet de l'ammoniac sur la composition, la digestibilité et la valeur alimentaire. Revue de l'Agric. 40 : 347.

(12) WÖHLBIER, W., KIRCHGESSNER, M. und SCHNEIDER, W. 1956. Die Zuverlässigkeit von experimenten mit Schweinen und Rindern ermittelten Verdauungsquotienten. Z. Tierphysiol., Tierernährg. u. Futtermittelkde 11 : 139.

(13) CHARLET-LERY, G. 1969. Methods for determination of digestibility coefficients of feeds for ruminants. EAAP Report n° 1 from the Study Commission on Animal Nutrition, pp. 33.

(14) SCHIEMANN, R., NEHRING, K., HOFFMANN, L., JENTSCH, W. und CHUDY, A. 1971. Energetische Futterbewertung und Energienormen. VEB Deutscher Landwirtschaftsverslag, Berlin, pp. 344.

(15) DACCORD, R. and SCNEEBERGER, H. 1986. Variability and repeatability of digestibility evaluated on sheep. J. Anim. Physiol. a. Anim. Nutr. 56 : 35.

(16) FORBES, E.B., ELLIOTT, R.F., SWIFT, R.W., JAMES, W.H. and SMITH, V.F. 1946. Variation in determination of digestive capacity of sheep. J. Anim. Sci. 5 : 298.

(17) RAYMOND, W.F., HARRIS, C.E. and HARKER, V.G. 1953. Studies on the digestibility of herbage. I. Technique of measurement of digestibility and some observations on factors affecting the accuracy of digestibility data. J. Br. Grassld. Soc. 8 : 301.

(18) BALCH, CC. 1969. In "Charlet-Lery, Methods for determination of digestibility coefficients of feeds for ruminants. EAAP Report N° 1.

(19) SCHIEMANN, R. 1981. Methodische Richtlinien zur Durchführung von Verdauungsversuchen für die Futterwertschätzung. Arch. Tierernährg. 31 : 1.

(20) OSBOURN, D.F., CAMMELL, S.B., TERRY, R.A. and OUTEN, G.E. 1975. Forage composition and the conduct of digestion trials for the comparative evaluation of laboratory procedures. J. Br. Grassld. Soc. 30 : 101.

(21) VAN ES, A.J.H. 1978. Feed evaluation for ruminants. I. The systems in use from may 1977 onwards in the Netherlands. Livest. Prod. Sci. 5 : 331.

(22) JORDAN, R.M. and STAPLES, G.E. 1951. Digestibility comparisons between steers and lambs fed prairie hays of different quality. J. Anim. Sci. 10 : 236.

(23) ALEXANDER, R.A., HENTGES, J.F.Jr., MCCALL, J.T. and ASH, W.O. 1962. Comparative digestibility of nutrients by cattle and sheep. J. Anim. Sci. 19 : 1302.

(24) RICHTER, W.J.F., BARANOWSKI, A. und KOCH, G. 1978. Zum Futterwert von aufgeschlossenem Stroh. 1. Mitteilung : Bertimmung der Enzymlöslichkeit von Stroh zur Bewertung der AufschluBwirkung durch Natronlauge. Das wirtschaftseigene Futter 24 : 198.

(25) RICHTER, W.J.F., BARANOWSKI, A. und KOCH, G. 1980. Zum Futterwert von aufgeschlossenem Stroh. 2. Mitteilung : Untersuchungen zur AufschluBwirkung von Ammoniak. Das wirtschafteigene Futter 26 : 165.

(26) BARBER, W.P., ALDERMAN, G., ADAMSON, A.H. and MANSBRIDGE, R.J. 1983. Chemical treatment of cereal straws by on-farm processes. Animals as Waste Converters, Proc. of an Int. Symp. Wageningen, 30 nov.-2 dec. 1983 p. 48.

(27) CHANDLER, P.T., JOHN E. and MILLER, C.N. 1975. Lactational response of dairy cows inoculated with live adapted rumen microorganisms. J. Dairy Sci. 58 : 1660.

(28) COOK, M.K., COOLEY, J.H. and HUBER, T.L. 1975. Performance of cattle inoculated with rumen bacteria. J. Anim. Sci. 41 : 396.

(29) SASAKI, M., YAMATANI, Y. and OTANI, I. 1973. Effects of abrupt feed change on the rumen contents. Nutr. Abstr. Rev. 43 : 707.

(30) MOSELEY, J.E., COPPOCK, C.E. and LAKE, G.B. 1976. Abrupt changes in forage-concentrate ratios of complete feeds fed ad libitum to dairy cows. J. Dairy Sci. 59 : 1471.

(31) XANDE, A. 1978. Valeur alimentaire des pailles de céréales chez le mouton. I. Influence de la complémentation azotée et énergétique sur l'ingestion et l'utilisation digestive d'une paille d'orge. Ann. Zootech. 27 : 583.

(32) LLOYD, L.E., PECKHAM, H.E. and CRAMPTON, E.W. 1956. The effect of change of the ration on the required length of preliminary feeding period in digestion trials with sheep. J. Anim. Sci. 15 : 846.

(33) SCHNEIDER, B.H. and FLATT, W.P. 1975. The evaluation of feeds through digestibility experiments. The University of Georgia Press, Athens, pp. 423.

(34) AXELSSON, J. and KIVIMAE, A. 1951. Comparison between accuracies of the direct and indirect methods in digestion trials with wethers . Acta Agr. Scand. 1 : 282.

(35) GREENHALGH, J.F.D., CORBETT, J.L. and McDONALD, I. 1960. The direct estimation of the digestibility of pasture herbage. II. Regressions of digestibility on faecal nitrogen concentration ; their determination in continuous digestibility trials and the effect of various factors on their accuracy. J. Agric. Sci. 55 : 377.

(36) TILLMAN, A.D., CHAPPEL, C.F., SIRNY, R.J. and MacVICAR, R. 1954. The effect of alfalfa ash upon digestibility of prairie hay by sheep. J. Anim. Sci. 13 : 417.

(37) VAN ES, A.J.H. and VAN DER MEER, J.M. 1980. Methods of analysis for predicting the energy and protein value of feeds for farm animals. Workshop on Methodology of analysis of feeding stuffs for ruminants, Lelystad (The Netherlands), 27-29 May 1980.

(38) INRA, 1978. Alimentation des Ruminants. Ed. INRA Publications 78000 Versailles.

(39) Den Braver, E.J. 1974. Determination of metabolisable energy in straw for ruminants by in vivo and in vitro methods. Swedish J. Agric. Res. 4 : 53.

(40) Givins, D.I., Dewey, P.J.S., Donaldson, E., Jones, D.I.H. and Adamson, A.H. 1987. Within and between centre variability in the measurement of in vivo organic matter digestibility of straw. EEC Workshop "Methods of evaluation of straws in ruminant feeding." INRA, Theix, France 2-4th June.

STRAW DIGESTIBILITY CALCULATION
AND DIGESTIVE INTERACTIONS

Daniel SAUVANT, Sylvie GIGER
STATION DE NUTRITION ET ALIMENTATION (INRA) DE L'INA PG
16, rue Claude Bernard - 75231 PARIS CEDEX 05

I - INTRODUCTION

The energy values of straws may vary a lot, because they depend on the vegetal species or varieties (ANDRIEU and DEMARQUILLY, 1985), on the technological treatment (CHENOST and DULPHY, 1987), on the nature of the associated feed (CHENOST, 1987) and of the level of intake (DULPHY et al., 1982a). As the organic matter digestibility (OMd) is the determinant factor of the straw energy value (figure 1), it is necessary to focus the attention on the experimental method which can be used to achieve these OMd values with a maximum of precision.

Numerous studies concerning the methodological aspects of in vivo digestibility measurements (animal preparation, faeces collection period duration, animals number, repetitions, feeding level...) have already been done (CHARLET-LERY, 1969 ; RRI, 1975 ; SCHNEIDER and FLATT, 1975 ; DEMARQUILLY and BOISSAU, 1976). In this paper, the attention will be mainly focused on problems associated with the methods available to calculate the digestibility coefficient.

II - OVERVIEW OF THE METHODS AVAILABLE TO CALCULATE THE DIGESTIBILITY COEFFICIENT

1. GENERAL PRINCIPLES

The estimation of the coefficient of digestibility (d) is based on the principle of additivity for the quantities of the different digestible nutrients. For example, when the organic matter (OM) is the considered constituent, the digestible organic matter intake (DOMI) of a diet including n ingredients i is :

$$DOMI = \sum_{i=1}^{n} DOMI_i \qquad (1)$$

Where $DOMI_i$ is the digestible organic matter intake of the ingredient i.

Equation 1 is equivalent with the following expression including the diet organic matter digestibility (OMd_d) :

$$OMd_d = \sum_{i=1}^{n} p_i . OMd_i \qquad (2)$$

Where p_i is the OM proportion of the ingredient i in the diet organic matter ($\sum_{i=1}^{n} p_i = 1$) and OMd_i is the OM digestibility coefficient of the ingredient i. The same approach can be performed to evaluate the digestibility of other constituents than OM, when using for p_i the percentage of the considered constituent for a given ingredient.

If straw (s) and concentrate (c) are the sole constituents of a diet, the equation (2) becomes :

$$OMD_d = p_s \, OMd_s + p_c \, OMd_c \qquad (2')$$

As the OM proportions of straw and concentrate in the diet are linked by the relationship : $p_s + p_c = 1$, the number of parameters can be reduced.

The various methods of the estimation of the OM digestibility are issued from the equations (2) and (2').

2. DESCRIPTION OF THE MAIN METHODS AVAILABLE TO CALCULATE THE DIGESTIBILITY COEFFICIENT

a. The difference method

If straw (s) is considered as the first ingredient in the equation (2), its OMd_s can be expressed as :

$$OMd_s = \frac{1}{P_s} \left(OMd_d - \sum_{i=2}^{n} p_i \cdot OMd_i \right) \qquad (3)$$

This way of calculation needs to experimentally measure the OMd_d and OMd_i values. If the ingredients i are forages (DULPHY, KOUASSI and BIENAIME, 1982b), their digestibilities have to be measured separately, but, if they are concentrates, two kinds of situations are encountered : specific experimental measurements with a forage chosen to minimize the digestive interactions (see latter) or the use of OMd_i table values. If the percentage of a constituent may vary between the m repetition j for a given ingredient (example : straw), we have proposed (GIGER and SAUVANT, 1983) to take this fact into account through a ponderated system :

$$OMd_s = \frac{\sum_{j=1}^{m} P_{sj} \cdot OMd_{sj}}{\sum_{1}^{m} P_{sj}}$$

Such a way of calculation includes the variations of the uncertainties related to the different values of p_{sj}.

When straw is combined at a proportion p_s in the diet with only an other feed, its OM digestibility is obtained from the relationship :

$$OMd_s = \frac{1}{p_s} \left(OMd_d - (1 - p_s) \, OMd_c \right)$$

b. The equation system method

This method consists in performing n measurements with
various values of p_i in order to obtain a system of n
equations (2) which can be solved to calculate the n OMd$_i$
values used as unknown variates. This method was described by
VON KNIEREM (1900) and GASNIER and VACHEL (1952) in the case
of two ingredients. For example, if they are straw (s) and
concentrate (c), and if two experimental measurements 1 and 2
have been done :

$$\begin{cases} OMd_{d1} = P_{s1}.OMd_s + P_{c1}.OMd_c \\ OMd_{d2} = P_{s2}.OMd_s + P_{c2}.OMd_c \end{cases}$$

from this system, the OMd$_s$ and OMd$_c$ values are calculated by
the expressions :

$$OMd_s = \frac{P_{c1}.OMd_{d2} - P_{c2}.OMd_{d1}}{P_{c2} - P_{c1}} \qquad OMd_c = \frac{P_{s1}.OMd_{d2} - P_{s2}.OMd_{d1}}{P_{c2} - P_{c1}}$$

c. The regression method

The context is similar to the previous ones but present data
are adjusted through a multiple regression procedure. In this
case, m trials j are carried out and data are adjusted with a
multiple regression model :

$$OMd_{dj} = \sum_{i=1}^{n} OMd_i.pi + ej$$

In the case of two ingredients, as for example, straw (s) and
concentrate (c), the equation is directly issued from the
equation (2') :

$$OMD_{dj} = \alpha \, c + \beta + ej$$

The data adjustement allows to estimate the parameters α and
β which are respectively equal to (OMd$_c$ - OMd$_s$) and OMd$_s$.

3. PRECISION OF THE METHODS

The precision is quantified by the standard deviation (SD(OMd$_s$))
or variance (SD^2(OMd$_s$)) which are linked to the experimental
OMd$_s$ data measurements. In this part, the imprecisions caused by
the digestive interaction are not considered. In the case of the
difference method (equation 3), if we assume that the various
OMd$_i$ values are independent, the precision is :

$$SD^2(OMd_s) = \frac{1}{P_s^2} . SD^2(OMdd) + \sum_{1=2}^{n} \left(\frac{P_i}{P_s}\right)^2 . SD^2(OMd_i)$$

This expression emphasizes the influence of the p_s values maximization and $SD(OMd_d)$ or $SD(OMd_i)$ values minimization to improve the precision of the OMd_s knowledge. Figure 2 illustrates this situation when $SD(OMd_d)$ and $SD(OMd_i)$ are equal to 2 and 3 points respectively.

When straw is combined with a concentrate the digestibility of which is considered as known with no imprecision, the previous expression becomes simpler :

$$SD(OMd_s) = \frac{SD\ (OMd_d)}{P_s}$$

When the equation system method is used for two ingredients and two levels of incorporation, the precision for the straw digestibility measurement is :

$$SD(OMd_s) = SD(OMd_d) . \left\{ \frac{P_{ci}^2 + P_{c2}^2}{(P_{c2} - P_{c1})^2} \right\}^{1/2}$$

This expression points out that the improvement in precision can be obtained by increasing both the mean straw proportion and the difference between the two levels of incorporation.

With the regression method, reliable OMd_i values depend first on the dependance level of the p_i values which must be minimized, and the regression calculation provides SD values for each digestibility coefficient. Moreover the e_j variations must be carefully studied to detect biases.

If the straw is combined, through the m trials j, with only an other ingredient, the precision is :

$$SD(OMD_s) = SD(OMd_d) \left\{ 1 + \frac{1}{m} + \frac{(1 - \bar{P}_s)^2}{\sum_j (P_{sj} - \bar{P}_s)^2} \right\}^{1/2} \quad \text{WITH} \quad \bar{P}_s = \frac{1}{m} . \sum_{j=1}^{m} P_{sj}$$

This expression emphasizes the necessity of maximisation of the mean proportion of straw (p_s), number of observation (m) and range of values around p_s to improve the precision on OMd_s value.

III - THE DIGESTIVE INTERACTIONS

1. GENERAL PRINCIPLES

A digestive interaction (I) can be considered as a lack of additivity between the digestible nutrients within a diet. For instance, when considering the OM, the equation (1) becomes :

$$DOMI = \sum_{i=1}^{n} DOMI_i + I$$

depending on the sign of the term I, positive or negative interactions are distinguished. Digestive interactions are of great importance in the straw digestibility evaluation, because this feed must be pratically associated with a complement which can induce a positive or negative interaction (XANDE, 1978 ; DULPHY, KOUASSI and BIENAIME, 1982b). The problem can be more complex when the sign of interaction depends on the percentage of concentrate (DULPHY et al., 1983).

Several aspects are involved in digestive interactions. They mainly deal with the reticulo-ruminal microbial activity variations (figure 3). These variations are caused by the presence of limiting factors of various natures of this activity : lack of essential nutrients (NH_3, amino acids, minerals...) or unfavorable influence of an ecological parameter (low pH...). Numerous works have dealt until now with these ruminal interactions (see for instance, MOULD, ORSKOV and MANNS, 1983).

The particulate transit is an other cause of lack of additivity. This phenomenon affects mainly constituents such as the cell wall (CW) which are slowly degraded in the rumen and present moreover lag phases of degradation which are proportional to the CW (SAUVANT et al., 1986). As a consequence, the difference between the potentially degradable CW (PDCW) and "effective" degradable CW (EDCW) with a 0.05 h^{-1} transit is not linear.

$$PDCW - EDCW^{0.05} = 0.202 \ (PDCW)^{1.22} \qquad (n = 24, R = 0.91)$$

Moreover, this difference between PDCW and EDCW increases with particulate removing rate.

2. QUANTIFICATION OF THE INTERACTION

The classical method used to quantify the digestive interaction is based on the interpretation of digestibility trials.

If the mixed diet is studied with only one level of straw incorporation and if the feed complement does not vary in digestibility, the interaction effect is entirely reported on the straw digestibility. This conventional method represents the classical way to test the influence of various feed complementation on straw digestibility (XANDE, 1978 ; DULPHY, KOUASSI and BIENAIME, 1982b).

The drawback of this approach is to carry back the interaction effect to only one of the diet constituent which is the straw in this case ; moreover, for a poor forage such as a straw, it is therefore necessary to indicate several digestibilities and energy values according to the complementation (table 1).

If the range of straw incorporation values allows to use the regression method, it becomes possible to use a quadratic model to take into account the interaction effect. The first Rowett Research Institute Report (RRI, 1975) proposed to fit the data by the model :

$$OMd_d = OMd_s \cdot p_s + OMd_c \ (1-p_s) + I \cdot p_s \cdot (1-p_s)$$

where the interaction term I represents the lack from linearity and must be statistically tested. GIGER and SAUVANT (1983) proposed to fit the data by the model :

$$OMd_d = a(p_s)^2 + b.p_s + c$$

Where the c parameter is equal to OMd_c , while OMd_s is equal to a + b + c. With such a model, it is possible to quantify the interaction as the maximum difference value between the linear and quadratic models. The same authors evocated the possibility to take into account the feeding level by adding it at a linear and quadratic level in the previous equation.

With the same kind of experimental data, it is possible to test the digestive interaction by comparing statistically the straw digestibility when given alone, with the predicted value extrapolated from the mixed diet digestibility data adjustement.

The in sacco procedure was frequently used to test the interaction effect on ruminal digestion activity. When a same feed is included as a repetition within a same diet, it must be noticed, the variations are not negligible (figure 4) ; it is consequently necessary to take care of the experimental device to be able to detect low differences in ruminal digestion capacity.

This approach was frequently used with straw used as standards in the nylon bags procedure in order to evaluate the influence of the diet forage/concentrate ratio on the rumen cellulolytic activity. Recently, (DULPHY, KOMAR and ZWAENEPOEL, 1984) and RAMIHONE and CHENOST (1987) have used it to test the unfavourable influence of the ammonia treatment on in sacco straw degradation ; moreover, the lattest authors demonstrated the favourable influence of fish meal complementation on ruminal digestion capacity. The same method was also applied to study the difference between the in vivo and in sacco cell wall digestion of diets (UDEN, 1984).

3. THE DIGESTIVE INTERACTION CONTROL

To maximize the straw digestion, it is necessary to decrease at the same time negative effects and to increase the positive ones by a suited diet formulation. The various new protein unit systems, such as the PDI one, present the advantage of taking into account the mean nitrogen and energy supplies to microbial population. They consequently allow to control at a certain level the digestive interactions, particularly those due to a lack of ruminal degradable protein in comparison with the energy ones.

However, these systems are now not able to practically prevent efficiently negative interactions which can occur during several hours per day consecutive to dynamic particularities of feed digestion or to feeding frequency. The first one will only be considered here, but buffer supplementation or feeding frequency effects on straw digestibility have already been studied by OSBOURN et al. (1970) and DULPHY and BIENAIME (1983).

It is nowadays possible to take partly into account some dynamic aspects of the reticulo-ruminal digestion with the in sacco method. In fact, through standardization with a diet such as lucerne hay combined with a concentrate blend, in a 75/25 ratio, the nylon bag method allows to approach the potential degradation rate of various feed constituents and to use it as a feed attribute. The knowledge of the feed composition permits to calculate the constituents quantities which disappeared from bags during the different incubation time intervals (t_i, t_{i+1}). Moreover, as particulate matter is submitted to transit, it is necessary to take this phenomenon into account by multiplying each quantity by the expression $(e^{kt_i}+e^{kt_{i+1}})/2$, where k is the particulate removing rate (KRISTENSEN, MULLER and HVELPLUND, 1982). Table 2 indicates, for a set of feed, the quantities of degraded crude protein ($DCP_{(t_i, t_{i+1})}$) during five time intervals with the assumption of a transit of $0.05h^{-1}$. The table 3 is similar to the previous one, but deals with the degraded organic matter ($DOM_{t_i, t_{i+1}}$) quantities. At each time interval, the $DCP_{(t_i, t_{i+1})}$ and $DOM_{(t_i, t_{i+1})}$ quantities are respectively able to sustain theorically by two ways the microbial crude protein synthesis ($MCP_{(t_i, t_{i+1})}$: $a.DCP_{(t_i, t_{i+1})}$ and $b.DOM_{(t_i, t_{i+1})}$. The effective $MCP_{(t_i, t_{i+1})}$ is equal to the minimum of these two values :

$$MCP\ (_{t_i,\ t_{i+1}}) = min\ \left[a.DCP\ (_{t_i,\ t_{i+1}}),\ b.DOM\ (_{t_i,\ t_{i+1}})\right]$$

Thus, each feed is characterized by its ability to promote MCP at different time intervals, from its DCP and DOM contents. If digestion beyond 48 hours is neglected, the proteosynthesis induced by a feed is equal to :

$$MCP = \sum_{i=1}^{n} MCP\ (_{t_i,\ t_{i+1}}) = \sum_{i=1}^{n} min\ \left[a.DCP\ (_{t_i,\ t_{i+1}}),\ b.DOM\ (_{t_i,\ t_{i+1}})\right]$$

In a first approach of the problem, the values of the parameter a is 1 g MCP/g DCP assuming the efficiency of DCP into MCP is 1 when available nitrogen is a limiting factor and the parameter b value is equal to 0.2 g of MCP/g of DOM. (DEMARQUILLY, ANDRIEU and SAUVANT, 1978).

These new feed characteristics can be used in diet formulation to try to obtain an harmonization between the nitrogen and OM available for microbial proliferation. Moreover, this latter can be more regularly controlled in time. For instance, a 50/50 blend of maize/soybean meal is able to promote a more regular microbial proliferation in time than a barley/groundnut meal one (table 4). The first blend is consequently, a priori, more suited for straw complementation than the second one.

From a practical point of view, the calculations become rapidly laborious, especially if various other diet characteristics must be taken into account. Therefore, we recommand to use a linear programming procedure to solve such a problem. For each time interval (t_i, t_{i+1}), the program uses a couple of equations :

$$\begin{cases} \sum_j (MCPN_{(ti, \, ti+1)})_{ij} \cdot X_j = MCPN_{(ti, \, ti+1)} \\ \sum_j (MCPOM_{(ti, \, ti+1)})_{ij} \cdot X_j = MCPOM_{(ti, \, ti+1)} \end{cases}$$

where :

. $MCPN_{(ti, \, ti+1)}$ is the microbial protein synthesis from nitrogen degradation of feed j during time interval (t_i, t_{i+1}) : $MCPN_{(ti, \, ti+1)} = DCP_{(ti, \, ti+1)}$,

. $MCPOM_{(ti, \, ti+1)}$ is the microbial protein synthesis from organic matter degradation of feed j during the time interval (t_i, t_{i+1}) : $MCPOM_{(ti, \, ti+1)} = 0.2 \, DOM_{(ti, \, ti+1)}$.

. X_j are the proportions of the ingredients j in the diet.

For the same time interval, an equilibrium between the diet MCPN and MCPOM must be respected to avoid, from one hand, ammonia losses and risks of toxicity due to an exces of NCPN relative to MCPOM and, from the other hand a pH drop and a nitrogen deficit for microbes due to an exces of MCPOM relative to MCPN

$$\begin{cases} MCPN_{(ti, \, ti+1)} - MCPOM_{(ti, \, ti+1)} \leqslant Y_{(ti, \, ti+1)} \\ MCPN_{(ti, \, ti+1)} - MCPN_{(ti', \, ti+1)} \leqslant Z_{(ti, \, ti+1)} \end{cases}$$

The $Y_{(ti, \, ti+1)}$ and $Z_{(ti, \, ti+1)}$ values must be as low as possible to avoid the above mentioned drawbacks.

The optimization procedure corresponds to a maximization of the microbial proliferation, as it must not be limited by a nitrogen lack we suggest to use the function :

$$Max \left[\sum_j MCPOM_{(ti, \, ti+1)} \right]$$

It is obvious that other contraints must be included in such a linear program model to take into account diet parameters such as :

. minimum of diet energy content,

. minimum of diet undegradable protein,

. etc...

IV - THE STRAW ENERGY VALUE CALCULATION

The straw metabolisable energy (ME) content is significantly determined by its OM digestibility, as the ME increase is of 0.148MJ/kg DM per point of OM digestibility (Rowett Research Institute Report n°4, RRI, 1984 ; figure 1).

A part this data, the straw energy value is calculated from its digestibility and the basis of the passage relationships used in the different energy systems. Figure 5 indicates that these various ways of calculation provide in some cases large differences of the straw energy value related to the barley one (VAN DER HONING and STEG, 1979).

V - CONCLUSION

The OM digestibility, and consequently the energy value, of the straw given alone present almost no practical significance. Consequently, straw digestion determination must be carried out within a diet.

The different methods of straw digestibility calculation which can be used depend on the experimental design and it seems necessary to adopt a design which enables the use of a calculation procedure testing the existence of a digestive interaction. The precision of the obtained values and the way of their obtention seem of great interest for the use of them.

As the digestive interaction is an important problem, more research is needed to explain more completely the implicated mechanisms and to control them in the right direction. A method of approach was presented on this aspect, but its interest needs to be experimentally confirmed.

BIBLIOGRAPHY

ANDRIEU J., DEMARQUILLY C., 1985 - p. 163-182, in "Les fourrages secs, récolte, traitement, utilisation". (C. DEMARQUILLY ed.) INRA, Paris (FRANCE), 689 p.

CHARLET-LERY G., 1969 - FEZ, Commission d'alimentation des animaux domestiques - n° 1068/63

CHENOST M., 1987 - p. 183-198, in "Les fourrages secs : récolte, traitement, utilisation". (C. DEMARQUILLY ed.). INRA, Paris (FRANCE). 689 p.

CHENOST M., DULPHY J.P., 1987 - p. 199-230, in "Les fourrages secs : récolte, traitement, utilisation". (C. DEMARQUILLY ed.). INRA, Paris (FRANCE). 689 p.

DEMARQUILLY C., ANDRIEU J., SAUVANT D., 1978 - p. 469-518 in "Alimentation des ruminants". (ed. R. JARRIGE). INRA, Versailles, (FRANCE). 597 p.

DEMARQUILLY C., BOISSAU J.M., 1976 - CRZV - INRA THEIX (octobre 1976) 6p.

DULPHY J.P., BIENAIME, 1983 - Ann. Zootech., 32, 81-92

DULPHY J.P., BRETON J., BIENAIME A., LOUYOT J.M., 1982a - Ann. Zootech., 31, 195-211

DULPHY J.P., BRETON J., LOUYOT J.M., BIENAIME A., 1983 - Ann. Zootech., 32, 53-80

DULPHY J.P., KOMAR A., ZWAENEPOEL P., 1984 - Ann. Zootech., 33, 321-342

DULPHY J.P., KOUASSY A., BIENAIME A., 1982b - Ann. Zootech., 31, 215-232

GASNIER A., VACHEL J.P., 1952 - Ann. Zootech., 1, 157-174

GIGER S., SAUVANT D., 1983 - Ann. Zootech., 32, 215-246

KRISTENSEN E.S., MULLER P.D., HVELPLUND T., 1982 - Acta Agric. Scand., 32, 123-127

MOULD F.L., ORSKOV E.R., MANNS O., 1983 - Anim. Feed Sci. Technol., 10, 15-30

OSBOURN D.F., TERRY R.A., CAMMELL S.B., OUTEN G.E., 1970 - Proc. Nutr. Soc., 29, 12A (Abstr.)

RAMIHONE B., CHENOST M., 1987 - 3èmes Journées des recherches sur les herbivores, Reprod. Nutr. Develop. (in press)

RRI, 1975 - First report, 1975, DAFS, Edimburgh (UNITED KINGDOM). 58 p.

RRI, 1984. Fourth report 1984, DAFS, Edimburgh (UNITED KINGDOM). 85 p.

SAUVANT D., DORLEANS M., DELACOUR C., BERTRAND D., GIGER S., 1986 - Reprod. Nutr. Develop., 26, 1B, 303-304

SCHNEIDER B.H., FLATT W.P., 1975 - p. 151-163, in "The evaluation of feeds through digestibility experiments". University of Georgia Press, Athens, (USA)

UDEN P., 1984 - Anim. Feed Sci. Technol., 11, 279-291

VAN DER HONING Y., STEG A., 1979 - p.23-26, in "Energy Metabolism". Ed L.E. MOUNT (BUTTERWORTHS)

VON KNIEREM K., 1900 - Landw. Jahr. 29, 489 cité par SCHNEIDER and FLATT, 1975

XANDE A., 1978 - Ann. Zootech., 27, 583-599

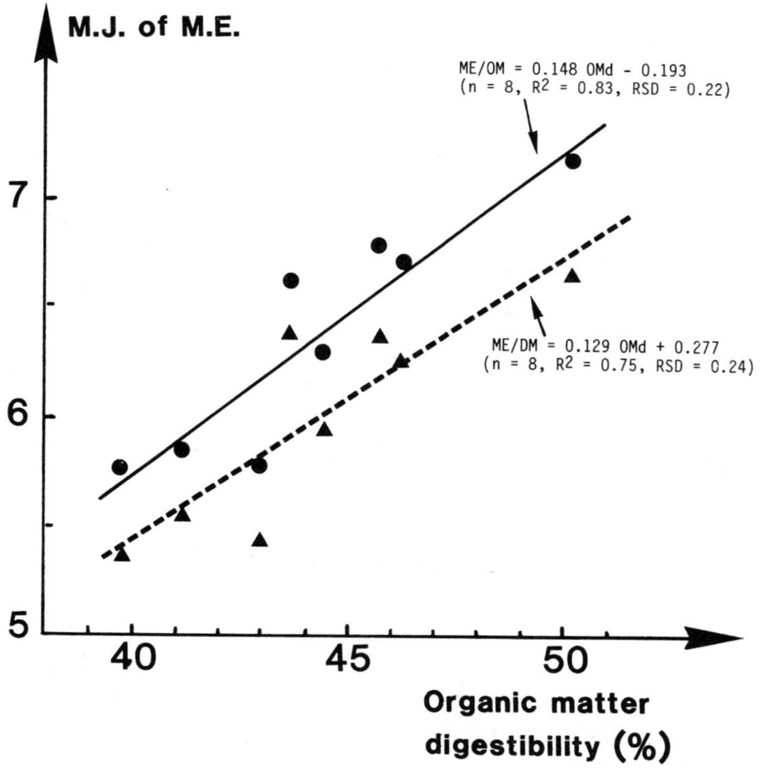
M.J. of M.E.
ME/OM = 0.148 OMd - 0.193
(n = 8, R2 = 0.83, RSD = 0.22)
ME/DM = 0.129 OMd + 0.277
(n = 8, R2 = 0.75, RSD = 0.24)
7
6
5
40
45
50
Organic matter
digestibility (%)

FIG. 1 - Relationship between the O.M. digestibility and metabolizable energy content of various straws (R.R.I. Report n° 4, 1984)

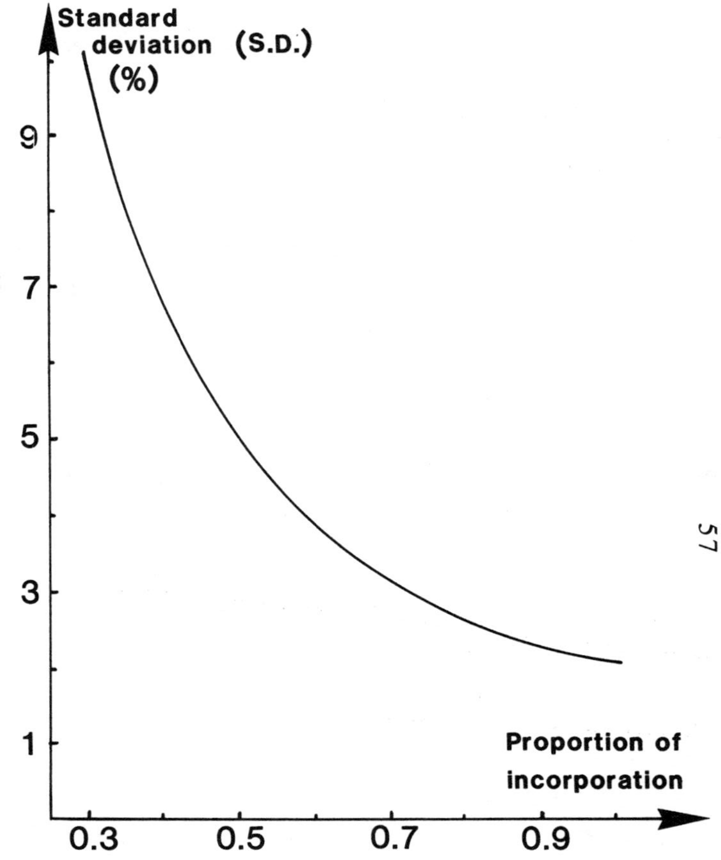
Standard
deviation (S.D.)
(%)
9
7
5
3
1
0.3
0.5
0.7
0.9
Proportion of
incorporation

ASSUMPTIONS : NO DIGESTIVE INTERACTION
DIET DIGESTIBILITY S.D. MEASUREMENT : 2 %
CONCENTRATE " " " : 3 %

FIG. 2 - Variation of precision of the straw digestibility value according to its incorporation level in the diet

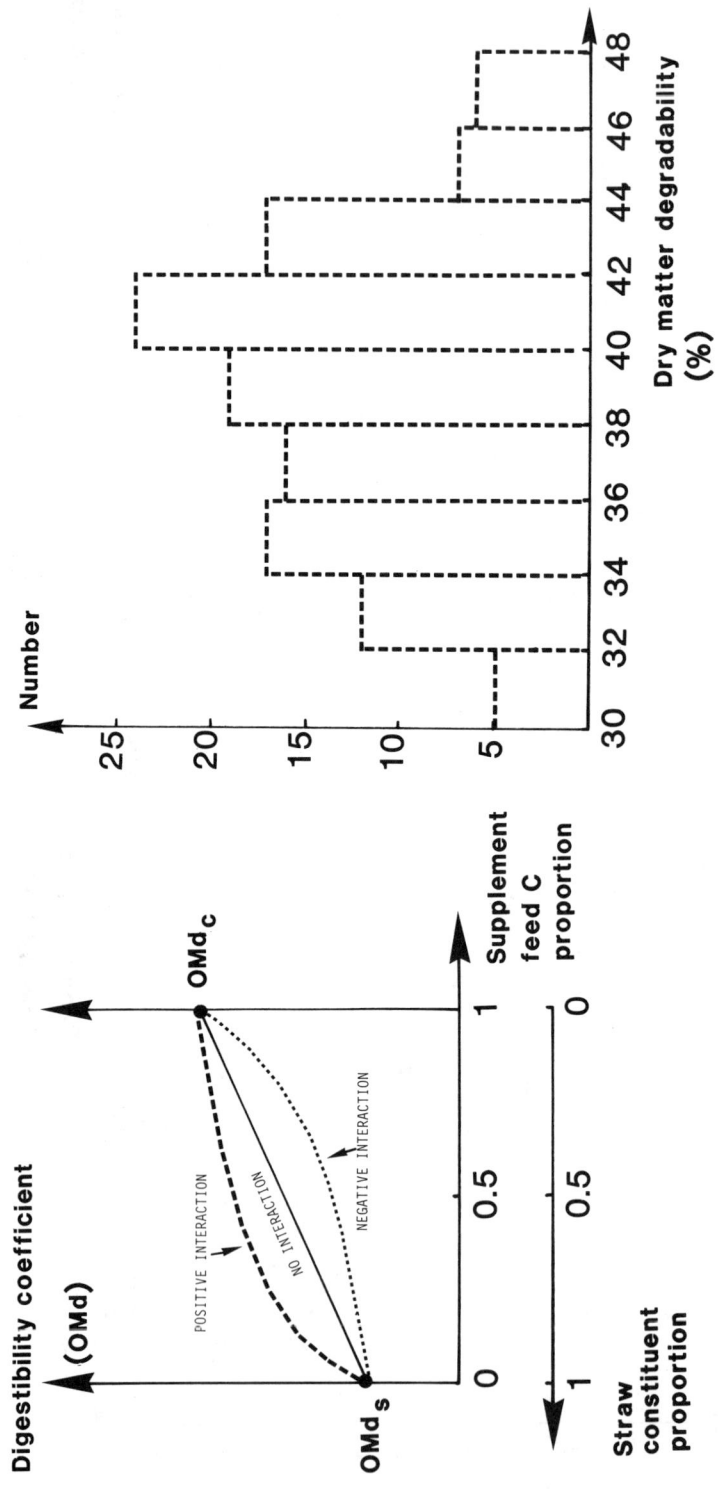

FIG. 4 - Variation of in sacco straw dry matter
degradability after 24 hours of incubation
within the same basal diet (Sauvant et Al., unpubl.)

FIG. 3 - Variation of the diet digestibility
in the case of interaction

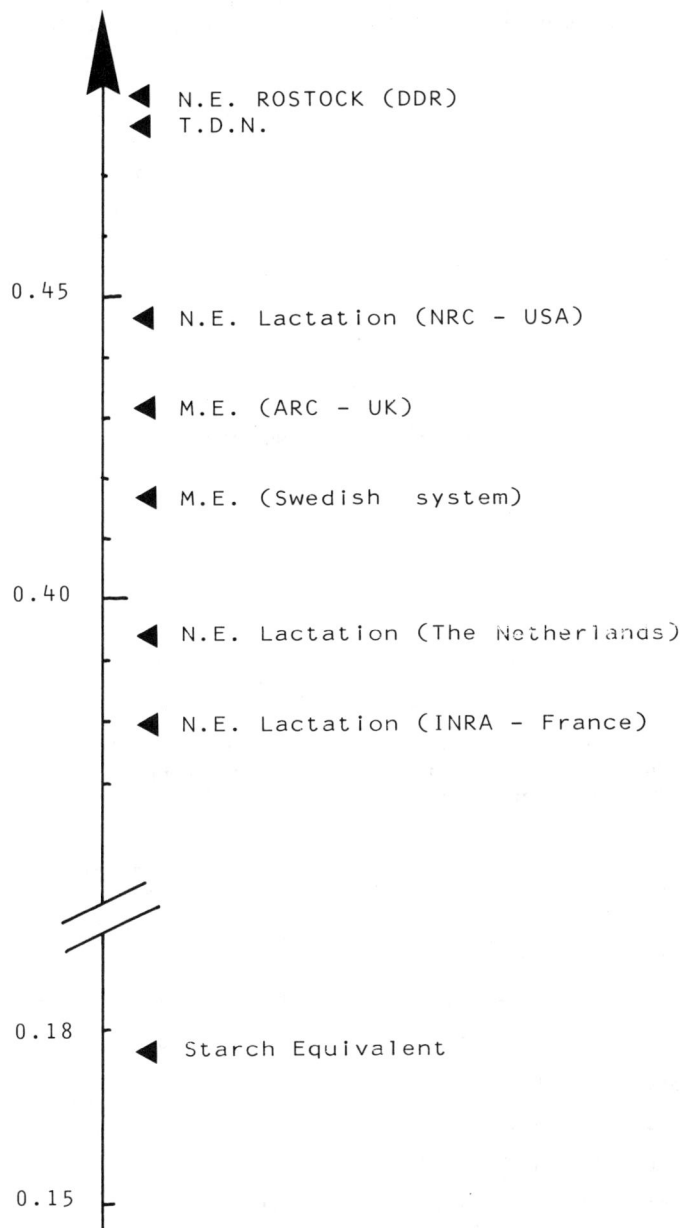

FIG. 5 - Energy value of wheat straw relative to barley according
to the feed evaluation systems
(Van der Honing - STEG, 1979)

Table 1: Variations of the straw O.M. digestibility according to the complementation in the INRA tables (DEMARQUILLY et al., 1978)

	ALONE (1)	WITH 25% OF CONCENTRATE
OAT STRAW	49	59
WHEAT STRAW	39	54
BARLEY STRAW	45	56

(1) Minimal complementation with N and minerals

(2) Blend of 50/50 maize grain/soybean meal

Table 2: Dynamic partition of the crude protein degradation in the rumen assuming a transit of 0.05 h^{-1}

	CP Content (g/kg DM)	degraded CP at different time interval					Undegraded CP (g/kg DM)
		0-1	1-6	6-12	12-24	24-48	
Wheat straw	35	3.4	1.2	2.3	1.6	0.7	25.8
Maize grain	106	15.6	11.1	6.5	6.5	8.7	57.6
Barley	117	28.2	32.3	13.6	4.7	1.0	37.2
Soybean meal	540	105.3	114.7	87.7	46.5	7.7	178.1
Groundnut meal	540	221.3	63.7	66.9	39.6	6.0	142.5
Fish meal	600	133.6	35.7	35.1	36.1	7.4	352.1
Maize/soybean 50/50	323	60.4	62.3	47.1	26.5	8.2	118.5
Barley/groundnut meal 50/50	328	124.7	48.0	40.2	22.1	3.5	89.9

Table 3: Dynamic partition of the organic matter degradation in the rumen assuring a transit of 0.05 h^{-1}

| | OM Content (g/kg DM) | OM degraded during different time intervals | | | | | Undegraded OM |
		0-1	1-6	6-12	12-24	24-48	
Wheat straw	926	90.0	31.5	60.0	43.5	18.5	681.5
Maize grain	984	143.9	119.0	97.5	120.4	37.2	466.0
Barley	974	472.9	221.0	39.0	12.9	3.5	225.0
Soybean meal	933	336.4	221.0	126.7	36.5	6.5	205.9
Groundnut meal	940	365.5	225.0	74.5	21.5	4.0	249.5
Fish meal	700	170.5	42.5	39.0	43.0	14.0	391.0
Maize/soya 50/50	958	241.0	170.0	112.0	78.5	22.0	334.5
Barley/groundnut 50/50	957	419.2	223.0	56.7	17.2	3.7	237.2

Table 4: Theoretical microbial crude protein synthesis (MCP) at various time intervals, comparison of   blends

| | TIME INTERVALS (HOURS) | | | | | TOTAL |
	0-1	1-6	6-12	12-24	24-48	
WHEAT STRAW (WS)	3.4	1.2	2.3	1.6	0.7	9.2
MAIZE + SOYA M. (MS)	48.2	34.0	22.4	15.7	4.4	124.7 ⎫
BARLEY + GROUNDNUT (BG)	85.0	48.5	13.4	5.1	0.7	152.7 ⎭
W.S. + M.S. (75/25)	17.7	13.2	13.5	7.8	2.6	55 ⎫
W.S. + B.G. (75/25)	33.7	12.9	11.8	6.3	1.4	66 ⎭

UNDERLINE D ⟶   MCP limited by N available.

WITHIN AND BETWEEN CENTRE VARIABILITY IN THE MEASUREMENT OF
IN VIVO ORGANIC MATTER DIGESTIBILITY OF STRAW

D I GIVENS
ADAS Nutrition Chemistry Feed Evaluation Unit, Stratford on Avon, UK

P J S DEWEY
Rowett Research Institute, Aberdeen, UK

E DONALDSON
East of Scotland College of Agriculture, Edinburgh, UK

D I H JONES
Welsh Plant Breeding Station, Aberystwyth, UK
and
A H ADAMSON
ADAS Nutrition Chemistry Department, Bristol, UK

Summary

Four centres assessed the within and between centre variability in
measuring the in vivo organic matter digestibility of untreated and
ammonia treated straw using sheep. Three evaluation methods were
used, straw fed ad libitum, straw fed with dried grass and the
digestibility values calculated by difference and straw fed at 2
levels with maize germ meal and the results calculated by regression.
The largest and smallest within centre variabilities were observed
using the difference and ad libitum methods respectively, both of
these occurring in the same centre. Significant differences in mean
values were observed between centres which could not be accounted
for by evaluation method and a significant interaction with ammonia
treatment was seen. The observed differences were unlikely to have
led to substantially different nutritional advice in practice,
although the difference method failed to identify any effect of
ammonia treatment.

1. INTRODUCTION

The reference point for the nutritive value of all forages in the
UK is the metabolisable energy (ME) value determined in vivo using sheep
fed at maintenance. However straw poses a number of problems, i) feeding
it alone is likely to lead to a deficiency of nitrogen in the rumen with
a consequent effect on its digestibility ii) feeding straw ad libitum
can lead to selective refusal (1) and iii) feeding with another feed and
calculating nutritive value by difference can lead to increased between
animal errors (2).

A comparison of ME measurements in straw using either the difference
technique or feeding ad libitum with urea and minerals has been reported
from Sweden (3) and indicated little difference between the two methods.
Since it is equally important that methods of evaluation can be reproduced
between different centres Barber et al (4) reported on UK work comparing
4 centres and 2 methods when measuring the organic matter digestibility

(OMd) of barley and wheat straw. These workers (4) concluded that there were significant between centre effects even when using the same method although the within centre variability was often as great as that between centres.

This paper represents the results of a further experiment involving 4 centres and 3 methods used to measure the OMd of barley and wheat straws, both untreated or treated with ammonia.

2. MATERIALS AND METHODS

Four centres (C 1-4) throughout England, Scotland and Wales participated in evaluating 1 untreated barley straw (UB), 1 ammonia treated barley straw (TB), 1 untreated wheat straw (UW) and 1 treated wheat straw (TW). Bulk samples of each straw were collected centrally and distributed to the centres, where it was chopped to approximately 2-4 cm.

Each straw was then fed to 4 castrated male sheep (40-90kg liveweight) as shown in table I.

Table I. Details of experimental diets.

Centre	Method of feeding straw	Base feed	Method of calculating digestibility
1	Ad lib	Nil	Direct
1	Restricted(500gd^{-1})	Dried grass(500gd^{-1})	Difference
2	Ad lib	Nil	Direct
3	Ad lib	Nil	Direct
4	Restricted to 80 or 60% of diet	Maize germ meal (180 and 360gd^{-1})	Regression

Where straw was fed ad libitum each animal was supplemented with 2.5gd^{-1} of sodium sulphate plus for untreated straw only, urea at 25g 100kg^{-1} liveweight. The animals were allowed an acclimatisation period of 10d followed by a balance period ranging from 8 - 15d. Table I also indicates the method used to calculate OMd.

3. RESULTS AND DISCUSSION

Table II shows the OMd of each sample by centre and method.

Table II. Organic matter digestibility of straw, arithmetic means and standard errors by centre and method.

Centre	Method	Organic matter digestibility of			
		UB	TB	UW	TW
1	Ad lib	0.441(0.008)	0.525(0.008)	0.487(0.006)	0.518(0.007)
1	*Diff	0.483(0.026)	0.463(0.013)	0.472(0.026)	0.476(0.016)
2	Ad lib	0.450(0.017)	0.520(0.012)	0.448(0.011)	0.506(0.006)
3	Ad lib	0.517(0.015)	0.565(0.015)	0.506(0.009)	0.536(0.010)
4	2 levels	0.488(0.010)	0.579(0.009)	0.508(0.009)	0.541(0.012)

* calculated by difference

Table III. Organic matter digestibility of straw, repeatability of
results within centres.

| Centre | Method | Each centre | | Overall | | Difference from |
		Variance	DF	Variance	DF	overall variance
1	Ad lib	1.99	12	9.22	62	$P < 0.001$
1	Difference	17.68	12	6.18	62	$P < 0.005$
2	Ad lib	5.34	12	8.57	62	NS
3	Ad lib	6.11	12	8.42	62	NS
4	2 levels	8.54	26	7.78	48	NS

Table III examines the repeatability of results within each centre
by comparing the between animal variance with the overall variance
excluding the one in question. It is evident that C1 using the ad libitum
method had a significantly lower variability than other centres and C 1
using the difference technique had a significantly poorer variability.
This greater between animal variability stemmed from the results of only
2 animals although the difference technique tends to magnify between
animal differences in whole diet OMd.
A regression model was used to examine reproducibility between
centres (identified as centre. method, since method and centre could not
be analysed separately) and the effect of other variables.
The summary of this analysis is shown in table IV.

Table IV. Organic matter digestibility of straw, reproducibility
between centres and effects of other variables.

Modification to regression model	DF	Variance ratio	Significance of variable(s)
+ NH_3 treatment	1	64.5	$P < 0.001$
+ Centre.method	4	18.3	$P < 0.001$
+ Straw type	1	0.6	NS
+ Centre.method.NH_3	4	5.0	$P < 0.01$
+ NH_3 . straw type	1	6.6	$P < 0.025$
+ Centre.method.straw type.	4	1.1	NS
+ Centre.method.straw type.NH_3	4	1.6	NS

The effect of ammonia treatment on OMd is clearly significant as
is the interaction between ammonia treatment and straw type. There is
also a very significant effect of centre.method indicating that on
average different results would be obtained amongst the centres using
their current method. The reason for a significant interaction between
centre.method and ammonia treatment is likely to relate to the fact that
unlike other methods, the difference technique did not identify effect of
ammonia treatment of the straw.
The mean OMd values calculated from the regression analysis for each
centre.method is shown in table V. The effect of centre.method referred
to above appeared to be essentially a difference between C 1 and 2 on the
one hand and C 3 and 4 on the other. There was no significant effect of
method within C 1 or between C 1 and 2. In addition there did not appear
to be any effect of method between C 3 and 4.

65

Table V. Organic matter digestibility (OMd) of straw. Predicted
mean OMd for each centre method.

Centre	Method	Predicted mean OMd
1	Ad lib	0.493^a
1	Difference	0.473^a
2	Ad lib	0.480^a
3	Ad lib	0.531^b
4	2 levels	0.530^b
	SED	0.015

a,b means with different superscripts are significantly
different (P<0.05)

The results of these experiments indicate that the within centre
variability can vary significantly between centres and in this work
repeatability was poorest using the difference technique. The work
has also shown that significantly different mean values can be obtained
between centres, that these differences may not always be explained by
the use of different methods and they may be modified by ammonia treatment. It is unlikely however that the differences would have given rise
to substantially different nutritional advice if applied in practice.

ACKNOWLEDGEMENTS
We wish to acknowledge the assistance of Hazel M Vint of the Rowett
Research Institute in carrying out the statistical analyses.

REFERENCES
(1) SHAND, W., SHEHATA, O., ØRSKOV, E.R. and MORRICE, A.F. (1987)
Studies on botanical preparations and nutritive value of varieties of
cereal straws and the ability of sheep to select the botanical part
with the greatest value. Anim.Prod.(Abstract). In Press.

(2) VAN SOEST, P.J. (1982). "Nutritional Ecology of the Ruminant".
O and B Books Inc. Corvallis, p.42.
(3) DEN BRAVER, E.J. (1976). Determination of metabolisable energy in
straw for ruminants by in vivo and in vitro methods. Swedish J.
agric. Res. 4, 53-59.
(4) BARBER, W.P., ALDERMAN, G., ADAMSON, A.H., MANSBRIDGE, R.J. and
WILLIAMS, T. (1984). Evaluation of untreated and alkali treated
cereal straw. In "Proceedings of Second Seminar on the Upgrading
of Crops and By-Products". Ministry of Agriculture, Fisheries and
Food, London. pp. 38-49.

PROTEIN EVALUATION OF TREATED STRAWS

T. Hvelplund
National Institute of Animal Science
Research in Cattle and Sheep
Forsøganlæg Foulum
8833 Ørum Sønderlyng
Denmark

Summary
Treatment of straw not only influences the digestibility, but
also the protein value of the straw. The influence of treatment on the protein value cannot be evaluated in a system based on digestible crude protein, but requires a system which
considers the actual nitrogen metabolism in the gastrointestinal tract. The different factors which determine the amount
of protein available for the animal, and therefore essential
for the protein value of the feed is discussed with special
reference to diets based on straw. Finally the protein value
of untreated, alkali treated and ammonia treated barley straw
is calculated in the AAT-PBV protein evaluation system, and
the significance of the PBV values in relation to practical
feeding with straw diets is discussed.

1. Introduction

Treatment of straw with chemicals like sodium hydroxide, calcium hydroxide, ammonia and ammonia precursors as urea to increase
the digestibility is used in many parts of the world. Such treatment generally increases both the rate and extent of fibre digestion in the rumen, which leads to a higher energy value of the
treated material as well as to a higher intake.

The potential increase in both rate and extent of digestion
can only be realised if other factors necessary to obtain this increase are not limiting. The most important factor in this context
is the quantity of nitrogen supplied to the rumen microorganisms
shown by Ørskov and Grubb (1). Treatment of straw will thus not
only influence fibre digestibility but has also a great impact on
nitrogen metabolism.

This paper describes important aspects of nitrogen metabolism
in the gastro-intestinal tract of ruminants with special reference
to diets based on treated straw.

2. Protein evaluation in general

The system based on digestible crude protein which still is
in use in many countries is unable to evaluate the protein value
of treated straw, because it does not consider the contribution
from the microbial protein produced in the rumen which on straw
diets is the main contribution to the intestinal protein flow.

Furthermore it does not express the nitrogen requirements of the rumen microorganisms. In protein evaluation of feeds it is necessary to consider the different aspects of nitrogen metabolism as done in the new protein evaluation systems proposed during recent years (2,3,4) where the protein value of the feed is separated in the contribution from undegraded feed protein and from microbial protein.

3. Protein contribution from undegraded protein in straw

The amount of amino acids absorbed from undegraded protein in a feedstuff is influenced by the crude protein content of the feed, rumen degradability of the protein, the amino acid content of the undegraded protein and finally the digestibility of amino acids in the undegraded protein.

3.1 Protein degradability in straw

The protein content in straw is generally low (app. 40 g CP/kg DM) but vary quite considerably both within and between variety. The major part of this protein is probably associated with the cell walls and therefore slowly degradable in the rumen, but approx. 25-30% of the protein in barley straw is found to be soluble in a mineral buffer, which implies that this fraction is also degraded in the rumen. The degradation of the protein associated with the cell walls is difficult to measure with the widely used nylon bag technique introduced by Mehrez and Ørskov (5) due to microbial contamination of the feed residues left in the bags after incubation in the rumen (6,7,8). The study of Varvikko and Lindberg (8) using ^{15}N labelled material indicates that the contamination of straw residues can be quite substential and they found a disappearance of only 5% based on nitrogen versus 72% based on ^{15}N after 24 h incubation in the rumen. A calculation of the protein degradability according to Kristensen et al. (9) on the values based on disappearance of ^{15}N and using buffer solubility, which in this study was estimated to 30.4%, as the soluble fraction, showed a degradability of 61% for the protein in untreated straw using a passage rate of 5% per h.

Treatment of straw to increase the fibre digestion probably also increases the protein degradation as the major part of the protein is associated with the cell walls. Results from our laboratory seem to support this as we found that the disappearance of nitrogen from nylon bags incubated at different time intervals with NaOH-treated barley straw was approx. 15 units higher than values obtained with untreated straw.

Treatment of straw with ammonia not only increases digestibility but also the nitrogen content in the treated material. Different reports indicate that not all the extra nitrogen added at treatment can be degraded but is so tightly bound to the straw that it is not released in the rumen (10,11). Similar results have been found for ammonia treated hay (12). This shows that the extra nitrogen bound to the straw during treatment can only be conside-

68

red as partly soluble in the rumen.

3.2 Amino acid content in undegraded protein from straw
Although the amount of undegraded protein entering the small
intestine on a straw diet is limited, the content of amino acids
in this fraction is essential for its potential value. In a diet
based on ammonia treated straw Møller and Hvelplund (13) found
that the proportion of amino acid N in duodenal NAN accounted for
only 58%. Considering that the majority of duodenal NAN is of microbial origin and contains approximately 70% amino acids in the
crude protein (14), this result indicates that the proportion of
amino acids in undegraded straw protein is rather low although
this value to some extent is influenced by the extra nitrogen
tightly bound to the straw due to the ammonia treatment. It seems,
referring to this result, that the content of amino acids in straw
crude protein shown in table I also can be applied to the undegraded protein without introducing any major error.

Table I. Nitrogen content and amino acid (AA) composition of
         barley straw (n=16)

	Mean	SD	Minimum	Maximum
Total nitrogen (% in DM)	0.8	0.3	0.47	1.51
Total AA-N (% of total N)a)	50.6	4.3	43.6	56.9
Essential AA-N (% of total N)	18.5	1.9	16.1	21.3
Non-Essential AA-N (% of total N)	32.1	3.2	25.7	36.5

a) Tryptophane was not estimated and consequently not taken into
account.

3.3 Digestibility in the small intestine of undegraded protein from straw
A high proportion of cell wall associated protein in the undegraded fraction entering the duodemum would indicate a low digestibility of this protein in the small intestine. This hypotesis
was tested in an experiment using the mobile nylon bag technique
to estimate intestinal digestibility (15). A sample of barley
straw and ammonia treated barley straw was incubated in the rumen
for 16 h to obtain samples representing rumen undegraded residues.
Prior to freeze drying the undegraded samples were treated in a
stomacher (16) to remove microbes attached to the feed particles
and after drying transferred to mobile nylon bags.
The extent of rumen degradation and the subsequent digestion
in the intestine of untreated and ammonia treated straw is shown
in table II. The table shows the already mentioned effect of ammonia treatment on nitrogen content and degradability in the rumen. From the figures it can be calculated that only 77% of the
ammonia bound to the straw is degraded in the rumen. The disappearance of both dry matter and nitrogen in the small intestine
from rumen undegraded material is limited and this indicates a low
value of the undegraded protein in straw.

Table II. N content in untreated and ammonia treated barley straw and in the undegraded residues after 16 h incubation in the rumen, the disappearance of DM and N in the rumen and in undegraded residues in the intestine estimated with nylon bag technique.

	Barley straw		Ammonia treated barley straw	
N content (% of DM) n=1				
Straw	0.48		1.32	
Rumen undegraded residue	0.37		0.72	
Rumen disappearance (%) n=1				
DM	24		44	
N	41		70	
Intestinal disappearance (%) n=7				
DM (Mean and SEM)	5.0	0.3	7.4	0.4
N (Mean and SEM)	31.7	1.2	35.7	2.4

4. Protein contribution from microbial protein

Microbial growth in the rumen is related to the amount of energy which is liberated during fermentation. On a straw diet the only source of energy for the rumen microbes is cell wall carbohydrates and the production of microbial protein is therefore mainly related to digestibility of the straw if other factors for microbial growth are not limiting. In a diet of treated straw the major limiting factor is probably nitrogen, but other factors for instance sulphur could also be limiting.

4.1 Nitorgen source for optimal microbial growth

Rumen microbial synthesis requires an adequate supply of nitrogen to achieve maximal effeciency. An important question in this connexion is whether ammonia or compounds, which after degradation yield ammonia (urea), can supply the sole source of N for maximal yield of microbial protein or whether preformed amino acids or peptides are required.

In vitro experiments by Maeng et al. (17) showed an increased microbial yield if 25% of the urea-N in a purified diet was replaced by an amino acid mixture. An increased digestibility of cellulose by substituting urea with protein sources such as low degradable fishmeal or peptides is demonstrated in several in vitro studies (18,19,20). These in vitro observations thus indicate, that the microbes in the rumen of animals eating low quality diets based on straw may have a reduced rate of cellulose digestion and consequently a reduced voluntary feed intake unless the diets are supplemented with preformed protein in a relatively undegradable form.

Several in vivo studies have shown an advantage to growth from supplementing straw rich diets with fishmeal (21,22,23). Whether this effect can be ascribed to an increased amount of undegraded protein passing to the intestine or is an effect on rumen digestion and thus support the findings in vitro is not clear.

An increased digestibility of cellulose in the rumen was observed by McAllen and Smith (24) in diets based on untreated and alkali treated barley straw when the supplement was fishmeal compared to urea. The same effect of fishmeal compared to urea a total organic matter digestibility of straw diets was also observed by Hovell et al. (23). In contrast to this Kellaway and Leibholz (25) concluded on their experiments that dietary requirement for rumen degradable protein can be supplied entirely as NPN provided that NPN intake is not too infrequent. Interesting in this context is also the results obtained with alkali treated straw by Fahmy and Sundstøl (26) where it was found that neither urea nor intact protein but a combination of these nitrogen sources resulted in the highest in vitro digestibility.

4.2 Expressing microbial yield in the rumen

Prediction of microbial protein synthesis in different feedstuffs is normally based on digestible organic matter corrected to a proportion digested in the rumen. In a study including 33 diets (27) it was found, that microbial amino acid synthesis could be predicted with the lowest error, when related to total digestible carbohydrates. The relation used and based on the largest amount of observations showed a production of 20 g microbial amino acid nitrogen per kg totally digested carbohydrates.

4.3 Digestibility in the small intestine of amino acids in microbial protein

The nutritional value of the microbial amino acids depends on their digestibility in the small intestine. Different estimates seems to agree upon that the true digestibility of microbial amino acids in the small intestine can be considered as a constant value of 85% for mixed rumen bacteria (15,28).

5. Calculations of the protein value in straw according to the AAT-PBV system

As already mentioned different new protein evaluation systems are proposed but in the calculation of the protein value in untreated and treated straw only the AAT-PBV system will be considered. In this system two protein values of the feed are calculated. AAT is the amount of amino acids truely absorbed in the small intestine and expresses the amino acid supply of the ruminant body. PBV is the protein balance in the rumen and expresses the nitrogen supply of the rumen microorganisms.

The factors used in the calculation and the protein values of three different straws are shown in tabel III. The contribution to the AAT value from both undegraded protein and microbial protein is also shown and from this it is obvious that the contribution from undegraded protein to the AAT supply can be neglected and

that the protein value of straw is related to the microbial protein synthesis and consequently to the digestibility of the straw.
This is clearly illustrated in the table where the microbial amino
acid synthesis on the treated straws is 30% higher than on untreated straw.

Table III. The factors used and the amount of AAT and PBV in
untreated, alkali treated and ammonia treated barley
straw. (The factors, unless otherwise indicated, are
mentioned in the text).

	Barley straw[a]		
	Untrea-ted	NaOH-treated	NH$_3$-treated
Factors used in calculation of AAT			
g crude protein/kg DM	21.3	21.3	88.3
1 - degradability	0.4	0.25	0.2[b]
proportion of AA in UDP	0.5	0.5	0.15[b]
digestibility of AA in UDP	0.3	0.3	0.3
g digested carbohydrates/kg DM	524	678	678
digestibility of AA in MP	0.85	0.85	0.85
Factors used in calculation of PBV			
g crude protein/kg DM	21.3	21.3	88.3
degradability	0.6	0.75	0.8
microbial AA from the relation to digested carbohydrates	65.5	84.8	84.8
proportion of AA in MP	0.7	0.7	0.7
Protein value (g/kg DM)			
AAT from UDP	1.3	0.8	0.8
AAT from MP	55.7	72.0	72.0
AAT	57	73	73
PBV	− 81	− 105	− 51

a) values for CP content and carbohydrates digested which is considered to be the same as OM digested are from Sundstøl and Coxworth (29).

b) corrected for that 20% of the ammonia is not degraded.
AA=amino acids, UDP=undegraded dietary protein, MP=microbial protein.

To achieve the AAT values shown in table III it is required
that the microbes in the rumen are supplied with sufficient nitrogen. The PBV values are all negative suggesting a deficit of nitrogen for microbial growth. The ruminant can however tolorate a
certain negative PBV because of recycling of nitrogen to the rumen. As feed intake on a diet of untreated straw normally is low,

the deficit in PBV can probably be met by recycling and this is in agreement with observations by Ørskov and Grubb (1). The same experiment also showed that supplementing NaOH-treated straw with urea both increased feed intake and digestibility. The high negative PBV value on NaOH-treated straw thus indicates that it is necessary to supplement with nitrogen if the potential increase of treatment is to be realised. Treatment of straw with ammonia reduced the negative PBV value with 50% compared to NaOH-treated straw which indicates that recycling can meet the requirement for nitrogen which also is in agreement with practical observations (13).

6. Conclusion

The protein value of treated straw cannot be evaluated in a system based on digestible crude protein. To do this it is necessary to consider the actual metabolism of nitrogen in the gastrointestinal tract.

The protein value of treated straw expressed as amino acids absorbed from the small intestine is entirely related to the extent of microbial protein synthesis in the rumen and thus to the digestibility of the organic matter in the straw as the contribution from the straw protein is insignificant.

The protein values calculated in the AAT-PBV system showed that the absorption of amino acids (AAT value) was 73 g per kg dry matter in treated straw. The protein balance in the rumen (PBV value) was negative for both ammonia – and alkali treated barley straw – 51 g and – 105 g respectively. This shows the necessity of supplementing with nitrogen unless recycling can meet this deficiency.

It is still uncertain whether slowly degradable protein, which shows a beneficial effect on digestibility of fibre in vitro also is required in vivo to obtain maximum fibre digestion in the rumen.

REFERENCES

(1) Ørskov, E.R. and Grubb, D.A. (1978). Validation of new systems for protein evaluation in ruminants by testing the effect of urea supplementation on intake and digestibility of straw with or without sodium hydroxide treatment. J. Agric. Sci., Camb. 91, 483-486.

(2) Verite, R., Journet, M. and Jarrige, R. (1979). A new system for the protein feeding of ruminants: The PDI system. Livest. Prod. Sci. 6, 349-367.

(3) ARC. (1984). The nutrient requirement of ruminant livestock. Suppl. no. 1. Agric. Res. Council, 45 pp.

(4) Madsen, J. (1985). The basis for the proposed Nordic protein evaluation system for ruminants. The AAT-PBV system. Acta Agric. Scand. Suppl. 25, 9-20.

(5) Mehrez, A.Z. and Ørskov, E.R. (1977). A study of the artificial fibre bag technique for determining the digestibility of fedds in the rumen. J. Agric. Sci. Camb. 88, 645–650.

(6) Mathers, J.C. and Aitchison, E.M. (1981). Direct estimation of contamination of food residues by microbial matter after incubation within synthetic fibre bags in the rumen. J. Agric. Sci., Camb. 96, 691–693.

(7) Rooke, J.A., Greife, N.A. and Armstrong, D.G. (1984). The effect of in sacco rumen incubation of a grass silage upon the total and D-amino acid composition of the residual silage dry matter. J. Agric. Sci., Camb. 102, 695–702.

(8) Varvikko, T. and Lindberg, J.E. (1985). Estimation of microbial nitrogen in nylon bag residues by feed ^{15}N delution. Br. J. Nutr. 54, 473–481.

(9) Kristensen, E.S., Møller, P.D. and Hvelplund, T. (1982). Estimation of the effective protein degradability in the rumen of cows using the nylon bag technique combined with the outflow rate. Acta Agric. Scand. 32, 123–127.

(10) Solaiman, S.G., Horn, G.W. and Owens, F.N. (1979). Ammonium hydroxide treatment on wheat straw. J. Anim. Sci. 49, 802–808.

(11) Borhami, B.E.A. and Johnsen, F. (1981). Digestion and duodenal flow of ammonia-treated straw, and sodium hydroxide-treated straw supplemented with urea, soybean meal or fish viscera silage. Acta Agric. Scand. 31, 245–250.

(12) Winther, P., Skovborg, E.B., Kristensen, V.F., Wolstrup, J., Holm, E. and Lund, A. (1983). Different methods for preservation of hay. 9. Ber. fra Fællesudvalget for Statens Planteavls- og Husdyrbrugsforsøg. 45 pp.

(13) Møller, P.D. and Hvelplund, T. (1982). Nitrogen metabolism in the forestomachs of cows fed ammonia treated barley straw supplemented with increasing amounts of urea or soyabean meal. S. Tierphysiol., Tierernährg. u. Futtermittelkde. 48, 46–57.

(14) Hvelplund, T. (1986). The influence of diet on nitrogen and amino acid content of mixed rumen bacteria. Acta Agric. Scand. 36, 325–331.

(15) Hvelplund, T. (1985). Digestibility of rumen microbial protein and undegraded dietary protein estimated in the small intestine of sheep or by in sacco procedure. Acta Agric. Scand. Suppl. 25, 132–144.

(16) Sharpe, A.N. and Jackson, A.K. (1972). Stomaching: a new concept in bacteriological sample preparation. Appl. Microbial. 24, 175–178.

(17) Maeng, W.J., Van Nevel, C.J., Baldwin, R.L. and Morris, J.G. (1976). Rumen microbial growth rates and yields: Effect of amino acids and proteins. J. Dairy Sci. 59, 68-79.

(18) Thomsen, K.V. and Johnsen, F. (1984). Availability of nitrogen in different protein sources, particularly as regards fish viscera silage for in vitro digestibility of starch and cellulose. Acta Agric. Scand. 34, 17-25.

(19) Thomsen, K.V. (1985). The specific nitrogen requirements of rumen microorganisms. Acta Agric. Scand. Suppl. 25, 125-131.

(20) Smith, R.H., McAllan, A.B. and Merry, R.J. (1986). Effect of dietary N on fibre digestion. IAEA symposium, 17-21 March, Vienna, 629-632.

(21) Smith, T., Broster, V.J. and Hill, R.E. (1980). A comparison of source of supplementary nitrogen for young cattle receiving fibre-rich diets. J. Agric. Sci., Camb. 95, 687-695.

(22) Ekern, A. (1982). Results from feeding trials and practical experience concerning protein feeding of ruminants in Norway. In protein Contribution of Feedstuffs for Ruminants: Application to Feed Formulation (ed. E.L. Miller, I.H. Pike and A.J.H. van Es) p. 86-102. Butterworth.

(23) Hovell, F.D. DeB, Ørskov, E.R., Grubb, D.A. and Macleod, N.A. (1983). Basal urinary nitrogen excretion and growth response to supplemental protein by lambs close to energy equilibrium. Br. J. Nutr. 50, 173-187.

(24) McAllan, A.B. and Smith, R.H. (1983). Factors influencing the digestion of dietary carbohydrates between the mouth and abomasum of steers. Br. J. Nutr. 50, 445-454.

(25) Kellaway, R.C. and Leibholz, J. (1983). Effect of nitrogen supplements on intake and utilization of low-quality forages. World Anim. Rev. 48, 33-37.

(26) Fahmy, S.T.M. and Sundstøl, F. (1984). The effect of urea and intact protein supplementation on the in vitro digestibility of untreated or alkali-treated barley straw. Z. Tierphysiol., Tierernährg. u. Futtermittelkde. 52, 118-124.

(27) Hvelplund, T. and Madsen, J. (1985). Amino acid passage to the small intestine in dairy cows compared with estimates of microbial protein and undegraded dietary protein from analyses on the feed. Acta Agric. Scand. Suppl. 25, 21-36.

(28) Storm, E.; Brown, D.S. and Ørskov, E.R. (1983). The nutritive value of rumen micro-organism in ruminants. 3. The digestion of microbial amino and nucleic acids in and losses of endogenous nitrogen from the small intestine of sheep. Br. J. Nutr. 50, 479-485.

(29) Sundstøl, F. and Coxworth, E.M. (1984). Ammonia treatment. In straw and other fibrous by-products as feed (ed. F. Sundstøl and E. Owen) p. 196-247. Elsevier.

75

DISCUSSION

Intake and digestibility (Rapporteur: J.M.C. RAMALHO RIBEIRO and B.G. COTTYN. Chairman: M. CHENOST)

Before undertaking intake and/or digestibility experiments one should first of all ask the following question: "What do we want to measure, and what for?"

Measuring digestibility is not an end in itself. It is a means of (a) either indicating the potential value of a given straw with a view of classifying straws relative to each other or (b) indicating the nutritive value of a straw in a given context (e.g. to give the farmer guidelines for feeding straw, within the context of a well-defined feeding system).

The first target, although very difficult to achieve, can in turn contribute to provide standard nutritional information which can be used for prediction purposes.

The second target is more relevant to specific environments ("local adaptation"). However, measurements done in this context should still respect the points raised in the Preamble, i.e. optimum cellulolysis conditions should be ensured.

It appears necessary to discriminate between the aspects relevant to the intrinsic properties of straws and those relevant to the roughage/animal interactions.

The participants agreed that all intake and digestibility data should be accompanied by a brief but precise description of the conditions in which these data were obtained (animals, rationing, feeding level, nature and quantity of supplements, etc.) in order to avoid confusion when applying these data in another context.

It seemed unlikely that a detailed common methodology for digestibility measurement could be recommended which would be adopted by all the countries represented at the workshop. The individual research or technical teams should be free to adopt their own experimental design, which takes into account the "local" constraints, provided it obeys the general rules presented in the Preamble.

These rules stress the need of carrying out digestibility measurements under conditions which allow optimum cellulolytic activity. Their importance was demonstrated in the paper by D.I. Givens showing considerable inter-laboratory variability in digestibility measurements.

Topics which require further research work are the quality and quantity of the nitrogen supplement for an optimum nutrition of the rumen microflora and the relation rumen volume / intake capacity of the animal.

Assessing digestibility and net energy value of straw within the total diet (Rapporteur: D. SAUVANT. Chairman: F. SUNDSTØL)

Among the three groups of methods available for measuring the digestibility of straw, i.e. difference, simultaneous and regression equations (from various levels of inclusion of supplement into the diet), it is agreed that the "difference" method is the easiest one to utilize while its precision is acceptable as far as straw (as the major part of the diet) is concerned.

This raises the problem of digestive interactions between supplements and straw. Since the concentrates to be incorporated into the diet must be rich in easily digestible cell-walls (see Preamble) it is likely that these interactions might not be a concern for such a calculation; more detailed discussion was later continued in a restricted group in which GIVENS, ADAMSON, STEG and VAN DER MEER doubted the importance of the interactions under standard circumstances. When interactions occur they are thought to be due to the animal and not due to the feed.

As straw is seldom fed alone, measurements of digestibility should always be carried out within a mixed diet to reflect the practical situation. However, there is a need for much more research to decide the best conditions in which straw digestibility should be measured and to assure that the data is applicable in practice.

Nitrogen value of straws (Rapporteur: T. HVELPLUND. Chairman: E. PFEFFER)

The discussion focussed on the need to measure microbial nitrogen net-synthesis which takes place in the rumen when straws, either untreated or treated, are correctly supplemented to optimize cellulolysis and on the difficulties encountered in these measurements. It was recognized that, in the case of poor quality roughages such as straw, the indirect measurement (measuring nitrogen degradability by means of the nylon bag technique) was rather imprecise in view of the relative importance of the microbial population which is attached to both straw particles and nylon bags. The direct measurement of microbial synthesis through the assay of nucleic acids or traced nitrogen incorporated in the diet is complex and time-consuming. Therefore, further research is still needed for a better evaluation of the actual nitrogen degradability.

The nitrogen solubility technique, although an interesting parameter for evaluating nitrogen degradability, has still to be improved.

Not only the amount but also the form in which nitrogen is required by rumen microorganisms of the microbes N requirement is still open to questions. Recent research has shown an effect of different amino acids, and even peptides, on the nutrition and, in turn, on the synthesis and degradation activity of these microbes.

It was also observed that the efficiency of nitrogen utilization in the case of NH_3-treated straw was low, as indicated by the high nitrogen content of excreted faeces. Three possible explanations for this low efficiency were proposed and discussed:

- Reduction of microbial activity/synthesis in the case of NH_3 treatment due to an inadequate and uneven supply of NH_3-N to the microbes which had been observed in several cases. However, this N-deficiency can be met partly by nitrogen recycled to the rumen.

- Fixation of part of the nitrogen on potentially digestible cell-walls which are not digested in the rumen because of the above reduction in cellulolysis and of the increased rate of passage, due itself to the positive effect of the NH_3-treatment on intake. These cell-walls could then be fermented in the hind gut where a secondary microbial synthesis would take place. Part of this microbial nitrogen, undigested, would thus increase the nitrogen content of faeces.

- Fixation of nitrogen on indigestibility cell-walls which pass into the faeces and increase their nitrogen content.

It was recognized that the fate of the added nitrogen was not known precisely enough and that further research was needed in this area.

The requirement of minerals for ensuring an efficient utilization of nitrogen by the rumen microflora formed another point of discussion. The supply of phosphorous and sulphur were seen to be the most critical. Especially the sulphur supply had to be both adequate and permanent and should be further studied.

Regarding the use of anhydrous ammonium or urea-generated NH_3 for the pretreatment of straws it was concluded that whenever water, temperature and the availability of urease equipment were not limiting factors, the simpler urea treatment should be preferred. Urea treatment was also less dangerous and cheaper than NH_3 treatment. Nevertheless the completion of the ureolysis reaction should be ascertained. An international working group on this topic was set up at a meeting in Firenze (Italy) in November 1987.

Topic B:

FEEDING TRIALS WITH PRODUCING ANIMALS: LONG TERM EFFECTS

LONG-TERM UTILIZATION OF AMMONIA-TREATED STRAWS FOR EWES IN MEDITERRANEAN COUNTRIES

R. CORDESSE
ENSA-Montpellier (France)
R. FACI, F. MUÑOZ and X. ALIBES
Sia-Inia, Apartado 727, 50080 Zaragoza (Spain)
F. GUESSOUS
Institut Agronomique Hassan II, Rabat (Maroc)

Summary

The results of two experiments are reported. Two flocks of ewes were fed over long periods with an ammoniated straw-based diet (about 100 days for ewes managed out in the open and over 8 reproductive cycles for housed ewes). When adequately supplemented with minerals and vitamins, the ammoniated straw diet satisfies the maintenance needs of the ewes. If supplemented with 300 g of a concentrate of barley + soya the intake of the treated straw is sufficient for the needs of pregnancy and insures for the suckling lambs a mean growth of 190 to 280 g per day.

1. INTRODUCTION

The treatment of straws with anhydrous ammonia improves the organic matter digestibility, the nitrogen value and the ingested dry matter (1,2,3,4,5,6).

The method proposed by Sundstøl (7) is convenient to be introduced in the farms and is well accepted by stock breeders. In temperate countries, this treatment is an easy way to enhance the value of straws because other foods are available to balance the diet of animals.

On the other hand, in mediterranean countries, where summer drought is quite systematic, the straws by-products of winter cereal cultures, are often the only available feeding.

We want here to specify two points :

- first, may the introduction of ammonia-treated straw in the diet of the animals resolve the problems of short term food scarcity ?

- secondly, will the feeding of ewes with ammoniated straw as roughage during several reproductive cycles, affect their productivity ?

Experiments were developed in Montpellier (France) and Zaragoza (Spain). The sheep is a good model for this kind of studies.

Indeed these animals have periods of high nutritional needs when ewes are lactating, and of low nutritional needs, when ewes are not pregnant or at the beginning of gestation.

In all the experiments which were developed in Montpellier, we used Arles Merino (AM) or crossbred F1 Arles Merino x Romanov (MA x Ro) ewes fed with wheat durum straw treated with 5 % anhydrous ammonia in airtight stacks.

In Zaragoza, Aragonese ewes were fed with barley straw treated with 3,5 % ammonia in stacks.

The moisture content of straws before treatment was at least 13 %. The animals were always supplemented with mineral additives enriched with sulphur, zinc and vitamins.

Experiment n°1 : feeding of AM and Fl ewes managed out in the open, throughout a pasture scarcity period.

Fifty five ewes were divided into two groups. Each of them used 4 paddocks of scrubland ("garrigue"). They stayed for 12 days on each paddock. Mating were planned near the 15th of October to get the lambing around the end of March or the beginning of April.

The regrowth of grass was hoped to satisfy the high needs of the lactating ewes.

When forage production (grass and bushes) was not sufficient, the ewes were penned to be fed with NH3-treated wheat durum straw supplemented or not, according to their physiological state.

Ammoniated straw was given in round bales. The twine was not removed to limit the wasting. The straw was renewed only when the previous distribution was exhausted. The weight of the given straw was noted over the whole period and the average quantity distributed to the ewes every day was calculated.

The losses were about 15-20 %.

We report here the results of two experiments developed during summer with dried ewes for the first one, and in the cold period with end-pregnant or lactating ewes for the second one.

- Summer period (100 days in 1982) (75 Arles Merino and Fl ewes)

The ewes were supplied with 1250 g per ewe per day of NH3 straw. 70 g of barley grains were distributed every day and completely eaten.

At the end of the 100 days period, the healthy state of the animals was good. The Arles Merino ewes maintained their weight of 40 kg, but the Fl ewes gained in average 2 kg.

We deduced from this trial that the nutritional value of the straw reached 0.53 UFL, 45 g of PDIE and PDIN, i.e lower values than those obtained with digestibility experiments. Therefore, the supplementation with barley was unuseful. We suppressed it at the time of the following food shortage.

- Winter period (111 days in 1984) (150 AM and Fl ewes)

NH3-straw was given "ad libitum". The animals were supplemented dayly with a concentrate (300 g/ewe/day) containing 200 g of barley grains and 100 g of soya bean cake "50".

We compared two mixed flocks of Arles Merino and Fl ewes. During summer, one group moved to new pasture in the Alps while the other one stayed over "garrigue".

During the last 40 days of gestation the ewes ingested a daily average of 300 g of concentrate and 1770 g of straw. No weighting was done throughout this period.

The lambing took place between the 13th of March and the 1st of April. It occured in good conditions. The lambs were weighted at birth. Then, all the animals were weighted the 4th and the 20th of April. The lactating ewes received 2650 g per animal and per day of ammoniated straw and the same quantity of concentrate as before lambing.

The performances are shown in the following table :

	Permanent flock		Transhumant flock	
Number of ewes	28 AM	27 F1	23 AM	26 F1
Ewe weight variation from the 4/04 to the 20/04 (g/day)	82 ± 148	154 ± 85	54 ± 103	118 ± 89
Fertility %	75	85	91	88
Prolificacy %	100	156	109	169
Daily gain (g) twins		120 ± 40	156 ± 80	145 ± 46
Daily gain (g) single	171 ± 45	223 ± 60	204 ± 38	281 ± 60

(average 10-30 days)

One can see that on the average, the ewes do not loose weight but the variability is important.

The fertility is acceptable and the prolificacy of the crossbred is high.

The growth of youngs from single lambing is reasonable for the used genotype, but the daily weight gain of twins remains slight.

Taking in account these results, we tried to assess the nutritional value of treated straws.

We calculate the nutritional value of NH3 straws, on the basis of a daily mean growth of 100 g for the ewes and of 150 or 250 g for the litter, and an evaluated true consomption of straw of 2 kg for the single lamb mothers and 2.2 kg for the twin lamb mothers.

The range is :

0.62 - 0.70 UFL for energy

56 - 69 g PDIN (Digestible protein allowed by nitrogen)

59-69 g PDIE (Digestible protein allowed by energy)

These values are high but close to those observed in other experiments (8)

The feeding of ewes in the same physiological conditions is achieved every year at that season. Recently we introduced fish meal as nitrogen source. The results are promising.

Experiment n° 2. Performances of ewes fed only with ammoniated straw as roughage, during several reproductive cycles.

We wanted to study the long-term effect of a diet containing only ammonia-treated straw as roughage and the less of supplementary foods allowing high performances.

In this experiment the ewes were housed and managed on the basis of 3 lambings over 2 years ; that is the reason why the feeding program had to avoid the loss of weight of the females during lactation. The NH3 straw accounted for 95 % of the whole diet over the maintenance period or the four first months of gestation, but 80 % on the fifth month and 55 % during lactation. The daily straw intake was constant and related to 1000 g of dry matter for Arles Merino ewes weighing 50-55 kg, and 800 g of dry matter for Aragonese ewes weighing 45 kg.

The concentrate contained cereals, soya bean cake, and sometimes peas. In all cases its composition was calculated to bring 1 to 1.2 UFL for the lactating period according to the INRA feeding standards (1978) (9). In Montpellier, 38 Arles Merino ewe lambs, which were 6 months old on the 15th of June, were divided into two groups (control and experimental n°1). They were mated at 10 months of age around the 15th of October after a heat synchronization with vaginal sponges and a 400 IU PMSG injection when sponges were removed. Subsequently 11 hoggets, from the first lambing of the group n°1, were mated in January when they were 10 months old (group n°2), simultaneously with their mothers.

The rams were fed with alfafa hay and oats as flushing and received the same ration as the ewes during mating.

Arles Merino rams were used for the two experimental groups of ewes and for the 3 first reproductive cycles of control ewes. The following matings of control ewes were achieved with Ile-de-France rams. As these rams are very sensitive to the season, we did not take in account the fertility parameter at the time of their utilization.

In Zaragoza two Aragonese ewe groups were choosen from 83 hoggets bred for a 550 day period during which they lambed twice. They weighted 25.5 kg at the experiment start, 35.8 kg at the firt mating and 42.6 kg at the second one on December of the same year. These weights did not differ significantly from those of the control ewes.

The feeding was fitted to the needs. The experimental group received 47 to 90 % of the ration as NH3 straw but the control one was fed with alfafa hay, untreated barley straw and grains.

As Arles Merino and Aragonese rams are not much seasonable, we emphasized the reproductive cycle number compared to the season in the presentation of the results (fig. 1 and table 1). One can notice a similar mean weight at mating for the 3 groups of AM ewes, and a good fertility rate for all groups, even after heat induction. Only three reproductive cycles show a fertility less than 70 %. The first mating out of season of young Aragonese ewes gave a low fertility rate of 74 and 75 % for experimental and control ewes respectively. The prolificacy (120 %) is good in the two groups. Inversely, when mating occured during the sexual season (2nd reproductive cycle) the fertility rate was higher (89 %) but the prolificacy was lower (100 %).

Some animal losses occured during the experimental period but they were not obviously connected with feeding : uterine malformation, accidental deaths, difficult lambing, thefts... In these conditions the last results of group n°1 and n°2 only concern 13 and 8 ewes respectively.

The weight of the lambs at birth is related to the weight of the mothers, but the super ovulation induced by PMSG treatment, gave multiple litters and low lamb weights, increasing weight variability.

For the Arles Merino breed, the mean lamb weight at birth is 3.55 ± 0.62 kg (all seasons and ages mixed). The mean lamb weight of the experimental ewes do not differ significantly. After birth, 1 or 2 lambs only were left with their mother.

In the following table we report for each reproductive cycle, the daily mean weight gain of lambs between 10 to 30 days of age - all groups mixed.

Breed	1	2	3	4	5	6	7	8
Arles Merino	143 ± 33	211 ± 31	226 ± 42	224 ± 36	238 ± 60	271 ± 52	284 ± 59	202 ± 95
Aragonese	199	219						

As a comparison, pure breed Arles Merino lambs housed in another farm near Montpellier have a daily growth of 212   63 g for the same period (10-30 days).

The daily weight gain of the Aragonese control lambs is 187 g and 221 g respectively for the 1st and the 2nd reproductive cycle. This growth is identical to that of the experimental group. Thus, we notice that the feeding of ewes with well treated NH3-straw accurately supplemented insures their maintenance needs whether they are pregnant or not ; the needs of lactating ewes are also reasonably covered.

We did not observe any decrease in the fertility rate or a loss of weight in the mothers over 8 reproductive cycles. The growth of the suckling lambs is in accordance with the potentialities of these rustic breeds.

2. CONCLUSION

Ammonia treatment of straws knows an important development in temperate areas. But its utilization in dry regions may allow to regularize livestock management.

In mediterranean countries hot and dry summers induce frequent food scarcities.

That is why matings, which usually take place between June an September, are not always fertilizing.

A more consistent animal feeding would surely improve reproductive conditions. Ammoniated straws may allow to offset nutritional lacks during the difficult periods of the year.

We showed that NH3-treated straws supplemented with minerals and vitamins may constitute the whole diet of sheep at maintenance or at the beginning of gestation. For lactating animals with higher needs, a balanced ration may be composed of ammoniated straws supplemented with concentrate. Ruminants accept well this kind of feeding, even over long periods.

Usually in mediterranean countries, straws and strubbles represent an important part of the ingested organ matter for ruminants (38 % in Marroco, (10)). Ammonia treatment of straws is yet widely used in northern countries. The economic effect of its utilization in mediterranean countries may be very important.

REFERENCES

(1) CHOMYSZYN, M., ZIOLECKA, A. (1972). Utilization of ammoniated feeds in ruminant nutrition, in : Tracer studies on non protein nitrogen for ruminants. IAEA-VIENNA FAO 153-161.
(2) HORTON, G.M. (1978). The intake and digestibility of ammoniated cereal straws by cattle. Can J. anim. Sci., 58, 471-478.
(3) SUNDSTØL, F., SAID, A.N., ARNASON, J. (1979). Factors influencing the effect of chemical treatment on the nutritive value of straw. Acta. Agric. Scand., 29, 179-190.
(4) WAISS, A.C., GUGGOLZ, J., KOHLER G.O., WALKER, H.G., GARRETT, W.N. (1972). Improving digestibility of straws for ruminant feed by aqueous ammonia. J. anim. Sci., 35, 109-112.
(5) CORDESSE, R., TABA-TABAI, M.M. (1981). Alimentation d'agneaux à partir d'une paille traitée à l'ammoniac. I. Valeur nutritive, croissance et composition corporelle. Ann. Zootech., 30, 137-150.
(6) ALIBES, X., MUÑOZ F., FACI R. (1984). Anhydrous ammonia treated straw for animal feeding. Some results from the Mediterranean Area. Anim. Feed. Sci. Technol., 10, 239-246.
(7) SUNDSTØL, F., COXWORTH, E., MOWAT, D.N. (1978). Amélioration de la valeur nutritive de la paille par le traitement à l'ammoniac. Rev. mond. Zootchn., 26, 13-21.

(8) ITCF. (1986). Rapport annuel Ruminant 1985. p.43.
(9) INRA, (1978). Alimentation des ruminants. ed. INRA Publications (Route de St-Cyr), 78000 Versailles. 597 p.
(10) GUESSOUS (1986). Personal communication.

Table 1. Fertility and prolificacy of ewes fed with an ammoniated straw diet during 8 reproductive cycles.
(Control animals received untreated roughages)

Experimental group		n°1		n°2	Control	
Ewe breed		Arles Merino	Aragonese	Arles Merino	Arles Merino	Aragonese
1st cycle	F	90.2	74	90.9	86.0	75
	P	122	120	120	128	120
2nd cycle	F	89.4	89	63.4	95	89
	P	140	100	100	135	100
3rd cycle	F	81.2		90.0	88.9	
	P	100		112	119	
4th cycle	F	94.7		90.0		
	P	172		111		
5th cycle	F	88.2		88.8		
	P	130		143		
6th cycle	F	81.2		50.0		
	P	161		100		
7th cycle	F	69.2				
	P	155				
8th cycle	F	72.7				
	P	125				

F : Fertility
P : Prolificacy

THE USE OF TREATED STRAW FOR FEEDING DAIRY CATTLE IN SCANDINAVIA

P. E. ANDERSEN, V. FRIIS KRISTENSEN and J. HERMANSEN
National Institute of Animal Science
Research in Cattle and Sheep
Forsøgsanlæg Foulum
8833 Ørum Sønderlyng
Denmark

Summary

Different methods of treatment of straw with alkali have greatly
increased the potential use of straw in cattle feeding. A series of
Scandinavian feeding experiments have illustrated different aspects of
using straw in the diet of dairy cattle. Results of these experiments
are summarized in this paper and conclusions about the optimum use of
straw as feed are drawn. Some factors and relationships concerning the
feeding of straw are briefly discussed. Treatment of straw with
sodiumhydroxide or ammonia increased the intake of straw, the milk
yield and the fat content of the milk of dairy cows. Chemically treated
straw could not replace high quality roughages without reducing milk
production in early lactation, even though the straw was supplemented
to reach the same level of energy and essential nutrients. High
yielding dairy cows require a high level of intake and at the same time
a great proportion of structure rich feed and digestible cell wall
constituents in the ration in order to supply the greatest possible
amounts of nutrients to the mammary gland. In the second half of the
lactation treated straw adequately supplemented with energy, protein,
fat, minerals and vitamins could partly or fully replace high quality
grass silage without effect on milk production. The relatively low rate
of digestion of treated straw makes the utilization of this feed
susceptible to the kind of supplemental carbohydrates. Supplements rich
in easily digestible cell wall constituents are better in milk
production than supplements rich in starch (barley). Also, fodderbeets
were better than barley. A good dairy diet based on by-products may be
obtained by mixing treated straw (roughly comminuted) with feeds rich
in easily digestible cell walls like beet pulp, citrus pulp or
cellulose pulp. In beef production the place of chemical treated straw
is limited for fast growing animals and it can not compete with good
quality grass silage, but in combination with silage it have some possibility. NH_3-treated straw gave less problems. For steers there are
possibilities in winter rations on lower growth rate. Problems with Mg
deficiency have been observed and must be dealt with giving more minerals to the animals when feeding NaOH-treated straw. In the diet of
replacement heifers, for which only limited growth rates are desired,
treated straw may constitute 60-80% of the total dry matter, provided
it is supplemented with easily digestible feeds containing the necessary nutrients.

1. INTRODUCTION
A great number of studies on chemical treatment of straw have been carried out during the last two decades and a new comprehensive book on treatment of straw and on feeding treated straw has been published (1). The digestibility of the organic matter in straw may be increased by 10-15 percentage units by treatment with ammonia and by up to 20 units by wet treatment with sodium hydroxide. New treatment methods have greatly increased the technical and biological possibilities for usage of straw as feed. In Denmark it has resulted in a fast increase in the use of chemical treatment. Based on the delivery of ammonia to farms during late summer and autumn it can be calculated that approximately 350,000 t of straw was treated with ammonia in Denmark in 1983. As smaller amounts have been treated with sodium hydroxide, the total amount of treated straw was between 350,000 and 400,000 t.

This paper gives a brief survey of Scandinavian feeding experiments with which it was attempted to illustrate 1) the effect of chemical treatment of straw on the performance of dairy cattle, 2) the effect of exchanging higher quality roughages with treated straw, and 3) the optimum supplementation of straw.

2. RATIONS FOR DAIRY COWS
Untreated chopped barley straw was compared in two experiments, one experiment with NH_3-treated straw and another with NaOH-treated chopped straw in rations for dairy cows (Table 1). The intake of straw was increased in both experiments by treatment. The milk yield and the fat content of the milk was significantly increased, when cows were fed treated straw.

Greenhalgh et al. (2) fed complete rations containing 50% concentrates and 50% either untreated or NaOH-treated (8% NaOH) barley straw. The DM intake was increased from 10.8 to 13.4 kg by treatment. The milk yield increased from 17.6 to 19.0 kg/d and the fat content of the milk from 3.54 to 3.74%.

Table 1   Daily feed intake, milk yield in dairy cows fed untreated and NaOH-treated, chopped barley straw (Kristensen, Hermansen and Andersen, 1984)

	Untreated	NH_3-treated	Untreated	NaOH-treated
Concentrates, kg DM	5.9	5.4	6.9	6.9
Beettop silage, kg DM	2.9	3.1	-	-
Molasses, kg DM	2.4	1.7	3.8	3.8
Fodderbeet, kg DM	2.4	2.0	-	-
Straw ad lib., kg DM	3.6	5.4	5.7	7.4
Milk, kg/d	20.1	20.7	24.0	24.6
Milk fat, %	3.89	4.12	3.34	3.64
4% FCM, kg	19.7	21.0	21.6	23.3

2.1 Treated straw versus higher quality roughages
The purpose of an experiment conducted by Kristensen, Hermansen and Andersen (3) was to compare the effects of feeding NH_3-treated barley straw versus grass silage to dairy cows in different parts of the lactation period, and to investigate the effects of changing from grass silage to

NH$_3$-treated straw. Four groups of cows in a continuous trial were fed as shown in Table 4. Grass silage and straw mixture were fed ad libitum. Concentrates, fodderbeets or molasses plus dried beef pulp and small amounts of grass silage or straw mixture were fed in fixed amounts. Grass silage contained in average 22% crude fibre.

There was only minor differences in feed intake. Straw gave a significantly lower yield than grass silage in the beginning of lactation. Change from grass silage to straw mixture at 12 weeks post partum also resulted in a significantly lower yield during the following 12 weeks. A change at 24 weeks post partum had a small and non significant affect on milk production.

Table 2 Comparison of NH$_3$-treated barley straw with grass silage in different parts of lactation (Kristensen, Hermansen and Andersen, 1984)

Weeks post partum	Group			
	1	2	3	4
0-12	grass sil.	grass sil.	grass sil.	straw mix.*
13-24	- " -	- " -	straw mix.*	- " -
25-	- " -	straw mix.*	- " -	- " -
	Intake of kg DM			
0- 4	5.7	5.1	5.1	6.4
21-24	6.3	6.3	6.9	6.5
	Yield of kg 4% FCM			
0-12	27.2	27.1	26.4	25.2
13-24	22.2	22.5	21.0	20.5
25-32	18.9	18.6	17.2	17.7
0-32	23.3	23.2	22.1	21.6

*) Composition, % of DM: NH$_3$-treated straw 62.6
Molasses   24.1
Soya bean meal   8.5
Minerals   3.7
Urea   1.1

The same level of energy and nutrients in all groups was aimed at by supplementing the straw with energy rich feeds plus protein, nitrogen and minerals. In spite of this the milk production was decreased in the beginning of lactation when cows were fed a diet with treated straw compared to grass silage. This effect is probably owing to the increased supplementation of very easily digestible feeds with a high proportion of cell contents, which stimulates anabolic processes in body tissues, leaving smaller amounts of nutrients for milk syntesis in the mammary gland. With higher quality roughages it is easier to obtain a high level of intake with a structure rich diet having a high content of digestible cell wall constituents, which gives the basis for the greatest possible supply of nutrients to the mammary gland.

In later lactation and for cows with moderate or low production treated straw partly or wholly can replace higher quality roughages with small or no effect on milk production. This has also been demonstrated in another experiment, the results of which are shown in Table 3, and it has been confirmed by Finnish and Norwegian results (4 and 5).

Table 3 Effect on ad libitum intake of NH_3-treated barley straw and on milk production of increasing amounts of grass silage (Kristensen and Andersen, 1980)

Nos. of cows	9	9	9
NH_3-treated straw, kg DM	6.0	3.5	1.2
Grass silage , kg DM	0	3.0	5.9
Concentrates , kg DM	6.3	6.2	6.2
Fodderbeets , kg DM	2.2	2.2	2.2
Milk, kg	20.9	20.6	21.4
Milk fat, %	3.87	3.79	3.86

Continuous trial, experimental period 10 weeks.

The intake of straw DM was decreased by 0.8 kg/kg increase in the amount of DM in grass silage (Table 3). The in vitro digestibility of the grass silage was 70% and that of straw 58%.

In the Finnish experiments the intake of long oat straw in cows was increased by 15% after treatment with NH_3 (4) (Table 4). In this experiment, the straw was supplemented with increasing amounts of grass silage. The intake of treated straw was decreased by approximately 0.6 kg DM for each additional kg DM given as grass silage. However, the amount of concentrate was reduced with increasing amounts of silage.

Table 4 Daily feed intake, milk yield and total live weight change in dairy cows fed untreated and NH_3-treated long oat straw in rations with varying amounts of grass silage (Rissanen and Kossila, 1977)

Straw	Un-treated	Treat-ed	Un-treated	Treat-ed	Un-treated	Treat-ed
Straw ad lib., kg DM	6.1	6.9	4.4	5.1	2.6	3.0
Silage, kg DM	–	–	3.2	3.2	6.5	6.3
Concentrates, kg	9.3	8.8	7.5	7.3	5.3	5.2
Dry molasses beet pulp, kg	2.0	1.8	2.0	1.9	1.8	1.9
4% FCM, kg	19.0	19.4	18.9	18.5	18.7	19.5
Milk fat, %	4.38	4.41	4.43	4.49	4.30	4.65
Weight change, kg	19	23	16	22	25	31

In the Norwegian experiment (5) replaced some high quality grass silage by NH_3-treated barley straw to dairy cows. The cows consumed 2.7 and 3.2 kg DM NH_3-treated long straw together with 5.2 kg silage DM plus 7.5 kg concentrate (Table 5). The straw replaced approximately 3.5 kg silage DM and was supplied with approximately 1 kg concentrate more than the pure silage. There was no significant effect on milk yield.

Table 5   Replacement of grass by NH_3-treated barley straw to dairy cows (Mo, 1978)

Group	Experiment I		Experiment II	
	1	2	1	2
Silage, kg DM/d	5.2	8.5	5.2	8.8
Straw, kg DM/d	3.2	–	2.7	–
Concentrates, kg/d	7.6	6.8	7.4	6.2
Milk, kg/d	21.4	21.8	20.3	20.4
Milk fat, %	3.64	3.61	3.69	3.77
4% FCM, kg/d	20.2	20.6	19.4	19.6

Garmo and Arnason (6) compared barley straw treated with alkali by different procedures. The straw was either treated with NaOH by soaking and washing of long straw (wet) or by mixing chopped straw with a concentrated alkali solution followed by storing (dry method). The third method was treatment with ammonia by adding liquid ammonia to a sealed stack of long straw. The three types of straw were given to dairy cows in different amounts giving equal calculated amounts of net energy (Table 6). There were no significant differences in milk yield.

Table 6   Comparison of different methods of alkali treatment of barley straw for dairy cows (Garmo and Arnason, 1980)

Group	Experiment I			Experiment II		
	1	2	3	1	2	3
Silage, kg DM/d	4.3	4.3	4.3	4.1	4.1	4.1
Straw, kg DM/d	3.3[1]	3.9[2]	3.8[3]	2.9[1]	3.7[2]	3.5[3]
Concentrates, kg/d	6.4	6.8	6.6	7.9	7.9	8.1
4% FCM, kg/d	18.2	19.4	18.4	19.8	19.3	19.0

1) NaOH (wet method). DOM in sheep: 74%
2) NaOH (dry method). DOM in sheep: 70%
3) NH_3 (dry method). DOM in sheep: 61%

It was concluded that high quality roughages should be reserved for the high yielding cows in early lactation, a smaller amount of treated straw can be used but may be a valuable roughage for supplementation in the last half of the lactation and for dry cows.

2.2 Supplementation of diets bases on straw

As mentioned before treated straw has a relatively low net energy value, and when fed to milking cows it must be supplemented by more energy rich feedstuffs containing easily digestible carbohydrates. Different carbohydrates have different depressive effects on the fermentation of cell wall constituents. It was, therefore, important to investigate the effect of different carbohydrate sources.

In an experiment (latin square design) with 16 cows in mid lactation barley grain and beet molasses were compared as supplements for NH_3-treated straw (7). The feed intake and yield are shown in Table 7. These supplements given in an amount of 3.5 to 4 kg DM did not affect feed intake or production differently.

Table 7 Effect of barley or beet molasses on ad libitum intake of NH$_3$-treated barley straw and milk production (Kristensen and Andersen, 1980)

Barley, rolled , kg DM	3.5	–
Molasses , kg DM	–	3.8
NH$_3$-treated straw, kg DM	6.0	6.0
Concentrates	5.1	5.1
Milk, kg	18.0	18.1
Fat, %	3.98	3.95

In another experiment (8) concentrated whey (hyperfiltrated, 20% DM) was compared to beet molasses. 10 cows per group in a continuous trial with 8 weeks experimental period were fed complete mixed diets with the following composition (% of DM):

    NaOH-treated straw   35
    Whey/molasses   35
    Concentrates   45

The results are given in Table 8. The intake of whey/molasses was 3.7 kg/d. There were no significant difference in feed intake or production.
    Hermansen (9) compared fodderbeets and beet molasses in greater amounts (app. 5.8 kg DM/cow/day) as supplements for both NH$_3$-treated straw and grass silage and found no significant differences in effect on milk yield.

Table 8 Effect of concentrated whey versus beet molasses on ad libitum feed intake and milk production (Andersen, 1984)

	Whey	Molasses
Feed intake, kg DM	18.5	18.4
Milk, kg	23.8	23.6
Fat, %	4.1	3.9

3. DIETS FOR GROWING CATTLE
    The utilization of chemically treated straw depends on the proportion of straw in the diet, the composition of the diet, and the level of feeding. Furthermore, the nutritional value of chemically treated straw may be affected by the chemicals or their residues.
    In some experiments the effect of alkali treatment on growth and energy utilization was found to be small when the diet contained only limited proportions of straw.
    In a Danish experiment (10) young bulls fed rations containing 20% and

40% untreated or treated (5% NaOH) barley straw to appetite did not respond to treatment at the low level of straw in the diet, but with 40% straw live weight and carcass gain were significantly improved by treatment (Table 9). In a 10-months experiment (11) bull calves were fed rations containing 25% untreated or NaOH-treated (4% NaOH) barley straw ad libitum in loose mixes. Other ingredients were 25% molasses and 50% concentrates. Live weight gain was significantly improved from 1121 g/day to 1202 g/day due to NaOH-treatment.

Table 9 Effect of NaOH-treatment at different levels of barley straw in pelleted diets for young bulls (Kristensen et al., 1977)

Straw in the diet, % of DM	Untreated straw		NaOH-treated straw	
	20	40	20	40
Nos. of animals	10	10	9	10
Days of experiment	158	176	166	159
Initial live weight, kg	224	234	222	233
Total DM intake, kg/d	7.8	8.5	7.8	8.5
Live weight gain, g/d	1374	1209	1336	1322
Carcass gain, g/d	736	624	707	685

In another experiment, H. Refsgaard Andersen, personal communication, young bulls were fed complete diets as loose mixes containing 20, 35 and 50% shredded NaOH-treated (4% NaOH) barley straw plus 25% molasses, the remainder being concentrates. These diets were compared to a control ration of pure concentrates supplemented with 1 to 2 kg of long straw and hay. The intake of diets containing treated straw was higher than expected and was considerably higher than that of the control ration. The feed efficiency however was poor. At 20% and 35% straw even negative net energy values for straw were calculated.

Thus the results of alkali treatment at low proportions of straw in the diet show some discrepancies. With small inclusions of straw the change in feeding value of the total diet resulting from alkali treatment of the straw will be small and therefore difficult to detect in feeding experiments. Additionally the discrepancies may partly be explained by differences in level of feeding and composition of the diet. If the diet contains a great deal of other roughages utilization of the straw would not be expected to be depressed as in a high concentrate diet.

Certain limitations on the utilization of alkali-treated straw may be due to reduced time of retention of feed particles in the forestomachs. This seems to be the case on treating with NaOH (12 and 13) or NH_3 (14). It results in an increased amount of potentially digestible feed escaping digestion in the rumen (15). The higher rate of passage may be due to the increased proportion of organic matter in straw solubilized after alkali treatment. Also in the case of NaOH-treatment (dry and semidry methods) water consumption is increased as a result of the high intake of sodium.

It may be concluded that at low proportions of straw and high proportions of easily fermentable carbohydrates, the effect of alkali treatment is small or even absent. Treatment therefore is probably not economic in these situations.

Arnason (16) decreased the amount of supplement fed with treated straw, when he compared untreated and NaOH-treated barley straw to young bulls (Table 10). In experiment K-131 food intake and weight gain were very high during the first 12 weeks of the experimental period, but serious health problems arose in the group fed treated straw. The animals developed diarrhoea and did not thrive. Their weight gain was reduced drastically although the feed intake remained high.

In the same experiment the blood serum concentrations of P and Mg were significantly reduced. In the other experiment (K-145) the serum Mg concentration was significantly reduced in animals fed NaOH-treated straw, but with reducing the gain. In experiment K-145, where straw was fed in restricted amounts, approximately 1 kg DM in concentrate could be saved without reeducing the gain, when the straw was treated.

Table 10 Comparison of untreated long and NaOH-treated[1] chopped straw for young bulls (Arnason, 1980)

Experiment	K-131		K-145	
NaOH-treatment rate, %	0	4.1	0	4.3
Digestibility of OM, %[2]	53	67	55	68
Initial weight, kg	175		275	
Days of experiment	247		176	
Food intake, kg DM/d				
Concentrate	3.8	2.1	3.2	2.3
Hay	–	–	0.9	0.9
Straw	3,0[3]	4.7	2.5[4]	3.4
Live weight gain, g/d				
0-12 weeks	1225	1225	–	–
Total exp. period	1056	937	906	948

1) Dry treatment
2) Data for straw alone. Determined in sheep fed restricted
3) First 12 weeks ad lib., thereafter max. 4 and 6 kg untreated and treated straw, respectively
4) Max. 3 and 5 kg of untreated and treated straw, respectively

Table 11 summarizes Norwegian experiments with NH_3-treated straw to growing bulls. In the trial by Arnason (17) the intake of treated straw was equal to that of grass silage, but the weight gain was lower on straw than on silage. In the trial by Kvåle and Homb (18) treatment of straw fed in a restricted amount (3.5 kg DM/d) increased daily live weight gain by 200 g, but in a similar experiment by Kvåle and Homb (19) no response to treatment appeared. In the experiment by Kvåle (20) treatment increased the intake of straw by 31% and the weight gain increased from 912 to 1024 g/day.

Table 11 Results of experiments with ammonia-treated straw in the diet of growing bulls in Norway

Experiment	Arnason, 1977		Kvåle and Homb, 1976		Kvåle and Homb, 1977		Kvåle, 1978	
Nos. of animals	20		28		28		28	
Days of experiment	174		151		172		134	
Initial live weight, kg	284		312		276			
Daily rations, kg								
Concentrates	2.0	2.0	2.0	2.0	2.0	2.0	2.4	2.4
Hay (Distillery slop)	1.0	1.0	2.0(25)	2.0(25)	(30)	(30)	(30)	(30)
Grass silage	4.34 (ad lib.)	–			6.5	6.5		
Untreated straw			3.5		3.4		3.5 (ad lib.)	
Ammonia-treated straw		4.48 (ad lib.)		3.5		3.4		4.6 (ad lib.)
Daily gain, g	1025	840	669	855	1161	1075	912	1024

Results of Norwegian experiments with NH_3-treated straw to steers are shown in Table 12. The straw was fed ad libitum and its intake was increased by 43%, 26% and 67% by treatment in experiments 1, 2 and 3, respectively (21, 22, 23). In experiment 3 the amount of concentrates fed to animals receiving treated straw was reduced. Daily weight gain was increased by 130 and 315 g in experiments 1 and 2 respectively, and in experiment 3 treatment increased weight gain by nearly 100 g/day even though concentrates were reduced by 1.6 kg/day.

Table 12   Results of experiments with amonia-treated straw in the diet of growing steers in Norway

Experiment reference and number	Pestalozzi and Matre, (1976) 1		Pestalozzi and matre, (1977) 2		Sundstøl and Matre (1980) 3	
Nos. of animals	8		10		28	
Days of experiment	84		112		168	
Initial live weight, kg	277		282		375	
Daily rations, kg						
Concentrates	2.0	2.0	2.0	2.0	1.9	0.25
Grass silage	5.0	5.0	3.0	3.0	–	–
Untreated straw	2.8	–	3.4	–	6.0	–
Ammonia-treated straw	–	4.0	–	4.3	–	10.0
Daily gain, g	530	660	215	530	349	434

4. STRAW FOR REPLACEMENT HEIFERS

For replacement heifers only limited growth rates (600–700 g/day) is desired during a great part of the rearing period. Medium or low quality roughages can, therefore, make up a great proportion of their diet. Treated straw, especially NH_3-treated straw, is a good source of energy for these animals. When straw makes up more than 50% of the diet dry matter, there is no significant problems concerning the effects of supplemental carbo-hydrates.

In dairy heifers fed 1.3 kg DM/day of molasses and fodderbeet and 0.6 kg/day soya bean meal, ammonia treatment increased the intake of long barley straw by 7% and daily live weight gain by 106 g from 635 to 741 g/day (24). In Norwegian experiments NaOH-treatment increased the intake of barley straw by 33% when at the same time the amount of concentrate was decreased by 1.3 kg DM/day. Daily weight gain was 707 and 772 on diets with untreated and treated straw respectively.

From these experiments it was concluded that treated straw may make up 60–80% of the total diet DM for heifers required to grow 600–800 g/day, pro-vided the straw is supplemented with easily digestible feeds containing the necessary nutrients.

In such fiber rich diets the source of nitrogen may affect the animal performance. Beneficial effects of supplementation with protein of plant or animal origin over non-protein-N on intake and growth rate have been report-ed from several experiments and reviewed by Kristensen (25).

REFERENCES

(1) SUNDSTØL, F. and OWEN, E., 1984. Straw and other fibrous by products as feed. Elsevier, Amsterdam, Oxford, New York, Tokio. 604 pp.

(2) GREENHALGH, J. F. D., PIERIE R. and REID, G. W., 1976. Alkali-treated barley straw in complete diets for lambs and dairy cows. Anim. Prod. 22: 159 (Abstr.).

(3) KRISTENSEN, V. F., HERMANSEN, J. and ANDERSEN, P. E., 1984. Economic use of treated straw in milk produktion, 35. Annual Meet. EAAP. The Hagne, The Netherlands.

(4) RISSANEN, H. and KOSSILA, V., 1977. Untreated and ammonized straw with or without silage to dairy cows. In: Quality of Forage. Proc. seminar NJF, 20-22 April, Uppsala, Sweden. Inst. Husdjurens utfodring och vård, Rapport No. 54: 177-180.

(5) MO, M., 1978. Ammoniakkbehandlet halm i forrasjonen til melkekyr. Paper presented at NJF seminar, 28-31 March, Middelfart, Denmark, 4 pp.

(6) GARMO, T. and ARNASON, J., 1980. Beckmann-luta, ammoniakbehandla og tørrluta (NaOH) halm som for til mjølkekyr. Husdyrforsøksmøtet 1980, Aktuelt fra Landbruksdepartementets opplysningstjeneste nr. 1, 405.

(7) KRISTENSEN, V. F. and ANDERSEN, P. E., 1980. Ammoniakbehandlet byghalm til malkekøer. Statens Husdyrbrugsforsøg, Copenhagen. Medd. No. 332, 4 pp.

(8) ANDERSEN, P. E., 1984. NaOH-treated straw to dairy cows. Notes to Annual Meeting at Nat. Research Inst. of Anim. Sci., Foulum, 1-5.

(9) HERMANSEN, J., 1984. NH_3 treated straw to dairy cows. Notes to Animal meet. at Nat. Research Inst. of Animal Science, Foulum, 4-6.

(10) KRISTENSEN, V. F., ANDERSEN, P. E., STIGSEN, P., THOMSEN, K. V., ANDERSEN, H. R., SØRENSEN, M., ALI, C. S., MASON, V. C., REXEN, F., ISRAELSEN, M. and WOLSTRUP, J., 1977. Sodium hydroxide treated straw as feed for cattle and sheep. 464. beretn., Statens Husdyrbrugsforsøg, Copenhagen, 218 pp.

(11) ANDERSEN, H. R., ANDERSEN, B. B., MØLLER, E., KLASTRUP, S., PHILIPSEN, H. and JENSEN, A. M., 1980. Fuldfoder med ludbehandlet (NaOH) kontra ubehandlet byghalm til ungtyre. Statens Husdyrbrugsforsøg, Copenhagen, Medd. No. 4 pp.

(12) COOMBE, J. B., DINUS, D. A. and WHEELER, W. E., 1979. Effect of alkali treatment on intake and digestion of barley straw by beef steers. J. Anim. Sci. 49: 169-176.

(13) BERGER, L. L., KLOPFENSTEIN, T. J. and BRITTON, R. A., 1980. Effect of sodium hydroxide treatment on rate of passage and rate of ruminal fiber digestion. J. Anim. Sci. 50: 745-749.

(14) OJI, U.I., NOWAT, D.N. and BUCHANAN-SMITH, J.G., 1979. Nutritive value of thermoammoniated and steam-treated maize stover. II. Rumen metabolites and rate of passage. Anim. Feed Sci. Technol. 4: 187-197.

(15) BERGER, L. L., KLOPFENSTEIN, T. J. and BRITTON, R. A., 1979. Effect of sodium hydroxide on efficiency of rumen digestion. J. Anim. Sci. 49: 1317-1323.

(16) ARNASON, J., 1980a. Tørrlutet (NaOH) halm som for til slakte okser. Sci. Rep., Agric. Univ. Norway, 59, (26), 18 pp.

(17) ARNASON, J., 1977. Halm i storfekjøttproduksjonen. Husdyrforsøksmøtet, Agric. Univ. Norway.

(18) KVÅLE, S. E. and HOMB, T., 1976. Forsøk med halm og drank til okser. Mimeographed paper, Dept. Anim. Nutr., Agric. Univ. Norway.

(19) KVÅLE, S. E. and HOMB, T., 1977. Produksjonsforsøk med avfall fra potetindustrien. Mimeographed paper. Dept. Anim. Nutr., Agric. Univ. Norway.

(20) KVÅLE, S. E., 1978. Oppdrettsforsøg med avfall fra potetindustrien som for til okser. Mimeographed paper. Dept. Anim. Nutr., Agric. Univ. Norway.

(21) PESTALOZZI, M. and MATRE, T., 1976. Forsøk med ammoniakkbehandlet halm til kastrater. Mimeographed paper. Dept. Anim. Nutr., Agric. Univ. Norway.

(22) PESTALOZZI, M. and MATRE, T., 1977. Forsøk med ammoniakkbehandlet halm til kastrater. Mimeographed paper. Dept. Anim. Nutr., Agric. Univ. Norway.

(23) SUNDSTØL, F. and MATRE, T., 1980. Bruk av ammoniakkbehandla halm i kjøttproduksjonen. Husdyrforsøksmøtet, Agric. Univ. Norway. 399–404.

(24) FOLDAGER, J., 1978. Halm til opdræt. Paper presented at NJF-seminar: Halm; håndtering, behandling og udnyttelse. 28–31 March, Middelfart, Denmark.

(25) KRISTENSEN, V.F. 1982. Effect of processing on nutrient content of feeds: Alkali treatment. In: Handbook of Nutritive Value of processed Food. Volume II: Animal Feedstuffs (Rechcigl, M., Jr., ed.), CRC Press, Inc., Boca Raton, Florida, 65–101.

THE INFLUENCE OF THE CHEMICAL TREATMENT OF STRAW ON

UTILIZATION OF MAGNESIUM BY DAIRY CATTLE

P. E. ANDERSEN and S. BOISEN
National Institute of Animal Science
Research in Cattle and Sheep
Forsøgsanlæg Foulum
8833 Ørum Sønderlyng
Denmark

Summary

From dairy cows fed NaOH treated straw in more than 1 lactation were taken blood samples. The analyses showed no influence in blood content of Na and K, but some influence on Ca and Mg. The latter in some cases being too low in 1st lactation. It was regulated in 2nd and latter lactations by increasing the mineral supply. The kidney and urine output was an excellent regulator of the big Na surplus.

1. INTRODUCTION

For many years the improvement of low quality roughages has been of great interest (1 and 2).

It is to a great extent the ligno-cellulose containing feedstuffs which are in question and it would mostly be grain straw from barley, oats, wheat and rice.

The chemical treatment with sodiumhydroxid, NaOH and ammonia, NH_3, is the most common used. In a previous lecture you have learned about the influence of NH_3 on the utilization of magnesium.

This paper would bring forward information from experiments with NaOH treatment of barley straw fed to dairy cattle. The purpose was to investigate the long time effect of an alkali-feed on the balance of acid-base in the blood and also measure the mineral level in the blood. It was a suggestion that the cow around calving would have an increasing difficulty with the balance of calcium and magnesium, when the cow was given alkali-treated straw.

2. EXPERIMENTAL DESIGN

The experiment had to be carried out for 2 to 3 lactations to obtain valid information of the acid-base balance and the mineral status and also the relationship with the health and fertility of the cow.

Information was obtained of the feed intake, and milk yield, together with the blood parametre which was taken at monthly intervals.

The treated barley straw (4% NaOH) was included in a complete feed with 40%, the rest was mostly concentrates, but also 20% molasses.

Before the first calf the heifers obtained only straw as roughages. A grain-protein mixture was given in quantity to obtain the same gain of the heifers.

The number of animals was:

Period	Treated straw (group 1)	Normal straw (group 2)
Heifers	20	20
1st calf	15	13
2nd calf	12	10
3rd calf	5	(9)

(new group)

Additional information was obtained after 4th calf from a few cows.
The blood samples were obtained regularly within each lactation to have an impression of the pattern or variation of these parametres within the lactation period. Also around the calving time additional blood samples were taken to see if there was any irregularity when the cow changed from a low to a higher requirement of minerals at the start of the milk production.

3. EXPERIMENTAL RESULTS

3.1 The "long" time experiment

Twenty heifers were started on the experiment 10 to 12 months before 1st calf on treated straw, and 20 heifers on normal straw.

3.1.1 The heifers period

	Treated straw (group 1)	Normal straw (group 2)
Straw, kg per day	7.0	6.1
Concentrate, kg per day	1.6	3.1
Gain, g per day	425	426
Blood parametre		
Calcium	2.54	2.49
Phosphorus	2.52	2.55
Magnesium	0.86	0.99

In the blood it was only in the magnesium there was a lower content from heifers given alkali-treated straw. All heifers were in good health.
After the first calving the number of animals was reduced to 15 and 13 respectively in group 1 and 2.
The cows on alkali-treated straw (NaOH) got a complete diet with 40% straw, and the control cows (normal staw) received a normal roughage ration with sugar beets, grass silage, a small amount of straw and concentrates according to yield.

3.1.2 The first lactation

Period*)	Experimental group (No. 1)			Control group (No. 2)		
	1	2	3	1	2	3
pH	7.43	7.39	7.35	7.45	7.40	7.35
Base excess	+4.73	+0.81	-3.30	+5.68	-0.37	-4.25
Cl mmol	96	98	102	98	101	106
Na "	140	139	133	142	140	137
K "	3.83	3.96	4.00	3.69	3.83	3.90
Ca "	2.21	2.12	2.26	2.29	2.23	2.39
Mg	0.84	0.81	0.84	0.92	0.86	0.91

*) Periods of 10 weeks

The feed intake of the experimental cows was ad libitum in the first periods and in the first half of the second period and then restricted feeding, or else the cow would be too fat before the next lactation.

The variation of pH, base excess (equilibration method) and chloride had a pattern within the lactation along with the milk yield or feed intake.

Sodium (Na) showed no difference in the blood. The intake of Na was increased from 32 g (control) to 196 g (experiment) per cow per day, but the cow could administrate it by kidney- and urine excretion. Also in the potassium (K) content, there were no significant differences.

In the content of calcium and magnesium is seen a small decrease. In the figures 1 and 2 it is obvious that the blood content is approaching the lower limit.

Some of the experimental cows showed blood values below this limit, but without serious illness as a result.

In the second and later lactation the differences obtained in the blood parametres were less than in the first lactation. Also because the level of Ca and Mg in the feed ration was raised with 20-30% above normal recommendation, which was the level used in first lactation.

The milk production and milk composition was normal for the cows at the experimental group or not significantly different from the cows in the control group.

The culling of cows in first and second lactation was caused by other factors than what could be related to the experimental feed. The level of fertility was equal of the experimental cows, 69% in calf of second insemination and 70% in calf of the control cows. The problem which is seen for cows fed alkali-treated straw in the feed ration goes along with a low feed intake and caused by other factors also seen by normal fed cows - mastitis, ketosis and milk fewer. But with the Ca and Mg in the blood approaching the lower limit more incidence can occur. Normally the feed intake would increase for cows fed alkali treated straw in bigger quantities.

When the cows after second and third calf was slaughtered the kidney and heart were removed for macro- and microscopical examinations. There was not in any case sign of major changes in the tissue of the kidney and heart.

From the tail a sample of bone was taken to measure the mineral composition, Ca, P, Mg and Na. A small but not significant increase of Na was observed in bone from the experimental cows.

101

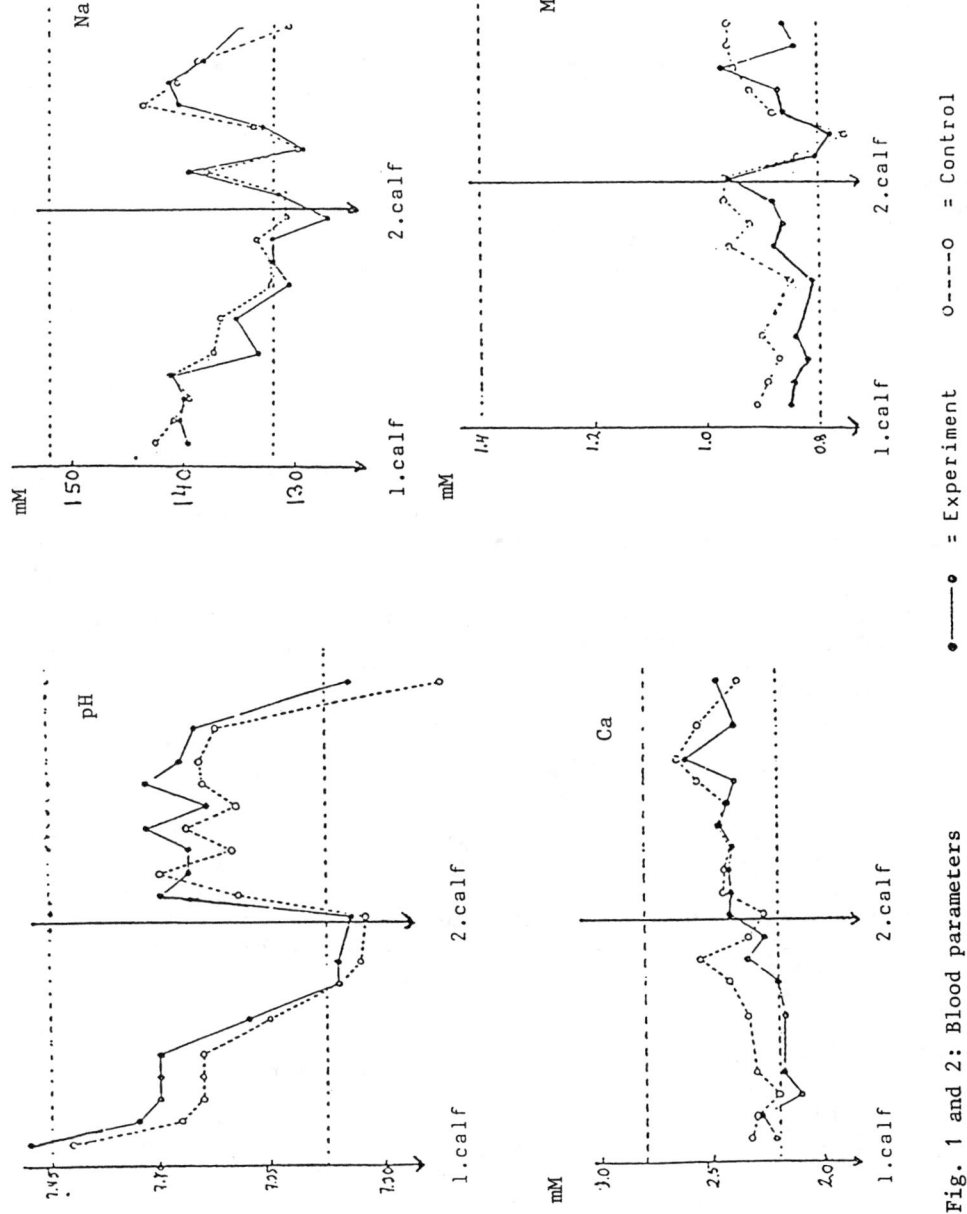

Fig. 1 and 2: Blood parameters

●———● = Experiment   ○----○ = Control

3.2 The "short" time experiment

The same tendency was also reported in two investigations with dairy cows and bulls in Norway (3 and 4). In these experiments (short time) was used deep-treatment of straw with NaOH (cows), and dry treatment (bulls):

Straw, kg	Dairy cow exp.			Bull calves exp.	
	0	3.0	8.3	Untreat.	NH$_3$-treat.
Blood parametre					
Base excess	+2.0	+5.7	+8.0	–	–
K, mmol	4.2	4.3	4.1	4.20	4.20
Na, "	134	137	134	147	146
Ca "	2.35	2.31	2.31	2.55	2.72
Mg, "	1.00	0.95	0.96	0.15	0.86
Urine samples					
pH	7.76	8.17	8.23	9.10	8.77
Na, mmol	76	236	272	21.4[1]	42.5[1]
Ca, "	5.1	1.3	1.7		
Mg, "	6.9	4.0	3.9	3.7[2]	24.4[2]

1) Water intake, kg per day   2) Urine per day

In the cow experiment there was an influence on the base excess, no influence on Na and K, and in both experiments a small influence on Ca and Mg in the blood. In the bull experiment there was a significant influence on Mg content.

The effort of the animal to regulate mineral balance is seen in the urine content, where at the same time a big increase in urine output must be regarded, which also can be seen from the results from the bull experiments concerning water intake and urine output.

The pH and Na is very much increased and the decrease in Ca and Mg would levelling out by the higher excretion of urine by the animals.

From a paper by Wamberg and Cooworkers (5) with results from a Danish experiment with bull calves fed NaOH-treated straw it could be sited:

Of major importance, however, is the remarkable capacity the normal kidney for quantitative excretion of the excessive loads of dietary-salts ensuring maintenance of normal or near-normal extracellular electrolyte and acid-base status by appropriate control of the fundamental processes of glomerular filtration and tubular reabsorption.

REFERENCES

(1) BECKMANN, E., 1919. Preussische Akademie der Wissenschaften, Berlin Sitzungsberichte 275.
(2) HOMB, T., 1984. Wet treatment with sodium hydroxide. In: chap. 6.1 p. 106-123. Straw and other fibrous by-products af feed. Editors: Sundstøl, F. and Owen E., publ. by Elsevier, Amsterdam, 1984.
(3) RANDBY, A. T., 1984. Dyppeluting av halm i forrasjonen til melkdyr. Aktuelt fra Statens Fagtjeneste for Landbruget, Husdyrforsøksmøtet nr. 3, 1984, 238-244.
(4) ARNASON, F., 1980. Dry treated (NaOH straw as feed for entire bulls. Med. fra Norges Landbrugshøjskole, Vol. 59, no. 26, 18p.
(5) WAMBERG, S. et al., 1985. Acid-base balance in ruminating calves given sodiumhydroxide-treated straw. British J. of Nut., 54. 655-667.

APPENDIX

Table 1 Daily feed (kg DM) and minerals (g)

	Feed	Straw	Na	K	Mg	Ca	P
Exp. group (1st lact.)	15.9	6.7	198	245	30	110	98
Control " (1st ")	12.7	1.8	32	178	29	86	82
Exp. group (2nd lact.)	19.0	8.0	257	382	59	134	127
Control " (2nd ")	17.6	2.1	52	342	26	91	75

Table 2 Annual yield

	Milk kg	Fat %	Butterfat kg	F.C.M. kg
Exp. group (1st lact.)	4936	4.13	204	5034
Control " (1st ")	4862	3.99	194	4834
Exp. group (2nd lact.)	5550	4.27	237	5774
Control " (2nd ")	5820	4.05	236	5871

Table 3 Mineral composition in milk, g/liter

	Na	K	Mg	Ca
Exp. group (1st lact.)	0.42	1.50	0.11	1.17
Control " (1st ")	0.41	1.58	0.12	1.26
Exp. group (2nd lact.)	0.44	1.54	0.11	1.16
Control " (2nd ")	0.42	1.66	0.11	1.17

DISCUSSION

Moderately producing animals in Mediterranean countries (Rapporteur: F. GUESSOUS. Chairman: X. ALIBES)

The two trials conducted in France by CORDESSE and in Spain by MUÑOZ and ALIBES, to examine the long-term effects of NH_3-treated straw as the major component of the diet, showed that the performance of ewes and lambs remained correct when treated straw represented 95% of total dry matter during maintenance, and 30% during lactation periods.

The question of the best energy supplement for the treated straw still remains open. Beet or citrus pulp or molasses, which are more available and less expensive in Mediterranean countries than cereals, seem to be best suited to improve the cellulolysis in the rumen.

Attention was drawn to the dangers of the production of toxic imidazole when treating with ammonia forages containing appreciable levels of nitrogen and soluble sugars. Imidazole would be transmitted to milk and would constitute a health problem for consumers. In Scandinavian countries, farmers are therefore encouraged not to treat their hay with ammonia. A maximum level of sugars in roughage beyond which no NH_3 treatment was to be applied should be recommended. The possibility of a relationship between imidazol production in NH_3-treated straw and the high temperature prevailing in e.g. Mediterranean countries was also raised.

High-producing animals in Scandinavian countries (Rapporteur: P.E. ANDERSEN. Chairman: X. ALIBES)

Also in the case of high-producing animals e.g. dairy cows, where the proportion of straw in the diet is less than 30%, one of the most important questions is the nature and quantity of the supplement to be used.

The theoretical aspects discussed earlier would logically lead to the use of feedstuffs rich in easily fermentable cell-walls. However, results obtained on both commercial farms and experimental stations provide evidence that barley, molasses or other sugar or starch-rich feeds can sustain correct milk production, provided these supplements are mixed with straw in form of a "complete ration". In addition, the Danish experiments show that they favour the cellulolytic fermentation.

The beneficial effect of treating straws when they form such a small portion of the feed, lies essentially in the increased voluntary intake of straw, as was observed by several authors attending this workshop, as well as by other authors in the literature.

- At low rates of incorporation of straw in the ration the beneficial effect of treating straws lies essentially in an increasing straw voluntary intake, as observed by several authors attending this seminar as well as literature work.

- It appears that feeding straw, untreated or treated, has now been well adopted and mastered by farmers in the Scandinavian countries. In France where the motivation of farmers may range from one extreme to the other, either using straw as a complement of the forage reserves, or as a basis of the winter feeding system, the adoption of NH_3 treatment (stack and Armako treatments, essentially) is also progressing: 20 000 t straw were treated in 1982 compared to more than 120 000 t in 1986. Results obtained by means of a farm survey (1) show that even when cereals and oil cakes were the only supplements used, growing heifers (dairy and beef types) had a growth rate of roughly 400 g/day and the weight loss of beef cows remained acceptable.

The scheme was such a success that a number of farmers in the survey had even decided to plough their pastures and to replace them by cereals. In such cases the winter feeding became entirely based on straw. Neither fertility nor animal health problems have yet been observed after 3 to 4 years with such feeding systems. The only concern might be, in the long term, a degradation of the soils under such farming systems.

The rate and nature of NH_3 treatment in Denmark has been commented upon by ANDERSEN. Anhydrous ammonia distribution and treatment is being handled by two private companies. The straw stacks are prepared beforehand by the farmers and are then injected by these companies. The economics of such a system are largely positive.

Both ANDERSEN and ADAMSON stressed, as a general remark, the need of being able to give the farmers general advice on how to treat, when and where, and how to best feed their animals depending upon the type of production required.

---

(1) GRENET, N., CHEVALIER, C., ROUDIER, J., LANGLOIS, J.P., PAYE, M., BINET, J.P., GAUTHIER, M., PIERRARD, M. and LATRON, J.P. (1985). C.R. ITEB, N° 85031, 27 pp.

In the U.K., the conventional forage-based system is still prevalent and the use of straw, although developing, is still being considered as an alternative for dry years only.

A tendency towards NaOH treatment is observed in some countries e.g. U.K. and Norway. In this respect, Dr. SUNDSTØL commented a new simple method being developed for NaOH treatment where alkali is recycled. The latter is shown on the following diagram:

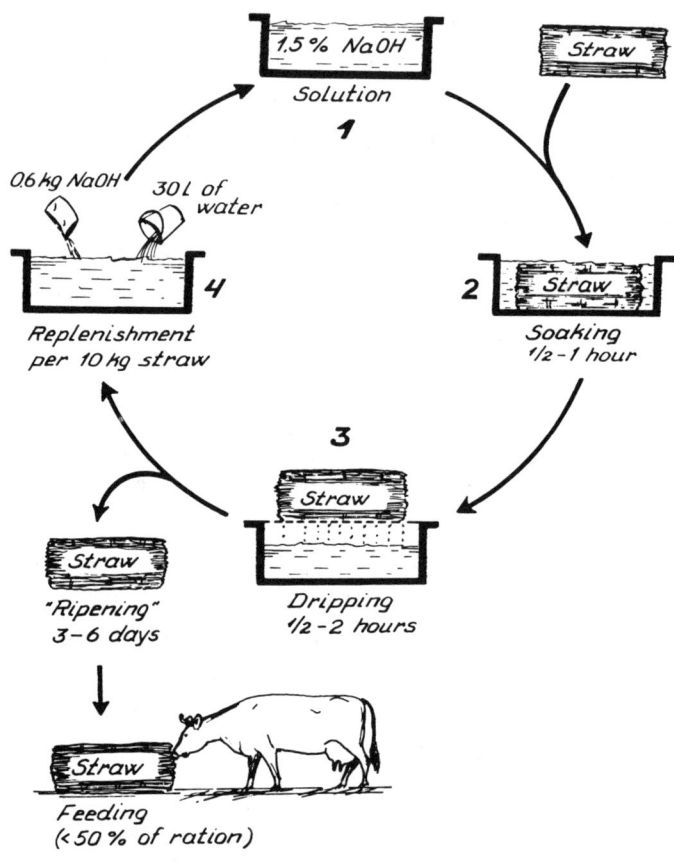

NaOH drip treatment of straw

Topic C:

IN VITRO METHODS FOR PREDICTING STRAWS DIGESTIBILITY AND INTAKE

PHYSICAL METHODS IN THE STUDY OF CELL WALL STRUCTURES AND CELL WALL DEGRADATION

J.M. van der Meer
Institute for Livestock Feeding and Nutrition Research
P.O. Box 160, 8200 AD Lelystad, The Netherlands

Summary

Characterization of polymeric cell wall structures can be effected through physical methods. The limitations of chemical methods occur because they measure only the content of cell wall components.
Available physical techniques are: -low voltage pyrolysis-mass spectrometry (pyMS) which can be used to show changes in the contents of phenolic substances as well as to study all changes in cell wall polymers.
Distribution of phenolics in cell walls can be studied with auto fluorescence, and energy dispersive X-ray analysis (EDXA).
Surface structures and bondings can be studied by X-ray and infrared spectroscopy (IR).
Orientation of carbohydrates and phenolic substances in the polymeric structure can be studied by pyMS and ^{13}C-nuclear magnetic resonance (^{13}C-NMR).
Near Infrared reflectance spectroscopy can best be used to follow changes in the structure during treatment or degradation.
These are specialised methods which should be used in combination in studies on structure of lignocellulosics.

1. INTRODUCTION

Ruminants can use lignocellulosic plant materials as a feed thanks to their symbiosis with micro-organisms in forestomach and large intestine. Voluntary intake and digestibility of these feeds mainly determine their feeding value for this kind of livestock.
Intake capacity of ruminants as to low quality feeds depends to a large extent on the rate of feed degradation in the mouth and in the forestomachs (1, 2). Particles longer than 0.1 cm are selectively withheld for a longer time in the forestomachs of sheep and goats (3), so reducing the possibility of renewed intake of feed. The reduction of particle size occurs through chewing, rumination and microbial degradation (4).
While maturing, all plants tend to increase the amount of (hemi) celluloses, lignins and sometimes tannins or silica in their stalks and leaves, as a result digestibility will decrease. The structural cell wall constituents are mainly polymeric in nature. These polymeric structures can be characterized by their mechanical, morphological, physical and chemical properties as well as composition, each of which influences digestibility and digestion rate by bacterial and fungal enzymes (Table 1).

Table 1. Characterization of plant fibres with relation to intake and digestibility

Cell wall properties methods	Treatments	Physiological: digestibility digestion rate
Mechanical - particle size, density, hardness, swelling, porevolume, ionexchange-capacity, absorption, pulping quality		
Morphological - histochemical, light microscopy, electron microscopy		
Physical - UV, IR, NIR, NMR, py.MS, ED, X-ray analyses, autofluorescence		
Chemical - Weende-, detergent methods, spectrophotometry (UV + visible), GC (IR), HPLC of sugars and phenols, analysis of acetyl- and methoxyl groups		

Chemical analysis only measures the contents of cell wall constituents (5-11). Composition of monomers of (hemi) celluloses, pectins and lignins does not provide information on the degree of polymerisation, branching, cristallinity, interwaving or encrustment of polysaccharides and phenols. Furthermore within the cell wall distribution of constituents is not uniform. Phloem contains highly digestible cell walls, the parenchym cells are only slightly slower digested. The remaining vascular bundles, with a composition and structure depending on its place in the morphological structure and on maturity, as well as epidermus are, almost, not degraded (12). Chemical (sodium hydroxide, lime, ammonia, sulphur dioxide) or physical (soaking, milling, steaming, exploding) treatments considerably change degradability in the digestive tract and often increase intake which however is poorly reflected in changes in the chemical composition (13-15). In Vitro and In Sacco incubations show the degradability but do not distinguish between morphological or physical structures (16).

A combined application of techniques is needed for a better understanding of the differences in the physical structure in relation with its morphological distribution and in its effects on degradation by bacterial- and free enzymes.
In this paper a selection of physical techniques recently applied for the study of cell wall structures are discussed for their possible contribution in the study of cell walls and illustrated with typical results.

2. SOME MECHANICAL FACTORS DETERMINING CELL WALL DEGRADATION

The pore size distribution of cellulose fibers can be measured by absorption of water after removal of the excess by centrifugation at 100 g. On immersion of dry fibers in a solution of polymers of a defined molecular weight in water penetration of the polymers is only a fraction of the absorption of water. When native cellulose is wetted with water the cellulose lattice is not penetrated or otherwise affected by the water in any way measurable with X-ray diffraction (17).

Deuterium oxide or titriated water are used to estimate the accessible OH-groups by subsequent infrared analysis of the transparant and not transparant carbohydrates respectively. It has been estimated that poresize is between 5 and 20 Angstrom. Hemicellulose is relatively less accessible than cellulose partly because of the strong internal hydrogen bonding between acetyl groups and neigbouring OH-groups.
This low accessibility will have its consequences for enzymatic degradation. The molecule size of cellulases are estimated at about 40 A. Although the conclusion will be that the carbohydrates showed a low accessibility to cellulase, in measurements the enzymatic degradation of cellulose proceeds without sudden changes in the reactivity (1st order reaction) that would suggest the early disappearance of a more accessible fraction on the surface of the fibers.

3. CHANGES IN THE ULTRA STRUCTURE ON DEGRADATION

Light microscopy provides information on plant histochemistry and can be used to survey large areas of samples rapidly and with less cost then with electron microscopy, thereby furnishing valuable information on forage anatomy related to degradation.
A section to slide technique is described for light microscopic observation of forage tissues digested by rumen micro organisms which will permit rapid evaluation (20).
Scanning and transmission electron microscopy (SEM and TEM) have provided data on the relative availabilities of specific tissues of forages for microbial degradation and on the manner in which cell wall digestion occurs and on the microbes involved. (21, 34). The resolution and in the case of SEM depth of field available with electron microscopy permits study of forage digestion from a perspective not available with light microscope.
Distribution of carbohydrates and lignins in the cell walls is dependent on the ultrastructure of the plant (20). Certain tissues, such as xylem cells, totally resist degradation by rumen micro organisms; these tissues stain positive for lignin with saturated phloroglucinol in 20% HCl (Weisnertest), the red-purple colour indicating the presence of coniferyl (cinnamaldehyde groups) (22). Other supportive tissues such as sclerenchyma ring and epidermis stain positive with hypochlorite followed by sodiumsulfite (or Maüle reagent), the rose-red colour reaction indicating the presence of syringyl (23). These tissues are not as resistant to attack as xylem cells, although they are poorly degraded.
Chemical treatment appears to make the chlorite-sulfite possitive tissues available for microbial attack but not the acid phloroglucinol staining tissues. It is suspected that the predominant phenolic monomers in these two types of lignin differ. p-Coumaric acid seems especially detrimental to forage digestibility and is also considered toxic to rumen micro organisms (24).
On staining cross sections of wheat straw stems for pectin with ruthenium red it seems under the light-microscope that ammonia treatment removes the uronic acids (24). From chemical studies it seems more probable that ammonia only alters the uronic acids.

The use of $KMnO_4$ and PaTAg as histochemical stains in electron micrsocopy enables the visualization of different cell wall components. Cellulose will appear as very fine black dotted lines on an amorphous fine granular (hemicellulose) background after PaTAg staining. The lignin stained by $KMnO_4$ shows a fibrillar skeleton due to the cellulose fibrils which are embedded in the lignin. These stains can be used in the study of bacterial activities (25).

The resolution in scanning electron microscopy (SEM) is determined by the electron spot diameter and the distance in the cell wall from which the secundary electrons are emitted. This problem is not met in transmission electron microscopy (TEM) on replica. The resolution that can be reached depends on the platina grains (25). Gordon et al. (26) applied TEM at freeze dried specimens embedded in white resin and the cut sections were stained with leadcitrate before examination.

Beside these histochemical studies on the anatomy of forages much work has been done on the rumen bacteria involved in the degradation (27, 28, 29). Recently the actions of protozoa (30) and rumen fungi (31, 32, 33) have been described.

The observations of Akin (34) showed that the fungi degrade sclerenchyma but Windham and Akin (35) did not find evidence for the breakdown of lignified tissues by these micro organisms. The production of (hemi) cellulolytic enzymes by fungi appears to be well established (36, 37, 38).

For ultra structural studies in the degradation of the plant cell walls in the rumen (27) fragments of tissues were incubated in nylon bags in the rumen of cannulated cows and degradation followed by electron microscope.

After 8 hours in the rumen the wheat straw fragments were largely colonized by rumen fungi under anaerobic conditions continuing until 48 hours. After 72 hours the fungi had disappeared. The penduncles of the many sporangia penetrated both the sclerenchyma cells, which form a ring around the stem and the underlaying parenchyma cells encrusted with lignin (phloroglucinol stain). It has also been observed that sporangia attached to the stem epidermus, the penduncle having probably penetrated the underlying sclerenchyma through a fissure. Colonization by anaerobic rumen fungi did not appear to be modified by ammonia treatment of the substrate (28).

Light microscopy has showed to be a technique which can be used in addition to other techniques.

Electron microscopy is a highly specialised technique but the information is very detailed and very relevant to the explanation of the degradation processes.

4. LOW VOLTAGE PYROLYSIS MASS SPECTROMETRY IN THE ANALYSIS OF CELL
   WALL CONSTITUENTS

The molecular aspects of the thermal dissociation of organic macro-
molecules and macromolecular complexes are not yet understood. The
repeatability of these processes in many different matrices and
samples is however evident from the now extensive literature on
pyrolyis mass spectrometry (39).
Comparative studies on curie point pyrolysis data from pyrolysis mass
spectrometry (pyms), pyrolysis gaschromatography (pygc) and pyrolysis-
gc-ms showed that the systems matched well (40) and have lead to modifications compared with the earlier models (39). A temperature controlled pyrolysis chamber has been introduced, which reduces the con-
densation of less volatile pyrolysate and results in excellent compa-
rability of py-gc-ms and pyms data.
Figure 1. shows schematic diagrams of the pyrolysis chambers used. In
pyms, the pyrolysis takes place in vacuo and the resulting pyrolysis
products expand in a heated gold coated expansion volume, which is
pumped down in about 20s through a leak to the ion source. This
arrangement precludes temperature resolved analytical data, but has
the advantage of short pyrolysis time (0.8s) and avoids high pressures
in the ion source. Ionization takes place at low electron voltages to
suppress molecular fragmentation, but the temperature regime maintained in the expansion chamber leads again to higher internal energies of
the molecules and therefore contributes to the fragment ion formation
(40).
In py-gc-ms, the pyrolysate is generated in the carrier gasstream and
swept immediately to the capillary column kept at room temperature.
Heavy fractions condens in the glas-liner around the ferromagnetic
probe. The carrier gas stream around the sample causes some cooling
compared to the vacuum conditions in pyms and hence somewhat longer
pyrolysis times (about 4s) are required. The capillary column ends in
the ion source of the mass spectrometer. Multivariate analysis of the
pyms data using factor analysis and discriminant analysis classifies
the pyrolysis spectra and extracts the characteristic information, defined as those corrected variables (mass peaks) which have the largest
outer variance (between group differences) and the best reproducibility (inner variance). The sets of correlated mass variables (discriminant functions) thus found are used to describe the relative difference between the samples (41, 42).

When samples of different species of bacteria or plants have been analysed, usually several discriminant functions are required to describe
the multidimensionality of the data. The chemical significance of the
mass peaks in pyrolysis mass spectra and discriminant function is
determined by pygcms. Pyrolysis products can be identified and their
contribution to the mass peak information in pyms can be estimated.
The classification based on pyms data are often found to correlate
with known chemical, biological or geological parameters. With adequate understanding of the chemical message in the pyrolysis data, the
distribution patterns found for the samples can be interpreted and
translated to their molecular architectures.
Isolated plant polymers, plant material, residues resulting from plant
decomposition have been studied by Curie point pyrolysis - mass
spectro metry (24-26) and pyrolysis-gc-ms techniques (43-45). Boon et

113

Figure 1: Schematic diagrams of the pyrolysis chambers

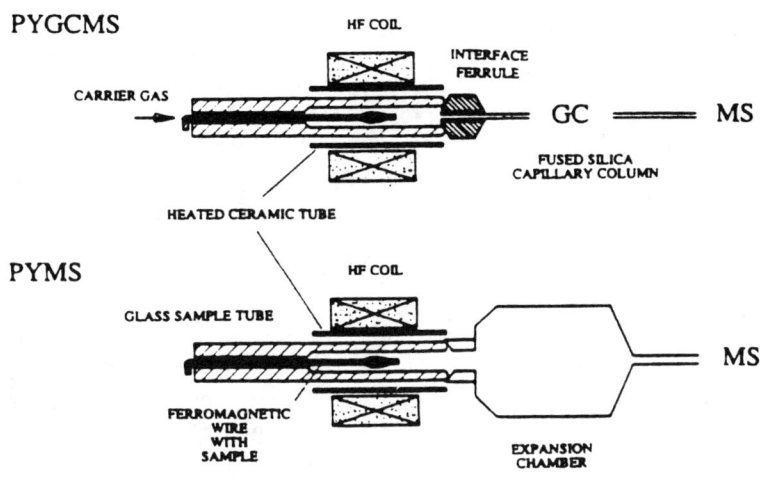

Figure 2: A typical mass spectrum of barley straw cell walls

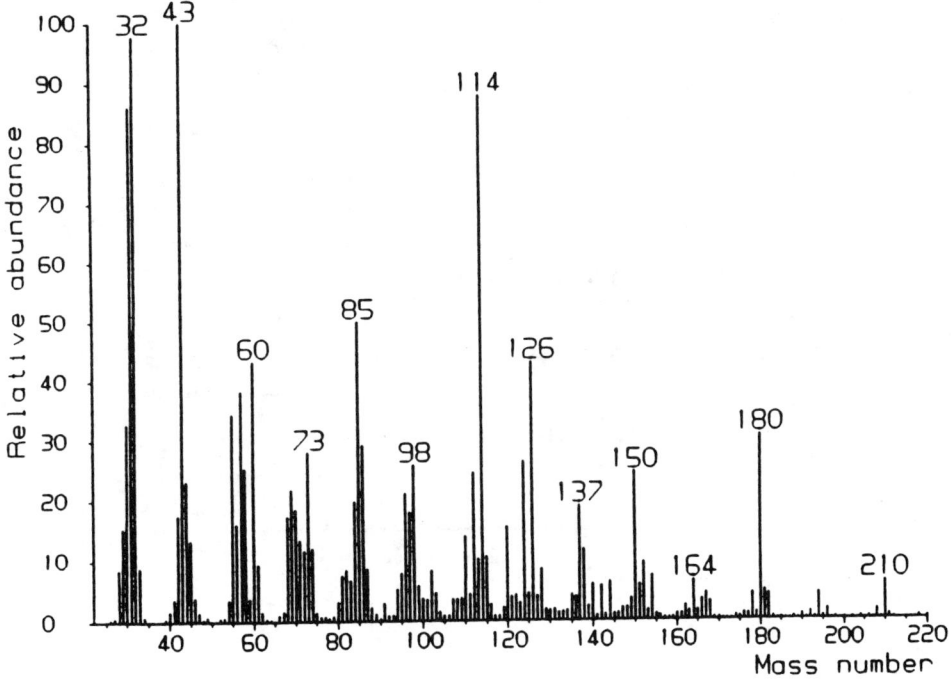

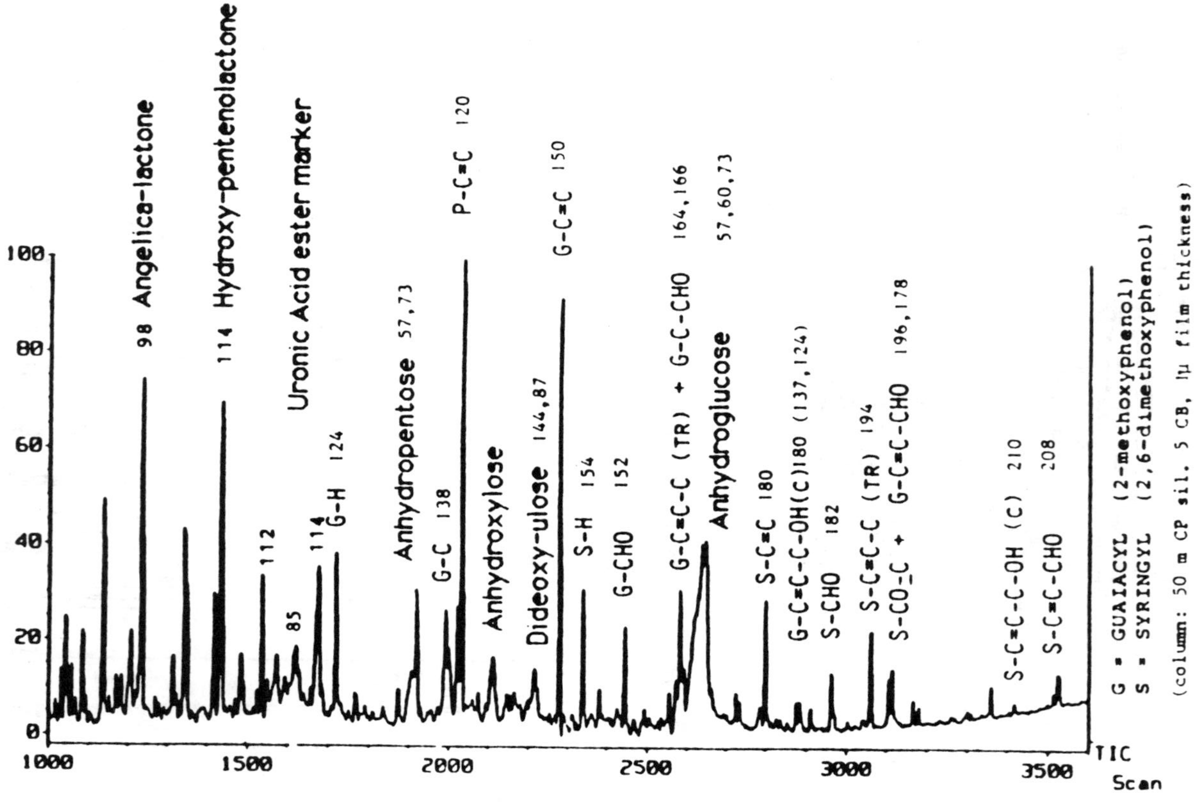

114

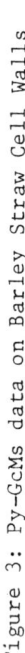

Figure 3: Py-GcMs data on Barley Straw Cell Walls

al. (30) have tabulated low voltage mass peaks indicative for the most common biopolymers.
Pyrolysis-gc-ms of amylose (50) and beech lignin (40) have revealed that some of the major peaks in low voltage electron-impact massspectra are fragment ion peaks, where as many of the mass peaks represent several chemical components.
To illustrate the data coming available with these methods in Fig. 2 a typical pyMS spectrum is shown of barley straw (46) containing the fragment sets originating from the phenolic acids (m/z, 120, 150, 180, 210 respectively for p. coumaric acid, ferulic acid, guaiacyl (coniferyl) alcohol and syringyl alcohol like structures. m/z 114 is specific for the pentosans and 126 for hexosans. Methyl uronic acid is characterized by m/z 85.
In fig. 3. a py-gc-MS, chromatogram of barley straw cell walls are shown analysed on a (50 m CP.sil 5CB) capillary column, 1 μ film thickness and curie pyrolysed at 510°C from a water suspension. The fragment m/z numbers from mass spectrometry are added have been placed next to the peak names (48). The carbohydrate and "lignin" fragments are clearly distinguished.
The increasing numbers of papers and applications is showing the importance of these methods. Combination with electron microscopy in the close future will enhance further detailed study of the cell wall structures.

5. ANALYSIS OF CELL WALL PHENOLICS BY AUTOFLUORESCENCE

Autofluorescence measurements are done with a Fluorescence microscope equipped with a mercury lamp and exciter filters. At an excitation wavelength of 366 nm the emission spectrum is recorded by measuring a sample area of 20 μm^2 with a RCA - photomultiplier tube operating at 1 kV. Maximal emission wavelength, intensity at maximal emission wavelength and decrease in intensity after 30 seconds (fading) are measured (51) (see fig. 4 for a typical spectrum).
In cell wall preparations after treatment with neutral detergent, acid detergent or in vitro incubation maximum emission was observed at 526, 508 and 480 mm respectively. In general removal of lignin from the cell walls (with organosolvents) is reflected in a decrease in intensity at Emax (50). On treatment of barley straw with ammonia a shift in the emission wavelength and intensity was observed in the parenchym tissue. In the cuticula tissue a wide peak maximum was obtained which also shifted to another wavelength on ammonia treatment. The maxima around 460-490 nm are from the fluorescence of the phenolic compounds like ferulic- and p. coumaric acid (50, 53).
The technique needs much more development in equipment and interpretation to improve the measurement and to explain observed effects. Photoreactivity is expected to cause changes in emission wavelength and intensity but cannot be interpreted yet.

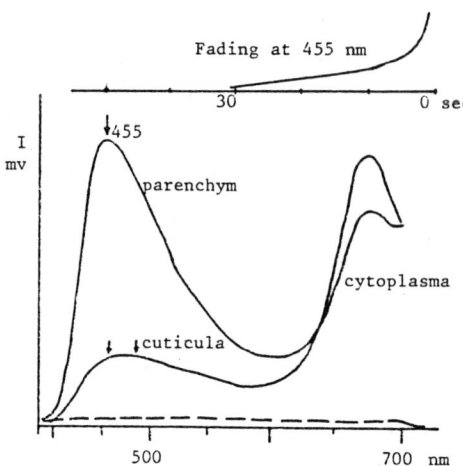

Figure 4: Autofluorescence spectrum of straw cell walls

6. ANALYSIS OF CELL WALL PHENOLICS BY ENERGY DISPERSIVE X-RAY

Combining scanning electron microscopy (SEM) or transmission electron microscopy (TEM) with energy dispersive X-ray analysis (EDXA) offers a combination of visual inspection with semi-quantitative information on the distribution of phenolics in cell walls (54).

In EDXA a specimen bombarded with electrons emit X-ray whose energies are characteristic for each element present. A silicon or other type of detector is used to capture and measure the intensity of the emitted X-rays. Generally the detection is limited to elements with an atomic number higher than neon. Therefor the use of this technique as a tool for lignin detection requires the incorporation of an element reacting specifically with lignin and having an appropriate atomic number. Bromine was found to satisfy both requirements.

Bromination was carried out in a non-aqueous system at room temperature. Under such conditions bromination of lignin takes place by addition to double bonds in side chain structures and/or substitution in aromatic nuclei, in particular, in phenolic structures.

In pine K_α (11,9 KeV) and K_β (13,3 KeV) emissions were observed, K and lignin were proportional. The use of ultra thin sections will also reduce the emitting area improving the resolution to 800 A, still it is difficult to match the morphological regions with the emitting area.

Measurements across the cell wall of pine showed the lignin distribution by SEM electron microscope and K_α-emission were in agreement with the expected distribution.

The permanganate stain technique with TEM was in close agreement with the SEM-EDXA findings.

Harbers et al. (24) and Gordon et al. (26) applied EDXA to localize silica and other minerals in the outer cuticularized epidermus of wheat stem (plasma ashed) and in the leaf hairs of rye grass. It was shown that ammonium hydroxide had no effect on the localization of silica in the cutille, expecting that rumen micro organisms would not penetrate this barrier.

7. ^{13}C-NUCLEAR MAGNETIC RESONANCE OF FORAGES.

The nuclei of certain atoms spin generating a magnetic moment along the axis of spin. If such an atom is placed in an external magnetic field its magnetic moment can be aligned with or against the external field. The amount of energy to flip over from the stable alignment to the instable one depends on the strength of the external field.

At a fixed radiation frequency for some value of the magnetic field strength the energy required to flip the nuclei matches the energy of radiation, absorption occurs and a spectrum is measured.

The number of signals tell about the kinds of nuclei, positions of the signals tell about the electronic environment of the nuclei, intensities of the signals are related to the number of nuclei of a kind, splitting of a signal in several peaks shows the environment with respect to other nearby nuclei. Chemical shifts arise from shielding and deshielding by electrons and are measured to a reference point, usually $(CH_3)_4Si(TMS)$.

Dissolved alkaline extracted hemicelluloses are analysed and showed to be glucoarabino.xylan (36). Barton suggested that the two hemicellulose fractions, xyloglucan and arabinoxylan, postulated by Albersheim (56) would be one structure only.

Grass lignins cannot be extracted free of sugars. There were notably differences in the spectra of the lignins from different species of grass (57). More carbohydrate tied up to p-coumaric acid in bermuda grass than to the lignin in fescue. Lignin is expected to be preferably associated with arabinose. The lignin complex in NDF was linked to xylo-araban with a xylose to arabinose ratio of 1:1 while the natural ratio is 3.5:1.

The need to dissolve samples limited the insitu analyses of structures with ^{13}C-NMR. With the 50 MHz equipment cross polarization-magic angle spinning (CP/MAS ^{13}C-NMR) enabled the analysis of spectra of solid materials.

Boer and Himmelsbach (58) used this technique to study the structural changes in cell walls on in sacco incubation. NDR and ADR fractions were prepared and spectra measured with polydimethylsilane (PDMS) as an internal reference.

Fig. 5 shows two spectra of the ADR fraction after 0 and 336 hrs of incubation. The spectra were taken with 16384 scans using a contact time of 2 ms. The signals in the region of 160-140 ppm are primarily due to phenolic carbons of phenolics esters and lignin, from 140-125 due to aromatic carbon from both protein and lignin sources. The signals between 108 and 60 ppm may be generally assigned to carbohydrates, since they are the overbearing constituent, although some aliphatic lignin signals do appear in this region.

For cellulose 105, 89, 84, 75-72, 64 and 62 ppm are respectively due to C1, C4(crystalline), C4(amorphous), C2, C3, C5, C6 (cristalline) and C6 (amorphous). Hemicellulose generally shows signals in the same regions as for amorphous cellulose with the 75-72 ppm region due to only carbons 2 and 3 and 62 ppm signed due to C5.

The signal at 56 ppm is due to methoxyl groups, mostly from lignin with some contribution from compounds like 4-0-methoxyglucuronic acid.

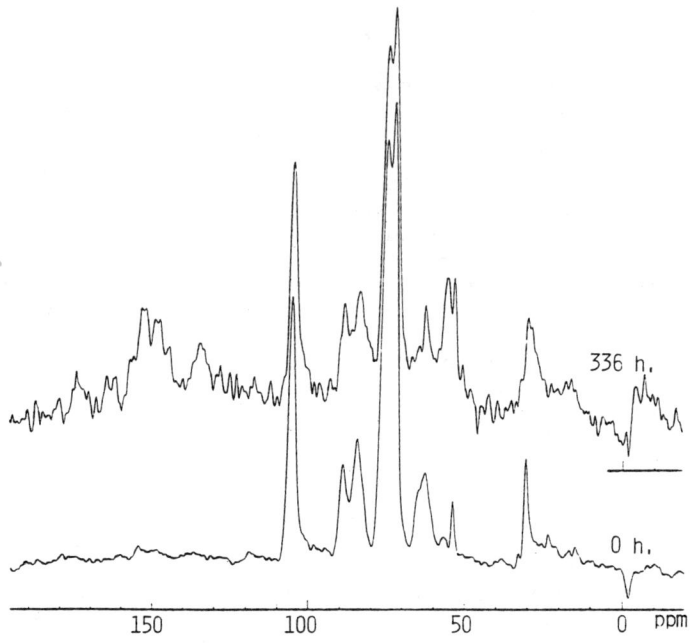

Figure 5: CP/MAS ^{13}C-NMR spectra of ADR fractions
(Grassilage) before and after nylonbag incubation for
336 hours

Two dimensional Fourier NMR spectroscopy is useful for studying
exchange rates of complex enzyme catalyzed reactions in the steady
state, following, the degradation and formation of individual nuclear
species (59).
Fourier transformation produces a 2 dimensional-spectrum which is a
function of two frequency variables F1 and F2. The substrate frequency
will be along the F1 (before reaction) and the product frequence along
F2. Changing the exchange period and repeating the measurements will
produce the 2D-plot with peaks related to the change of substrate to
product symmetrically at the intersections of the perpendiculars along
F1 and F2. Unchanged structures will result in a zero value in the
plot.

8. NEAR INFRARED REFLECTANCE SPECTROSCOPY TO ANALYSE CELL WALL
   COMPONENTS.

NIR uses radiation from the near infrared region (1100-2500 nm) of the
electro-magnetic spectrum. The diffuse reflectance of a sample is used
to determine spectro-photometrically the chemical concentrations or
physical properties of a sample. Because NIR uses a series of multiple
linear regressions to deduce automatically corrections for background
or sample-matrix interferences, it can analyze many sample types that
would be difficult by other spectroscopy techniques. The sample can be
in the form of powders, other solids (whole grain feeds) or
semisolids. Transflectance is normally used to analyze particulate

suspensions and turbid liquids (milk) where the sample is partially transmissive and partially reflective (60, 61).
Generally NIR after calibration with sufficient samples with known chemical composition can be used to measure the cellwall components NDF, ADF and ADL or the contents on digestible organic matter by In Vitro T&T, Cellulase or digestible NDF by In Vitro van Soest, provided these are predicted in vivo values.
Problems which arise are the selection of the standard samples and the boundaries set by these for the samples to be analysed.
In fig. 6 a calibration line for acid detergent insoluble nitrogen (ADIN) of a nonrestricted set of samples is shown which has a low correlation. Restriction of the dataset to product groups will improve this relation considerably. Identification of wheat varieties by NIR followed by principal component analysis and multiple discriminant analysis was done by Bertrand (62).
In combined In Vitro-NIR studies spectral changes from straw samples at different incubation times will show where important changes in composition of the straw occur.
Comparison of changes in 2nd derivative spectra at wavelength 2295 and 2325 nm show the decrease in cellulose and increase in indigestible fiber (fig. 7).

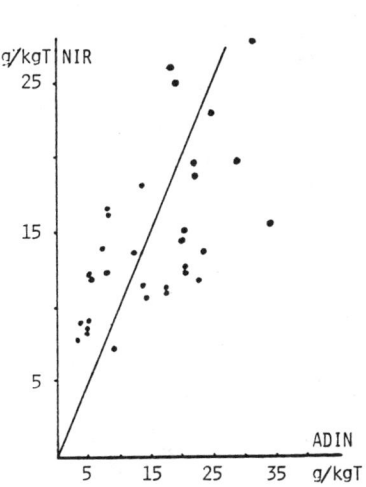

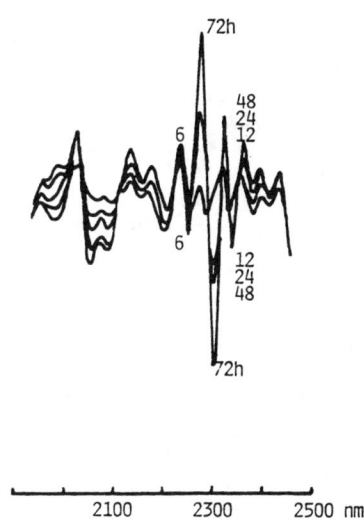

Figure 6: Plot of acid detergent insoluble nitrogen vs NIR.

Figure 7: NIR 2nd derivative of straw after different incubation periods

From the difference spectrum of ammoniated minus untreated straw Barton et al. (16) concluded that the wavelength 2070 mm/s related to the change in digestibility and they assumed that the bonding responsible was $R(CO)NH_2$.
Generally 1st and 2nd derivative spectra are useful in the study of the degradation of straw.

9. CONCLUSIONS.

Application of not one technique on its own will give adequate information to derive the cellwall structures and to explain differences in degradability.
It is expected that all information together could build and confirm the general rules of the construction and degradation of cell walls.
Application of physical techniques have shown to produce information especially on the nature of polymers. But these techniques often require expensive equipment and qualified scientists not only to measure but also for the interpretation. Another complication is that research with these instruments are expensive and already involved in research programms.

ACKNOWLEDGEMENT: The author is greatly indebted to dr. E. Grenet, prof.dr. M.T.M. Willemse, dr. J.J. Boon, dr. ir. H. Boer for their contributions to the results on microscopy, autofluorescence, pyrolytic-MS- spectrometry and NMR.

REFERENCES

(1) NICHOLSON, J.W.G. (1984). Digestibility, nutritive value and feed intake. In: Straw and other fibrous by-products as feed. (Sundstol, F. and Owen, E., Eds) Elsevier, Amsterdam 340-372.
(2) MINSON, D.J. (1985). Fibre as a limit to tropical animal production. Proc. 3rd EAAP Animal Science Congress, Seoul, May 1985, vol. 1, 108.
(3) HELLER, R., et al. (1985). Physiological aspects of using lignocellulosic materials for animal feed. In: Improved utilisation of lignocellulosic materials for animal feed. OECD, Paris, p. 76.
(4) WELCH, J.G. (1982). Rumination, particle size and passage from the rumen. J. Anim. Sci. 54: 885-894.
(5) VAN SOEST, P.J. (1978). Dietary fibers: their definition and nutritional properties. Am. J. of Clin. Nutr. 31: 512.
(6) BAILEY, R.W. (1978). Plant cellwall fractionation and structural analyses. Am. J. of Clin. Nutr. 31: 577.
(7) GAILLARD, B.D.E. and NIJKAMP, H.J. (1968). Calculation of the digestibility for ruminants of roughages from their contents of cellwall constituents. II Time saving method of analysis. Neth. J. Agric. Sci. 16: 21.
(8) ENGLYST, H. (1978). Procedure for analysis of free sugars, starch and unavailable carbohydrates. EEC/IARC working party. Cambridge 13-XII-78.
(9) WINDHAM, W.R. (1983). HPLC analysis of component sugars in NDF for representative warm and cold season grasses. J. Agric. Food Chem. 31: 471-475.
(10) HARTLEY, R.D. and BUCHAN, H. (1979). High perfomance liquid chromatography of phenolic acids and aldehydes, derived from plants or from the decomposition of organic matter in soil. J. Chromatography 180: 139-143.
(11) THEANDER, O., UDEN P. and AMAN, P. (1981). Acetyl and phenolic acid substituents in timothy of different maturity and after digestion with rumen micro-organisms or a commercial cellulase. Agriculture and Environment 6: 127-133.

(12) BRICE, R.E. et al. (1985). Ammonia treatment of barley straw. Characterisation of untreated and ammonia treated straw by light and electron microscopy. (to be published).

(13) SOLAIMAN, S.G., HORN, G.W. and OWEN, F.N. (1979). Ammonia hydroxide treatment on wheat straw. J. Anim. Sci. 49: 802-808.

(14) HERRERA-SOLDANA, R., CHURCH, D.C. and KELLERNS, O. (1983). Effect of ammoniation treatment of wheat straw on in vitro and in vivo digestibility. J. Anim. Sci. 56: 939-942.

(15) WANG, P.J., BOLKER, H.I. and PURVES, E.B. (1964). Ammonolysis of uronic ester groups in birch xylan. Can. J. Chem. 42: 2434-2439.

(16) BARTON II, F.E., WOLSINK, J.H. and VEDDER, H.M. (1986). Near Infrared Reflectance spectroscopy of untreated and ammoniated barley straw. Anim. Fd. Sci. Techn. 15: 189-196.

(17) RANBY, B. (1984). Recent progress on the structure and morphology of cellulose. In: Cellulases and their applications 139-151.

(18) MANN. J. and MARRINAM, H.J. (1956). The reaction between cellulose and heavy water. Part 3. A quantitative study by Infrared. Trans Faraday Soc. 52: 492.

(19) SUMI, Y., HALE, R.D and RANBY, B.G., (1963). The accessibility of Native Cellulose microfibrils. TAPPI 46: 126.

(20) AKIN, D.E. (1982). Section to slide technique for study of forage anatomy and digestion. Crop Science 22: 444-446.

(21) AKIN, D.E. and ROBINSON, E.L. (1982). Structure of leaves and stems of Arrow leaf and Crimson Clovers as related to In Vitro digestibility. Crop Science 22: 24-29.

(22) VANCE, C.P., KIRKWOOD, T.K. and SHERWOOD, R.T. (1980). Lignification as a mechanism of disease resistance. Annual Review of Phytopathology 18: 259-288.

(23) AKIN, D.E. and BURDICK, D. (1981). Relationship of different histochemical types of lignified cell walls to forage digestibility. Crop Science 21: 577-581.

(24) HARBERS, L.H. et al. (1982). Ruminal digestion of ammonium hydroxide treated wheat straw observed by scanning electron microscopy. J. of Animal Sci. 54: 1309-1319.

(25) ENGELS, F.M. (1986). Changes in the physical/Chemical structures of cell walls during growth and degradation. In: Proceedings COST84-bis Workshop 1 March 1986, Lelystad. (Eds. J.M. v.d. Meer, B. Rijkens and .. Ferrantie). Publ. Elsevier.

(26) GORDON, A.H., LOMAX, J.A., DALGARNO, K. and CHESSON, A. (1985). Preparation and composition of Mesophyll, Epidermis and Fibre cell walls from leaves of Perennial Rye grass (Lolium perenne) and Italian Rye grass (Lolium multi florum). J. Sci. Food & Agric. 36: 509-519.

(27) STEWART, C.S., DINSDALE, D., CHANG, K.J. and PANIAGUA, C. (1979). The digestion of straw in the rumen. In: Straw decay and its effect on disposal and utilization p. 123130. Proceedings, april 10-11th (Ed. E. Grossbard). Publ. Wiley Interscience.

(28) BRYANT, M.P. (1959). Bacterial species of the rumen. Bact. Rev. 23: 125.

(29) AKIN, D.E. (1980). Evaluation by electron microscopy and anaerobic culture of types of rumen bacteria associated with digestion of forage cell walls. Applied and Environmental microbiology. 39: 242-252.

(30) AKIN, D.E. and AMOS, H.E. (1979). Mode of attack on orchard grass leaf blades by rumen protozoa. Applied and Environmental microbiology 37: 332-338.

(31) GRENET, E. and BARRY, P. (1987). Etude microscopique de la digestion des parois végétales des tequments de soja et de colca dans la rumen. Repr. Nutr. Dévelop 27: 246-248.

(32) GRENET, E. and BARRY, P. (1987). Colonization of thick walled tissues by anaerobic rumen fungi. Anim. Feed Sci. Technol. : 00.00

(33) THEANDER, O. and AMAN, P. (1984). Anatomical and chemical characteristics. Dev. Anim. Vet. Sci. 14: 45-78.

(34) AKIN, D.E. (1983). Electron microscopie studies of fiber degradaton by rumen fungi. In: Proceedings 41st Annual Meeting of the electron microscopy society of America. p. 814-815 (Ed. G.W. Bailey). San Francisco Press. Inc.

(35) WINDHAM, W.R. and AKIN, D.E. (1984). Rumen fungi and forage fiber degradation. Appl. Environ. Microbiol. 48: 473-476.

(36) PEARCE, P.D. and BAUCHOP, T. (1985). Glucosidases of the rumen anaerobic fungus Neocalli mastix frontalis grown on cellulosic substrates. Appl. Environ. Microbiol. 49: 1265-1269.

(37) FONTY,G. et al. (1987). Isolement et caractérisation des champignons anaerobics stricts du rumen de moutons. Premiers resultats. Repr. Nutr. Develop. (In Press).

(38) FONTY, G., GONET, Ph. and SANTE V. (1987). Influence des interactions entre champignons et bacteries méthanogènes du rumen sur la cellulolyse in vitro. Results preliminaires. Repr. Nutr. Develop. (In Press).

(39) MEUZELAAR, H.L.C., HAVERKAMP, J. and HILEMAN, F.D. (1982). Pyrolysis mass spectrometry of recent and fossil biomaterials. Compendium and Atlas. Elsevier, Amsterdam, 293 pp.

(40) GENUIT, W.J.L., BOON, J.J. and Faix, O. (1987). Characterisation of beech milled wood lignin by pyrolysis gaschromatography photoionization mass spectrometry. Anal. Chem. Vol. 59, in press.

(41) WINDIG, W., HAVERKAMP and KISTEMAKER, P.G., (1983). Interpretation of sets of pyrolysis mass spectra by discriminant analysis and graphical rotation. Anal. Chem. 55: 81-88.

(42) HOOGERBRUGGE, R., WILLIG, S.J. and KISTEMAKER, P.G. (1984). Discriminant analysis by double stage principal component analysis. Anal. Chem. 55: 1711-1712.

(43) BOON, J.J., EYKEL, G.B. and BEST, E.P.H. (1983). Study of the seasonal change in composition in roots and shoots of Phragmites Australis by pyrolysis mass spectrometry combined with multivariate data analysis. In: Proc. Int. Symp. Aquat. Macrophytes, Nijmegen, 18-23 sept. 1983.

(44) HARTLEY, R.D. and HAVERKAMP, J. (1984). Pyrolysis-Mass spectrometry of the phenolic constituents of plant cellwalls. J. Sci. Food Agric. 35: 14-20.

(45) VAN DER MEER, J.M., and BOON, J.J. (1987). To be published.

(46) SAIZ-JIMENEZ and LEEUW, J.W. de (1985). Pyrolysis gas chromatography mass spectrometry of isolated, synthetic and degraded lignins. Org. Geochem. 6: 417-423.

(47) OBST, J.R. (1983). Analytical pyrolysis of hardwood and softwood lignins and its use in lignin-type determinations of hardwood vessel elements. J. Wood Chem. Technol. 3: 377-397.

(48) HARTLEY, R.D. and BOON, J.J. (1987). To be published.

(49) BOON, J.J., POUWELS, A.D. and Eykel, G.B. (1987). Pyrolysis high resolution gas chromatography- mass spectrometry studies on beech wood: capillary high resolution mass spectrometry of a beech lignin fraction. Biochem. Soc. Transactions 15: 170-174.

(50) GENUIT, W.J.L. and BOON, J.J. (1985). Pyrolysis gas chromatography-photoionization-mass spectrometry a new approach in the analysis of macromolecular materials. J. Anal. Appl. Pyrol. 8: 25-40.

(51) WILLEMSE, M.T.M. (1972). Changes in the autofluorescence of the pollen wall during microsporogenesis and chemical treatments. Acta. Bot. Neerl. 21: 1.

(52) WILLEMSE, M.T.M., (1981). Changes in autofluorescence of lignin. In: Cellwalls'81 - Proc. of the 2nd Cellwall Meeting, Göttingen, April 8th-11th, 1981 (Eds. Robinson, D.G. and H. Quader).

(53) HARRIS, P.J. and HARTLEY, R.D. (1976). Detection of bound ferulic acid in cellwalls of the Gramineae by Ultraviolet fluorescence microscopy. Nature 259: 508-510.

(54) SHIRO SAKA, THOMAS, R.J. and GRATZL, J.S. (1984). Lignin distribution by energy disposal. In: Dietary Fibers: Chemistry and Nutrition, 15-29.

(55) BARTON II, F.E., AKIN, D.E., WINDHAM, W.R. and HIMMELSBACH, D.S. (1983). Methods of forage analysis-Quantitative and Qualitative aspects. In: wood and agricultural residues (ISBN 0-12-654560-x), 167-202.

(56) ALBERSHEIM, P., NEIMS, R.J., ENGLISH, P.D. and KARZ, A. (1967). Carbohyd. Res. 5: 340.

(57) HIMMELSBACH, D.S. and BARTON II, F.E. (1980). ^{13}C-nuclear Magnetic Resonance of Gran Lignin. J. Agric. Food Chem. 28: 1203.

(58) BOER, H. and HIMMELSBACH, D.S. (1987). To be published.

(59) FERRETI, J.A. and BALABAN, R.S. (1984). The measurement of enzyme catalysed rates of reaction by 2D NMR spectroscopy. Trends in Anal. Chem. 3: 148-151.

(60) HONIGS, D.E. (1985). Near Infrared Analysis. In: Analytical Instrumentation 14: 1-62.

(61) Symposium in Norwich, U.K., 1983: Near Infrared Analysis - Today or Tomorrow? Anal. Proc. 20: 65-83.

(62) BERTRAND, D., ROBERT, P. and LOISEL, W. (1985). Identification of some wheat varieties by Near Infrared Reflectance spectroscopy. J. Sci. Food Agric. 36: 1120-1124.

BIOCHEMICAL EVALUATION OF STRAW AS A FEEDSTUFF FOR RUMINANTS

A. CHESSON and SANDRA D. MURISON
Rowett Research Institute, Bucksburn, Aberdeen, AB2 9SB, UK.

Summary

Lignin content and degradability of straw, whether determined in vivo as OMD, in vitro using cell-free enzymes, or by the nylon bag method, are rarely sufficiently well correlated to be used predictively. Analysis of the mechanism of cell wall degradation by rumen microorganisms suggests that this is because the extent of lignin-carbohydrate bonding is also important in determining the rate and extent of cell wall degradation. As no routine chemical methods exist to measure lignin-carbohydrate bonding, biological or enzymatic measures of degradability are an essential element of any evaluation scheme. "Cellulase" enzyme preparations are being increasingly used for this purpose. Commercial preparation show considerable variation both between products and between batches. If use of this method is to continue, standards should be established which give the minimum levels of activities such preparations should contain. Existing chemical methods of evaluation, unlike biological measures, cannot be applied directly to alkali-treated straws. Additional methods have been proposed to overcome this difficulty and their value is discussed. Predicting the likely response to treatment is also difficult. For alkali-treated straws increases in degradability following treatment is inversely correlated (r = 0.71) with the degradability of the untreated straw, implying that alkali-labile lignin-carbohydrate linkages are fewer in number in straws of high digestibility.

1. INTRODUCTION

Cereal straws differ in two important respects from the vast majority of other plant materials offered as feed to ruminant and non-ruminant animals. Although carbohydrates account for 70-80% of straw dry matter, they are found only in the form of the structural polysaccharides which form the greater part of all plant cell walls (1). The water-soluble carbohydrates and starch found commonly in other plant materials fed to animals are virtually absent from cereal and other straws. Although the gross energy content of carbohydrates are the same whether present as low molecular weight sugars, storage or structural polysaccharides, their susceptibility to microbial attack in the digestive tract differs considerably. Structural polysaccharides invariably are degraded at slower rates than other forms of carbohydrate.

The second feature of straws which distinguishes them from most other plant-based feedstuffs relates to their maturity at time of harvest. Straws are considered and treated as agricultural by-products, not as the primary product. Straw harvest is dictated by the maturation of the grain and not by the nutritive value of the vegetative part of the cereal plant. As a consequence the process of lignification which accompanies the maturation of all plants is considerably more advanced in straw than is found in forage plants which are grazed or harvested well before grain filling. Virtually all cells within straws are dead, devoid of the cell contents which add to the nutritional value of forage plants and are uniformly and extensively lignified. Digestion of straw by the microorganisms inhabiting the ruminant digestive tract is thus effectively synonymous with the digestion of straw cell walls.

While both of these properties make straw a useful model with which to study the effect of lignification on cell wall breakdown by gut microorganisms, they substantially reduce the value of straw as a feedstuff. Straws must be considered of marginal value, capable at best of providing only maintenance levels of nutrition when fed alone to ruminants. However there are a number of strategies which can be employed to maximise their value in animal production. The term "straw" covers a wide range of plant species and varieties whose digestibility can vary by as much as 30% (2,3). Selection of suitable straw varieties can do much to improve the value of straw without carrying the cost of poorer grain yields. There is some evidence that farmers are beginning to recognise this fact. In the UK, one variety of spring barley, Corgi, which produces a straw with a high digestibility value, is being increasingly grown by farmers intending to feed straw to beef cattle. Plant parts also differ in their digestibility. Leaves of cereal straws are invariably more digestible than the stem and the stem nodes usually more digestible than internodes (4,5). This situation is apparently reversed in rice straw because of the high silica level generally associated with the leaves (6). Various methods can be employed to maximise the recovery of leaf at harvest or to minimise the length of the straw internode and add to the quality of the straw.

Finally straws can be chemically treated to enhance their degradability and hence their nutritive value. Methods involving the application of alkaline (NH_3, NaOH), acidic and oxidative (SO_2, O_3 alkaline H_2O_2) reagents have all proved effective, at least on a laboratory scale, when applied to monocotyledenous straws (7-10). However only the more severe oxidative treatments have proved effective for dicotyledenous straws such as rape straw (11).

Methods of straw evaluation are thus required which allow the digestibility of different straws to be quickly, accurately and cheaply determined and which are capable of taking account of the effects of any chemical treatment applied to enhance digestibility. Other methods which allow the effects of treatment to be predictedwithout the need for actual treatment would also be of value. Many farmers have available straws of different varieties. Foreknowledge of which to treat and which to feed in an unmodified form could be of considerable practical benefit.

2. LIGNIN AND THE PLANT CELL WALL

There is now no doubt that the level of lignin is the overriding factor in determining the accessibility of the cell wall polysaccharides to microbial attack (12). The broad relationship that exists between lignin content and degradability of plant materials shown in Figure 1 has been demonstrated on many occasions (13). However the relationship can rarely be used to differentiate a group of residues with similar lignin values, particularly if the samples cross species boundaries. Fifteen varieties of spring barley with lignin values ranging from 8.7 to 12.7% of dry matter gave correlation values (r) of only 0.118 and 0.144 when related to 48 h and 72 h nylon bag estimates of degradability respectively. Similarly the correlation found between acid lignin content and neutral detergent cellulase digestibility (NCD) for the straw samples shown in Figure 1 was found to be r = 0.619. The relationship was little changed when _in vivo_ organic matter digestibility values were substituted for those obtained by the NCD method (r = 0.698). These results simply exemplify the well recognised fact that lignin values alone are insufficient to allow prediction of nutritive value however this is expressed. Evidently there are factors present, in addition to the amount of lignin _per se_, which are capable of influencing the rate and extent of cell

Table 1. Activities of various commercial "cellulase" enzyme preparations shown against a range of isolated plant polysaccharides. Names of the commercial preparations have been excluded with the exception of the preparation marketed as a laboratory reagent by BDH Ltd.

Polysaccharide	Units g^{-1} cellulase preparation[a]				
	BDH	1.	2.	3.	4.
Avicel	11	17	20	16	17
Carboxymethylcellulose	58	88	72	53	54
Xylan (ex oats)	184	200	300	104	160
Xylan (ex larchwood)	207	156	200	92	132
Galactan (ex L. albus)	8	12	82	69	131
Arabinan (ex beet)	0	9	65	9	4
Polygalacturonic acid	2	25	150	200	147
Pectin (citrus)	0	30	121	150	94
Starch (rice)	7	23	21	2	0

[a] 1 unit = amount of enzyme required to release 1 μmol reducing group equivalent min^{-1} at 40°C, pH 5.0.

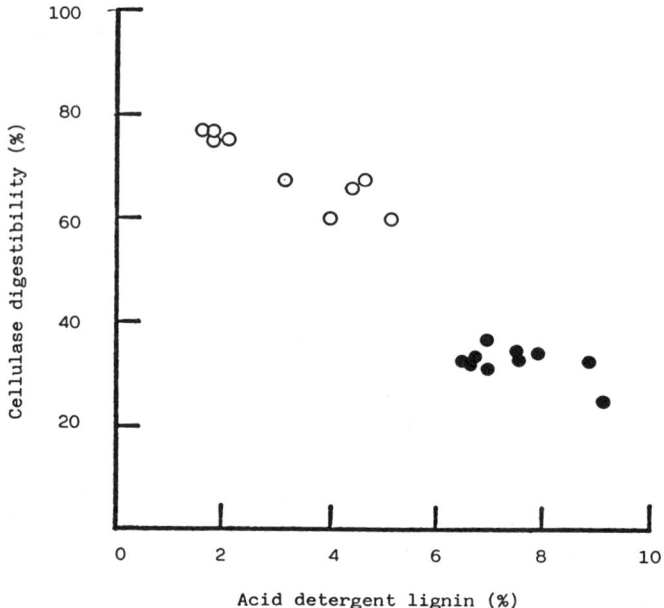

Figure 1.   Relationship between cellulase digestibility (NCD) and acid detergent lignin content of samples of grass (O) and wheat, barley and oat straws (●).

wall degradation. Results from several investigations of cell wall structure and degradability suggest that the "missing" factors relate to interactions formed between lignin and the polysaccharides of the cell wall.

During the peroxidase-mediated polymerisation of lignin precursors within the maturing cell wall, linkages appear to be formed between the developing lignin macromolecule and other wall components, notably carbohydrate, but probably also protein (14,15). The lignin-carbohydrate complexes so formed have been described for a wide variety of plant materials. Those isolated from grass and cereal straws have been shown to contain the pentose sugars and uronic acid typical of glucuroarabinoxylan, the major hemicellulosic polymer of monocotyledons (16,17). Nitrogen also is invariably detected in complexes isolated from the plant and in the soluble lignin-carbohydrate complexes found in the rumen (18,19). Fragments of complexes akin in structure to those containing phenolic acids and carbohydrate (20,21), have yet to be isolated and the nature of the bonding conclusively established. However indirect evidence points to the presence of at least three types of linkages (22), present in amounts which reflect the phylogenic origin of the material under investigation. In the lignin-carbohydrate complexes of monocotyledons, ester linkages are believed to predominate because of the response shown by Gramineae to alkaline reagents, while in dicotyledenous material, ether linkages would appear to be more numerous (11).

The availability of structural polysaccharides to attacking microorganims is thus a product of two factors, the amount of lignin present and the extent to which it is bonded to cell wall polysaccharides. Analytical methods, however imperfect, exist for the former but not for the latter although the extent of bonding may be an equally important factor in the control of the digestive process. Physico-chemical techniques applied to the analysis of the surface layer of straw cell walls undergoing digestion by rumen microorganisms give results which suggest that lignin accumulates at the cell wall surface following the selective removal of polysaccharide from the outermost layer of the wall (23). During the course of degradation this gradual preferential retention of lignin leads to the formation of a modified surface layer, largely phenolic in character, which cannot be degraded by the attacking microorganisms. Once formed, this layer prevents digestion and serves to protect underlying polysaccharide from further attack. While the amount of lignin initially present in the wall in an important factor in determining the rate at which the modified surface layer is formed, the extent to which lignin is bonded to other components of the wall is an equally important factor influencing the stability of the modified surface layer.

Chemical methods for estimating the extent of lignin-carbohydrate interactions are only partially established (24), and those that are available are far too laborious for use on a routine basis. Yet if rapid non-biological methods for the evaluation of straw are to be effective, they must take countenance of the nature and extent of the linkages formed between lignin and the structural polysaccharides of the cell wall. Instrumental approaches seem the most likely to provide the methods of the future. It is possible, for example, that some of the absorbancies selected by NIR users on a purely pragmatic basis may prove to have their origin in this form of bonding.

3. CELL FREE ENZYMES

It is no accident that predictive equations containing a biological measure of "digestibility" in addition to chemical parameters are invariably more robust than equations developed using values derived only from chemical estimations. All existing biological measures, by broadly mimicking rumen digestion, are affected by factors not currently measured by chemical techniques. In the case of straw and other lignified materials this includes the effect of lignin and its association with cell wall polysaccharides.

Various biological methods for the estimation of degradability exist. With a single exception, all are dependent on the use of live rumen microorganisms. The exception is the use of cell-free enzyme preparations, commonly, if inaccurately, referred to as the "cellulase assay". Substrates for this assay may be the straw itself (cellulase digestibility, CD) (25) or, now more usually, neutral detergent fibre produced from the straw (NCD) (26). Use of this method is increasing and is likely to continue to do so as public pressure and government legislation limit the availability of experimental animals. A cause for concern, however, is the ad hoc manner in which the technique is being introduced. There is no universally agreed source of cell-free enzyme preparation and although use of the cellulase marketed by BDH Ltd. is becoming standard in Europe, and was the enzyme of choice in recent ring tests. No quality control is, however, applied to the enzyme preparation itself. It is well recognised that the efficient degradation of plant cell walls requires the concerted action of many different enzyme activities and is not a product of "cellulase" activity alone. Enzyme manufacturers, however, formulate enzyme preparations to meet the activities declared on the label and are rarely concerned with the presence or absence of other activities. A wide range of commercial products carry the label "cellulase" although they originate from relatively few microbial species. As Table 1 shows, even a superficial examination of the presence and levels of activities other than "cellulase" which are important in cell wall hydrolysis shows the wide variation found between different commercial products. Further variation is likely to be found between batches of enzyme produced by the same manufacturer. The UK advisory service, ADAS, recognising that batch to batch variation in enzyme preparations was introducing an unacceptably high error into their NCD assay, now standardise their results against a series of reference feedstuffs. This is one approach. There remains the need to define the minimum activities and levels of activities necessary to fully degrade cell wall material which any enzyme preparation used for NCD determinations should possess.

4. EVALUATION OF TREATED STRAWS

Many straws are treated to enhance their nutritive value. Methods of choice, at present, centre on the application of alkali either in the form of sodium hydroxide or more usually ammonia. Hydrothermal methods, such as the Canadian STAKE process, may also be used at an industrial rather than on-farm level. Routine chemical methods of feed evaluation are not generally applicable to those straws treated by alkali. Although lignin and other components are solubilised by alkali to an extent which determines the increase in degradability alkali soluble products are not washed from the straw during processing. Acid lignin (ADL, CL) and other chemical determinations thus give identical values for both treated and untreated straw. No chemical methods which measure specifically the extent of cleavage of lignin-carbohydrate linkages necessary to achieve solubilisation are currently available. There remains only the biological methods which are equally applicable to both treated and untreated residues.

The need for alternative approaches to the evaluation of treated straws has been recognised and a number of additional rapid methods have been proposed.

Application of sodium hydroxide to cereal straw results in the solubilisation of a fraction of the lignin initially present in the straw (28). The extent to which lignin is solubilised is strongly correlated with enhanced degradability and is determined by the amount of alkali applied (Fig. 2). As can be seen from Figure 2, there is a maximum response which can be

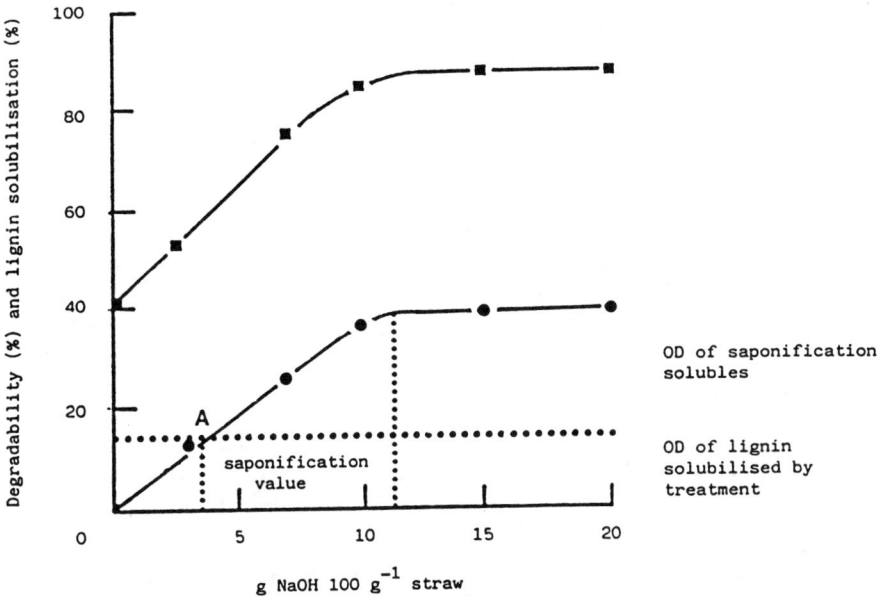

Figure 2. Effect of sodium hydroxide application level on the water-solubility of acid detergent lignin (●) and 72 h nylon bag degradability (■) of barley straw. An arbitrarily selected treatment level "A" is shown to demonstrate the rationale underlying proposed OD and saponification value measurements.

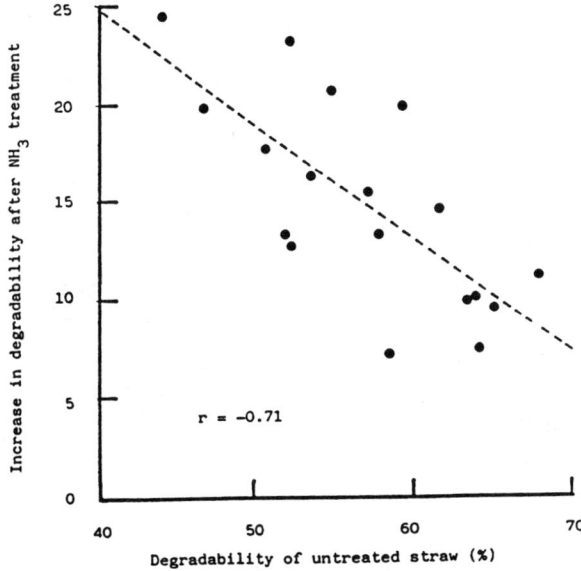

Figure 3. The relationship between degradability of untreated barley straw and the increase in degradability found after treatment with ammonia by the oven method (3 g NH3 100 g^{-1} straw).

achieved, which for most cereal straws occurs at application levels of 8-10 g NaOH 100 g^{-1} straw. Thereafter, increasing the application level does not release additional lignin or further improve degradability. Several direct and indirect methods of estimating the extent to which lignin has been made water soluble have been proposed as a means of determining the efficacy of treatment (29-31). These are represented diagrammatically in Figure 2 for an arbitrarily chosen treatment represented on the curves by point "A".

The first, and simplest method proposed, extracts the lignin solubilised by treatment either by washing with buffer or neutral detergent and measures the optical density of the extract at 280 nm; one of the wavelengths at which phenolic compound show maximum absorbance. Absorbance values of both buffer and neutral detergent solutions have been reported to be positively correlated with in vivo organic matter digestibility (neutral detergent solubles, r = 0.792). Neutral detergent extraction appears more reliable than buffer extraction and has the added advantage that it can both provide values for NDF and material suitable for an NCD determination. In this laboratory, the OD of buffer extracts prepared from 20 ammonia treated barley straws could not be correlated with the improvement in degradability measured by the nylon bag methods, although absorbance values were weakly, but postively, correlated (r = 0.473) with the amount of phenolic material solubilised as determined by the acetyl bromide method. The latter would suggest that OD determined at a single wavelength is probably unable to sufficiently discriminate between phenolic compounds and other material absorbing at the same wavelength. Use of FTIR, and multiple absorbancies might improve the discrimination.

Two other proposed measures, saponification value and OD of the solubles released by saponification (29,30), provide indirect measures of lignin solubilisation. Both are dependent on the fact that there is a maximum response shown to sodium hydroxide addition (Fig. 2). Treated straws are saponified with a known amount of excess alkali and the saponification extract back-titrated with acid to measure the amount of alkali consumed to give the "saponification value" expressed as meq base consumed g^{-1} straw. The OD at 280 or 314 nm of the neutralised extract also provies a possible measure of the amount of alkali-soluble lignin remaining in the straw. Both measures are negatively correlated with digestibility since both measure alkali-soluble lignin which the treatment has failed to release. The relative merits of the two methods is shown by the agreement achieved with in vivo OMD values for the treated straws. Correlation coefficients of r = -0.918 have been reported for saponification values compared to values of r = 0.579 and -0.557 for OD determinations made at 280 and 314 nm respectively (31).

Oxidative reagents degrade both the alkali-soluble and alkali-insoluble fractions of straw lignin. As a consequence, saponification values and associated methods are unlikely to be of value for straws treated with ozone, sulphur dioxide and similar reagents or those subjected to composting with selected fungi (32). However, although oxidation has been shown to be a highly effective means of upgrading straw (9,10) and despite the interest in the use of combined oxidative and alkaline treatment (33,34), the costs and practical problems involved make it unlikely that these methods will be adopted on an industrial or farm scale in the foreseeable future.

5. PREDICTION OF THE RESPONSE TO TREATMENT

Estimation of the bioavailability of cell wall polysaccharides, whether present in treated or untreated straw can be accommodated within existing evaluation schemes; the problems being those associated with the evaluation of any low quality roughage. None of the existing or proposed measures, however, provides a/means of predicting the effect of any treatment without first treating the straw. Given the large variation in the digestibility of straws and other by-products it would be of considerable practical benefit to be able to rapidly and cheaply estimate the likely outcome of any treatment applied. An interesting observation first made by Ørskov and his colleagues (3) and presented in slightly different form in Figure 3, suggests that ammonia-treated straws show much the same degradability after treatment regardless of the degradability of the untreated straw. The extent to which the degradability of straws is improved by ammonia treatment thus is negatively correlated with their initial degradability (Fig. 3) and response greatest in the poorest quality straws. This observation raises a number of theoretical considerations, not the least being the extent to which sodium hydroxide and ammonia treatments can be considered as having a common mode of action.

It is possible to speculate that ammonia, at levels normally applied to straw, is adequate to hydrolyse most ester linkages with the release of acyl groups and the cleavage of lignin-carbohydrate ester bonds. If this is the case then straws with a higher intrinsic degradability must have fewer alkali-labile lignin-carbohydrate linkages than straws of lower degradability. This would suggest that the greater response shown by most straws to the stronger alkali sodium hydroxide must be a product of the cleavage of some lignin internal linkages (35) in addition to the hydrolysis of lignin-carbohydrate ester bonds. If this is the case it is questionable whether saponification values obtained by saturating the sytem with sodium hydroxide are applicable to straws treated with ammonia.

The account given above of some of the problems associated with the evaluation of straw as a feedstuff for ruminants is, of necessity, limited in scope. Little has been said of straws other than cereal straws, of treatment methods other than alkali, and most importantly, of animal effects. Degradability of straw is only one facet of the factors determining animal performance. Certainly of equal importance are the factors determining intake.

REFERENCES

(1)   GORDON, A.H., LOMAX, J.A. and CHESSON, A. (1983). Glycosidic linkages of legume, grass and cereal cell walls before and after extensive digestion by rumen microorganisms. J. Sci. Food Agric. 34, 1341-1350.

(2)   PEARCE, G.R., BEARD, J. and HILLIARD, E.P. (1979). Variability in the chemical composition of cereal straws and in vitro digestibility with and without sodium hydroxide treatment. Aust. J. Exp. Agric. Anim. Husb. 19, 350-353.

(3)   TUAH, A.K., LUFADEJU, E. and ØRSKOV, E.R. (1986). Rumen degradation of straw. 1. Untreated and ammonia-treated barley, oat and wheat straw varieties and triticale straw. Anim. Prod. 43, 261-269.

(4)   THIAGO, L.R.L. de S. and KELLAWAY, R.C. (1982). Botanical composition and extent of lignification affecting digestibility of wheat and oat straw and paspalam hay. Anim. Feed. Sci. Technol. 7, 71-81.

(5)   RAMANZIN, M., ØRSKOV, E.R. and TUAH, A.K. (1986). Rumen degradation of straw. 2. Botanical fractions of straw from two barley cultivars. Anim. Prod. 43, 271-278.

(6)   JACKSON, M.G. (1978). Rice straw as livestock feed. The Green Revolution, pp 95-98.

(7)   SUNDSTØL, F. and OWEN, E. (1984). Straw and other fibrous by-products as feed. Elsevier, Amsterdam.

(8)   HARTLEY, R.D. and JONES, E.C. (1978). Effect of aqueous ammonia and
       other alkalies on the in vitro digestibility of barley straw. J. Sci. -
       Food Agric. 29, 92-98.

(9)   BEN-GHEDALIA, D. and MIRON, J. (1981). Effect of sodium hydroxide,
       ozone and sulphur dioxide on the composition and in vitro digestibility
       of wheat straw. J. Sci. Food Agric. 32, 224-228.

(10)   KERLEY, M.S., FAHEY, G.C., BERGER, L.L. GOULD, J. and BAXTER, M.
       (1985). Alkaline peroxide treatment unlicks energy in agricultural
       by-products. Science, 230, 820-822.

(11)   ALEXANDER, B.W., GORDON, A.H., LOMAX, J.A. and CHESSON, A. (1987).
       Composition and rumen degradability of straw from three varieties of
       oilseed rape before and after alkali, hydrothermal and oxidative
       treatment. J. Sci. Food Agric. (in press).

(12)   BRICE, R.E. and MORRISON, I.M. (1982). The degradation of isolated
       hemicelluloses and lignin-hemicellulose complexes by cell-free
       hemicellulases. Carbohydr. Res. 101, 93-100.

(13). MINSON, D.J. (1982). Effect of chemical composition on feed digesti-
       bility and metabolizable energy. CAB Nutrition Abstr. 52, 592-615.

(14)   WHITMORE, F.W. (1982). Lignin-protein complex in cell walls of Pinus
       elliottii: amino acid constituents. Phytochemistry 21, 315-318.

(15)   DILL, I., SALNIKOW, J. and DRAEPELIN, G. (1984). Hydroxyproline-rich
       protein material in wood and lignin of Fagus sylvatica. Appl. Environ.
       Microbiol. 48, 1259-1261.

(16)   TANNER, G.R. and MORRISON, I.M. (1983). Phenolic-carbohydrate
       complexes in the cell walls of Lolium perenne. Phytochemistry 22,
       1433-1439.

(17)   FORD, C.W. (1986). Comparative structural studies of lignin-carbohy-
       drate complexes from Digitaria decumbens (Pengola grass) before and
       after chlorite delignification. Carbohydr. Res. 147, 101-117.

(18)   NEILSON, M.J. and RICHARDS, G.N. (1978). The fate of the soluble
       lignin-carbohydrate complex produced in the bovine rumen. J. Sci. Food
       Agric. 29, 513-579.

(19)   LOMAX, J.A., CONCHIE, J. and HAY, A.J. (1984). Methylation analysis of
       soluble lignin-carbohydrate complexes from the sheep rumen. In: Plant
       Polysaccharides, Structure and Function, INRA/CNRS, Nantes pp.
       227-229.

(20)   SMITH, M.M. and HARTLEY, R.D. (1983). Occurrence and nature of ferulic
       acid substitution of cell-wall polysaccharides in Graminaceous
       plants. Carbohydr. Res. 118, 65-80.

(21)   KATO, Y. and NEVINS, D.J. (1985). Isolation and identification of
       (O-ferulolyl-α-L-arabinofuranosyl)-(1-3)-O-β-D-xylopyranose as a
       component of 2ea shoot cell-walls. Carbohydr. Res. 137, 134-150.

(22)   MORRISON, I.M. (1974). Structural investigations on the lignin-carbo-
       hydrate complexes of Lolium perenne. Biochem. J. 139, 197-204.

(23)   CHESSON, A. (1986). The evaluation of dietary fibre. In Feedingstuffs
       Evaluation. Modern Aspects, Problems, Future Trends (ed. Livingstone,
       R.M.). FEEDS publication 1, Aberdeen, pp. 18-25.

(24)   CHESSON, A., GORDON, A.H. and LOMAX, J.A. (1983). Substituent groups
       linked by alkali-labile bonds to arabinose and xylose residues of
       legume, grass and cereal straw cell walls and their fate during
       digestion by rumen microorganisms. J. Sci. Food Agric. 34, 1330-1340.

(25)   DOWMAN, M.G. and COLLINS, F.C. (1982). The use of enzymes to predict
       the digestibility of animals feeds. J. Sci. Food Agric. 33, 689-696.

(26) DE BOEVER, J.L., COTTYN, B.G., BUYSSE, F.X., WAINMAN, F.W. and VANACKER, J.M. (1986). The use of an enzymatic technique to predict digestibility, metabolizable and net energy of compound feedstuffs for ruminants. Anim. Feed Sci. Technol. 14, 203-214.

(27) WAINMAN, F.W., DEWEY, P.J.S. and BOYNE, A.W. (1981). Compound Feedingstuffs for Ruminants. Rowett Research Institute, Aberdeen and Department of Agriculture and Fisheries for Scotland, Edinburgh.

(28) CHESSON, A. (1981). Effects of sodium hydroxide on cereal straws in relation to the enhanced degradation of structural polysaccharides by rumen microorganisms. J. Sci. Food Agric. 32, 745-758.

(29) LAU, M.M. and VAN SOEST, P.J. (1981). Titratable groups and soluble phenolic compounds as indicators of the digestibility of chemically treated roughages. Anim. Feed Sci. Technol. 6, 123-131.

(30) VAN SOEST, P.J., MASCARENHAS FERREIRA, A. and HARTLEY, R.D. (1984). Chemical properties of fibre in relation to nutritive quality of ammonia-treated forages. Anim. Feed Sci. Technol. 10, 155-164.

(31) KJOS, N.P., SUNDSTØL, F. and McBURNEY, M.I. (1987). The nutritive value of weather-damaged and good-quality straw of barley, wheat and oat, untreated and treated with ammonia or sodium hydroxide. J. Anim. Physiol. a. Anim. Nutr. 57, 1-15.

(32) AGOSIN, E., TOLLIER, M.T., BRILLOUET, J.M., THIVEND, P. and ODIER, E. (1986). Fungal pretreatment of wheat straw: effects on the biodegradability of cell walls, structural polysaccharides, lignin and phenolic acids by rumen microorganisms. J. Sci. Food Agric. 37, 97-106.

(33) BEN-GHEDALIA, D., SHEFET, G. and MIRON, J. (1980). Effect of ozone and ammonium hydroxide treatment on the composition and in vitro digestibility of cotton straw. J. Sci. Food Agric. 31, 1337-1342.

(34) DRYDEN, G. McL. and LENG, R.A. (1986). Treatment of barley straw with ammonia and sulphur dioxide gases under laboratory conditions. Anim. Feed Sci. Technol. 14, 41-54.

(35) JOHANSSON, B. and MIKSCHE, G.E. (1972). Über die benzyl-arylätherbindung im lignine. II. Versuche on modellen. Acta Chem. Scand. 26, 289-230.

PREDICTION OF THE ORGANIC MATTER DIGESTIBILITY OF AMMONIATED AND UNTREATED

STRAW BY DENSITOMETRY: COMPARISON WITH OTHER PREDICTORS

BESLE J.M*, SIGNORET C.**, CHENOST M.*, AUFRERE J*, JAMOT J.*
*INRA de THEIX - 63122 CEYRAT (FRANCE)
** Centre d'Etudes Nucléaires de Grenoble, BP 85X - 38041 GRENOBLE (FRANCE)

Summary
        Samples of 28 straws (25 wheat, 2 barley, 1 oat), of which 16
were untreated (US) and 15 were ammonia treated (AS), of known in
vivo organic matter digestibility (OMD) were used to study OMD
prediction methods. Densitometric methods were tested, modified (MOD)
to improve precision and compared to cell-wall predictors, cellulase
solubility (COMS) and in vitro digestibility (IVOMD).
        Among the various conditions studied to establish MOD (e.g.
buffer and ammonia extraction for US, temperature, time of extraction
and filtration for all samples, ultrafiltration (0.1 µ) increased the
precision of prediction, more particularly with AS (P < 0.001), as
compared with paper filtration. MOD gave the highest precision of OMD
prediction for AS (R = 0.87 , Syx = 1.61 , P < 0.001) and for all (US
+ AS) samples (P < 0.001 , R = 0.87 , Syx = 2.66) but not for the US
samples (P < 0.01 , R = 0.69, Syx = 3.08). COMS was the best predictor
for US samples (R = 0.79, Syx = 2.61). The precision of OMD
prediction with other methods were, in decreasing order : IVOMD,
lignin, CB and ADF.

1. INTRODUCTION

        The range of organic matter digestibility (OMD) values of cereal
straws, even within a given species, is wider than it can be expected for a
classical forage of a given physiological growth stage. Prediction of OMD
is useful but difficult due to the complexity of chemical (1) and animal
(2) factors governing straw degradability.
        Chemical characteristics of cell-walls, i.e. crude cellulose or
lignocellulose are in poor relationship with OMD. However lignin content is
relatively more satisfactory (3, 4). Biological criteria (in vitro
digestibility, 5 ; in sacco disapearance, 6 ; cellulase solubility, 7, 8)
are better OMD predictors but are time consuming compared to chemical
methods. In addition, except for the in sacco methods (9), they are less
useful for treated than for untreated straws (10,4).
        Prediction methods based on saponification index (11) or on the
optical density of various buffer extracts (12, 13) have the advantage of
rapidity. Saponification index is correlated with OMD but with a degree of
precision which varies greatly depending upon the authors and whether or
not straws are treated. Densitometry allows a better prediction for treated
than for untreated straws (14, 15). However the interest (and limits) of
this method and causes of discrepancy versus treatment are not well
established. For treated straws, it is likely that prediction is based on
absorbance of (among other products) solubilised alkali-labile lignin (16)
and some phenolic acids (17, 18). Absence of these compound in extracts of
untreated samples can explain poor results obtained by some workers.
Nevertheless a satisfying correlation is likely to exist between OMD data
for untreated samples before and after treatment (19). We can thus propose
that, for untreated samples, extraction with alkali would be superior to
neutral buffer for the prediction of OMD. For these reasons, in this study
of OMD prediction for untreated and ammonia treated straws, we tested known
densitometric methods (12, 13) and tried to improve their precision by
firstly optimising extraction conditions such as temperature, time, buffer

composition for all samples and, especially for untreated samples, extracting with ammonia solution and, secondly, modifying the filtration method to select the molecular size of filtrates best correlated with OMD. These densitometric methods were then compared to other chemical, enzymatic and microbiological predictors mentioned above.

2. MATERIAL AND METHODS

2.1. Straws
Twenty-eight samples of straw (25 wheat, 2 barley, 1 oat) were obtained, of which 16 were untreated and 12 ammonia treated by various techniques (table 1).

2.2. Organic matter digestibility measurement
OMD of these straws were measured using groups of 6 adult male sheep fed experimental diets in limited quantity (30 g/kg $P^{0.75}$) allowing 15 days for adaptation and 6 days for faeces collection. Diets were composed of treated straw alone or untreated straw plus sufficient soybean oilmeal to reach the level of 10 % total N x 6.25 on dry matter basis. Supplementary minerals and vitamins were given to meet requirements.

2.3. Predictive measures
2.3.1. Densitometric
2.3.1.1. Reference methods. The first method tested was one proposed by LAU and VAN SOEST (12) and involved extraction of samples by reflux with phosphate – EDTA buffer, followed by filtration on Whatman 41 paper and measurement of absorbance at 280 and 320 nm. For the second method extractions were for 20 h at ambient temperature as proposed by VAN SOEST, MASCARENHAS FERRERA and HARTLEY (13) but the rest of procedure (e.g.- buffer and filtration) was as above.
2.3.1.2. Modified procedure.
. Overall straw samples : the ground (0.8 mm screen) straw sample was weighed (0.5 g) and introduced in a 100 ml erlenmeyer flask. Phosphate buffer pH 7.0 (Na_2HPO_4 12 H_2O : 10.75 g, KH_2PO_4 : 3.15 g, distilled water to bring to 1 l) was added and mixed with sample. The flask was stoppered with a glass bubble and stired for 20 h at ambient temperature (20°C). The mixture was then either filtered on a Whatman 41 paper (without washing the sample) or ultrafiltered through a cellulose nitrate membrane of 0.1μ porosity (SARTORIUS). The filtrate was diluted and its absorbance at 280 and 350 nm measured (a tenfold dilution was generally required when using an optical pathlength of 1 cm).
. Untreated straws : Extraction was with ammonia 0.025 N instead of the phosphate buffer. The rest of the methodology was unchanged.
. Precautions : UV light must be avoided, readings must be made preferably on fresh extracts (within hours).
. Expression of data. Measured optical density for an optical pathlength of 1 cm ($OD_m^{1\ cm}$) is then corrected ($OD_c^{1\ cm}$) as follows :

$$OD_c^{1\ cm} = \frac{OD_m^{1\ cm} \times d \times V}{W \times DM\ \% \ /100}$$

V = volume of the extractive solution (50 ml)
d = dilution of filtrate
DM % = dry matter percentage
W = weight (g) of sample

2.3.2. Chemical. Crude cellulose was determined by the Weende method (20). Lignocellulose and lignin corrected or not for ash, were determined by acid detergent method of GOERING and VAN SOEST (21).

2.3.3. <u>Enzymatic</u>. Organic matter solubility in cellulase was measured using the commercial enzyme Onozuka R10 in acetate buffer either without pretreatment (COMS, 7) or after pretreatment of the sample with either a 0.1 N HCl (22) or a N HCl (8) pepsin solution (respectively P 0.1N-COMS and P1N- COMS).

2.3.4. <u>Microbiological</u>. The <u>in vitro</u> OMD (IVOMD) method used was that of TILLEY and TERRY (5).

3. RESULTS

3.1. Densitometric methods, justification of modifications

Experimental conditions were tested to obtain the best precision (correlation and residual standard deviation, RSD) for the prediction of OMD.

<u>Extraction</u>. In a first run with 12 samples extracted 20 h at ambient temperature, phosphate buffer (simpler than VAN SOEST, MASCARENHAS FERREIRA and HARTLEY's buffer) was compared with phosphate-EDTA buffer (12). As the precision of OMD prediction was very similar the simple phosphate buffer was adopted.

When compared with 1 h reflux, modified 20 h ambient temperature extraction gave results very close with untreated samples and slightly better (but unsignificatively) with treated samples (table 2).

When untreated samples were extracted (at ambient temperature) with ammonia solution, absorbances reach the same level as that obtained with treated samples extracted with neutral buffer. Increase of precision in OMD prediction however was small (RSD decreased from 3.15 to 3.08). The regression curve (slope, intercept) was different from that obtained with treated samples.

<u>Filtration</u>. Ultrafiltration produced a highly significant (P 0.001) increase in the precision of OMD prediction for treated samples (principally at 350 nm) when compared with paper filtration (Whatman, 41) while, for untreated samples, precision remained low. Regression equations of both populations had the advantage of being very similar (fig. 1). As a consequence, the correlation coefficient obtained for the overall samples was high (0.87) and standard deviation relatively small (2.69).

<u>Readings</u> of optical density obtained at 280 and 350 nm were generally better than those obtained at 315 nm and more particularly those at 400 nm. Thus, the first two wavelengths were found to be preferable.

3.2. Comparison between overall methods (table 2)

Densitometric methods are particularly convenient in the case of treated samples, especially using ultrafiltration and measuring at 350 nm. Cellulase and IVOMD methods are significatively less accurate ; cell-wall predictors remain at an unsignificant level.

In the case of untreated samples, the highest OMD prediction was obtained by using COMS (RSD = 2.61). The correlation coefficient was significantly better than when using PO.1N-COMS and still better than P1N-COMS . Densitometric methods were less satisfactory even when using ammonia extraction. Of the cell-wall constituents, undemineralised lignin content was the most closely correlated, with a RSD close to that attained by PO.1N-COMS. Other cell-wall constituents were only weakly correlated.

For all samples, the proposed method (ultrafiltration/350 nm) gave the best precision, followed by COMS.

4. DISCUSSION

For all samples, the precision of OMD prediction by densitometric methods (Whatman 41 filtration) was very close to that obtained by GUILLERMIN, CORDESSE and DULPHY (15) (extraction with neutral detergent solution, 12). In our case, however, semilogarithmic transformation of data was not needed.

Within this limited study, our results show that, especially in the case of treated straws, the correlations obtained are little influenced by the extraction conditions studied but are influenced by the method of filtration. The results obtained by using reflux are likely due to the difficulty in reproducing identical treatment conditions (temperature variations, duration of cooling) for all samples. In fact, the repetability of this method was always lower than the method at ambient temperature. Advantages of modified extraction conditions would then be principally its simplicity and the lower cost of the equipment required.

Among the treated straw water-soluble substances absorbing in UV, it has been shown that alkali-labile phenolic acids (17, 18) and lignin (16) are highly correlated to OMD. The increase of the correlation coefficients with ultrafiltration indicates that small molecules are more significant than high- molecular weight material retained by the membrane , especially at 350 nm.

The highest precision of the OMD prediction obtained for all samples with the proposed method (R = 0.87, RSD = 2.66) is still not ideal but very near to the maximum obtained when taking various variables (OD 280, OD 315, OD 350 and COMS) (R = 0.88, RSD = 2.65). We probably attained a threshold that, either other factors than those studied, or poor precision in in vivo measurement of OMD, are allowing. In an effect, RSD values of OMD measurement of treated (RSD = 2.1) and untreated (RSD = 3.45) straws are high compared with those obtained with other better quality forages (1.3 - 1.7).

Straws contain other aromatic substances such as flavonoïds and, in addition, those produced by the treatment (eg Maillard reaction products). These substances are mainly responsible for the yellow to brown color of straws (as shown by absorbance at 400 nm). They were not well correlated to OMD, as judged by poor results obtained both at 400 nm for all straws, and at all utilised wavelengths for the neutral extracts of untreated straws, which do not contain appreciable quantities of free water-soluble lignin or phenolic acids (18). Ammonia extraction only little increased the precision of prediction, which is not in agreement with the observed relation between untreated and treated straws (19). However it is likely that a more marked increase would be obtained if working with a larger population.

Results using COMS on all samples were in agreement with those of GUILLERMIN, CORDESSE et DULPHY (15). Discrepancies with pepsin-HCl-cellulase method can be due, in latter procedures, to lower level of enzyme or to pretreatment, that beside are very useful in the case of good forages samples (8). COMS is particularly convenient for untreated samples. It is possible that with treated samples the phenolic compounds released by treatment would inhibit cellulase activity. This inhibition was however not observed by REXEN and VESTERGAARD THOMSEN (23).

Relationships between OMD and IVOMD are not as good as observed by other (3, 23). In addition, the correlations between IVOMD and other methods, particularly COMS, were found to be poor (fig. 2). Reason for this might be found in the fact that our data were obtained by using different donor animals, thus the correction used with a standard forage might have been inadequate. Nevertheless, relationships between OMD and IVOMD seem linear (fig. 3). In agreement with SUNDSTOL et al.,(3), IVOMD values are not systematically higher than OMD ones as observed by BERGER, KLOPFENSTEIN and BRITTON (10) with sodium hydroxyde treated straws. Of the cell-wall components, lignin is the best predictor but, as shown in fig. 4, and in agreement with VAN SOEST, MASCARENHAS FERREIRA and HARTLEY (13), regression curves for untreated and treated samples are distinct and parallel.

5. CONCLUSION

It seems that none of the criteria considered here will satisfactorily predict digestibility of both treated and untreated samples. Densitometric methods are particularly convenient for first group, especially when ultrafiltration is used. Extraction at ambient temperature, which gives slightly better results than refluxing at higher temperatures has the main advantage of simplicity. These methods are very rapid as compared with biological ones but they remain unsatisfactory for untreated straws. We recommand thus, for these samples, a complementary measurement using COMS. Further research is needed in order to improve the knowledge with regard to relationship between ultrastructure and degradation of cell-wall. Anyhow the highest level of precision will still be limited by the precision in the in vivo digestibility measurement itself.

LITERATURE

(1) BESLE, J.M. (1988). Digestion de la lignine en relation avec celle des parois, le point des connaissances. To be published.
(2) CHENOST, M. (1982). Adaptation digestive. Bull. Techn. CRZV, Theix, INRA, 47, 69-72.
(3) SUNDSTOL, F., KOSSILA, V., THEANDER, O., VESTERGAARD THOMSEN, A., (1978). Evaluation of the feeding value of straw. Acta Agric. Scand., 28, 10-16.
(4) DEMARQUILLY, C., ANDRIEU, J. (1987). Prévision de la valeur alimentaire des fourrages secs au laboratoire, 243-275 . in Demarquilly C., Les fourrages secs : récolte, traitement, utilisation, INRA Paris.
(5) TILLEY, J.M.A., TERRY, R.A. (1963). A two-stage technique for the in vitro digestion of forage crops. J. Br. Grassld Soc., 18, 104-111.
(6) CHENOST, M., GRENET, E., DEMARQUILLY, C., JARRIGE, R. (1970). The use of the nylon bag technique for the study of forage digestion in the rumen and for predicting feed value. Proc. XIth Intern. Grassld Congr., 697-702. Univ. Queensland, Sta Lucia, Australia.
(7) REXEN, B. (1977). Enzyme solubility - a method for evaluating the digestibility of alkali-treated straw. Anim. Feed Sci. Technol., 2, 205-218.
(8) AUFRERE, J. (1982). Etude de la prévision de la digestibilité des fourrages par une méthode enzymatique. Ann. Zootech., 31, 111-130.
(9) ORSKOV, E.R., KAY, M., REID, G.W. (1988). Prediction of intake of straw and performance by cattle from chemical analysis, biological measurements and degradation characteristics. in EEC COST 84 bis, Workshop on evaluation of straws in ruminant feeding. June 2-4, 1987. Clermont-Ferrand, France, in press.
(10) BERGER, L.L., KLOPFENSTEIN, T.J., BRITTON, R.A. (1980). Effect of sodium hydroxide treatment on rate of passage and rate of ruminal fiber digestion. J. Anim. Sci., 50, 745-749.
(11) GAILLARD, B.D.E. (1966). Calculation of the digestibility for ruminants of roughages from the contents of cell-wall constituents. Neth. J. Agric. Sci., 14, 215-223.
(12) LAU, M.M., VAN SOEST, P.J. (1981). Titratable groups and soluble phenolic compounds as indicators of the digestibility of chemically treated roughages. Anim. Feed Sci. Technol., 6, 123-131.
(13) VAN SOEST, P.J., MASCARENHAS-FERREIRA, A., HARTLEY, R.D. (1983/84). Chemical properties of fibre in relation to nutritive quality of ammonia-treated forages. Anim. Feed Sci. Technol., 10, 155-164.

(14)   Mc BURNEY, M.I., VAN SOEST, P.J. (1984). Laboratory methods for estimation of digestibility and chemical and physical properties of fibrous forages. OECD Workshop on "Improved utilization of lignocellulosic materials with special reference to animal feed", September 19-21, Braunschweig, RFA.

(15)   GUILLERMIN, P., CORDESSE, R., DULPHY, J.P. (1988). Prévision de la digestibilité des pailles et des foins à partir de mesures de laboratoire. Ann. Zootech., in press.

(16)   FORD, C.W., ELLIOTT, R. (1988). Biodegradability of mature grass cell-walls in relation to chemical composition and rumen microbial activity. J. agric. Sci., Camb., in press.

(17)   HARTLEY, R.D. (1972). p-coumaric and ferulic acid components of cell-walls of ryegrass and their relationships with lignin and digestibility. J. Sci. Fd Agric., 23, 1347-1354.

(18)   CHESSON, A. (1981). Effects of sodium hydroxide on cereal straws in relation to the enhanced degradation of structural polysaccharides by rumen microorganismes. J. Sci. Fd Agric., 32, 745-758.

(19)   CHENOST, M., DULPHY, J.P. (1987). Amélioration de la valeur alimentaire (composition, digestibilité, ingestibilité, des mauvais foins et des pailles par les différents types de traitement, 199-230. in Demarquilly C., Les fourrages secs : récolte, traitement, utilisation. INRA Paris.

(20)   WEENDE, official method, 1977. Détermination de l'indice d'insoluble dit "cellulosique", NF V 03040.

(21)   GOERING, H.K., VAN SOEST, P.J. (1970). Forage fiber analyses (Apparatus, Reagents, Procedures and Some applications). Agriculture Handbook, 379, Agricultural Res. Service, U.S., Dept of Agriculture.

(22)   AUFRERE, J., MICHALET-DOREAU, B. (1983). In vivo digestibility and prediction of digestibility of some by-products. in "Feeding value of by-products and their use by beef cattle". Séminaire Melle Gontrode 1983, 25-33. Commission of the European Communities, Brussels.

(23)   REXEN F., VESTERGAARD THOMSEN, 1976. The effect on digestibility of a new technique for alkali treatment of straw. Anim. Feed Sci. Technol., 1, 73-83.

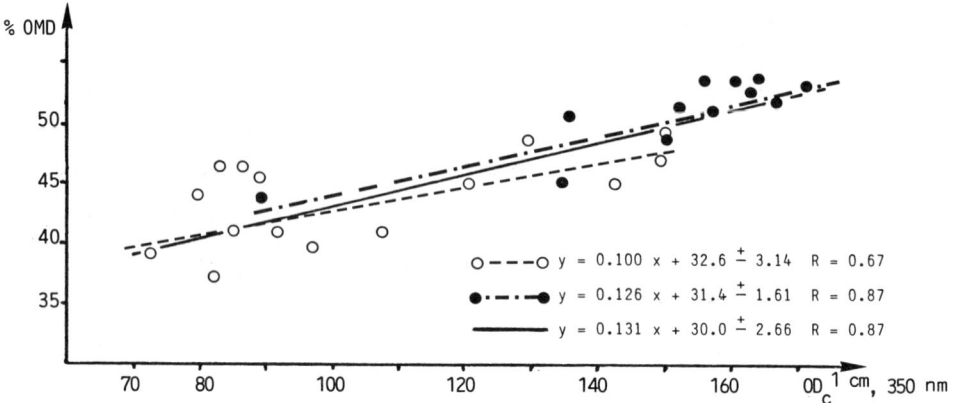

Figure 1 : Relationship between organic matter digestibility (OMD) and corrected optical density at 350 nm ($OD_c^{1\ cm}$,350) of a buffer extract (ambient temperature, ultrafiltered)

O‒‒O untreated straws ;   ●‒‒● treated straws ; ——— all samples

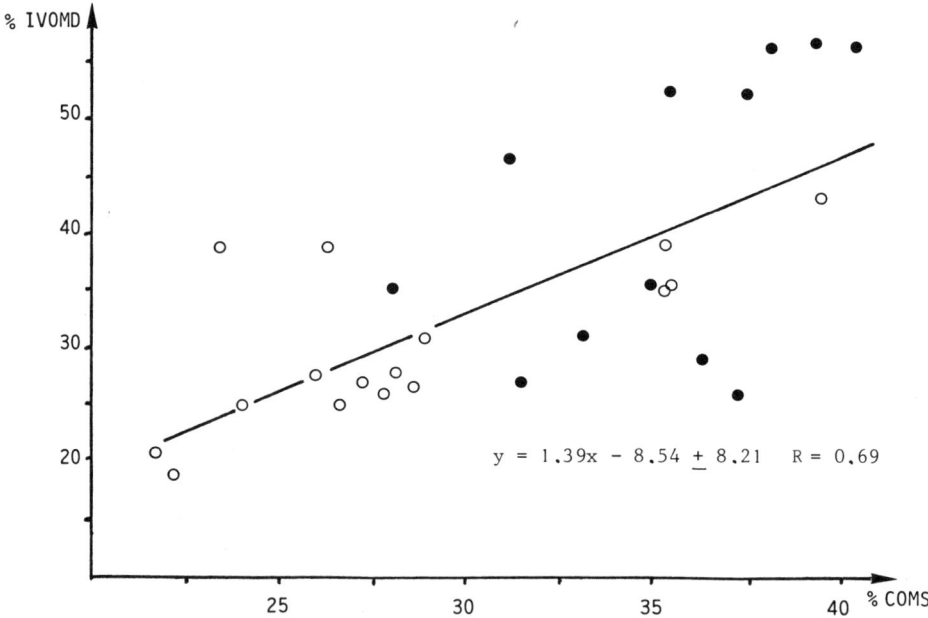

Figure 2 : Relationship between in vitro, organic matter digestibility (IVOMD) and cellulase solubility of organic matter (COMS)

o untreated straws ; ● treated straws

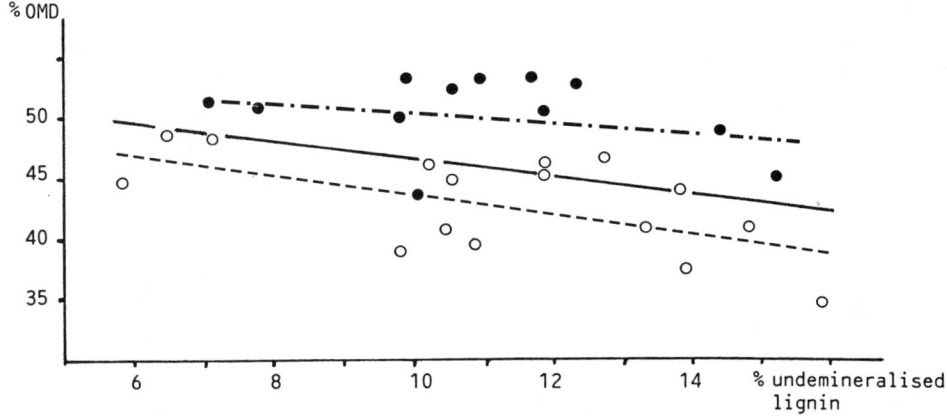

141

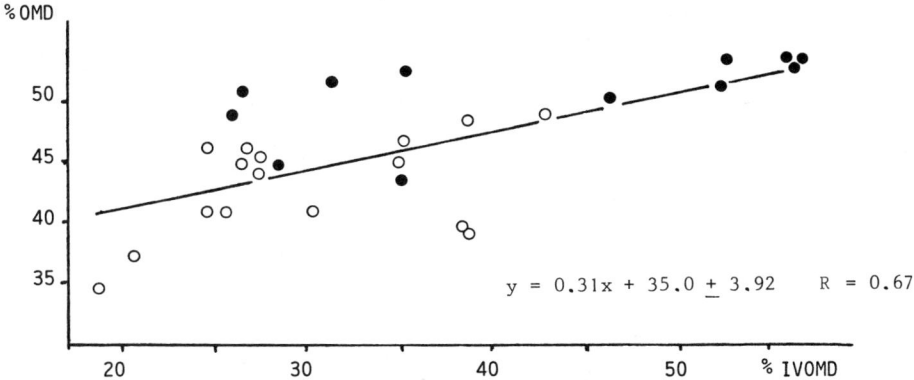

Figure 3 : Relationship between organic matter digestibility (OMD) and in vitro organic matter digestibility (IVOMD)

    o untreated straws ;   ● treated straws

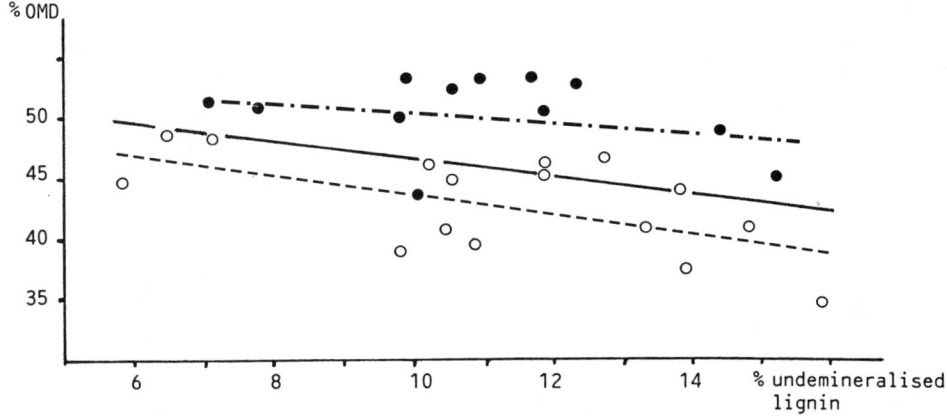

Figure 4 : Relationship between organic matter digestibility (OMD) and undemineralised lignin.

o———o untreated straws $y = -0.87 x + 52.6 \pm 3.34$ R = - 0.62
●—·—● treated straws $y = -0.45 x + 55.2 \pm 3.14$ R = - 0.33
——— overall samples $y = -0.79 x + 54.9 \pm 4.87$ R = - 0.40

Table 1 : Botanical origin, treatment and organic matter digestibility (OMD) of straws.

BOTANICAL ORIGIN	TREATMENT	NUMBER	OMD extreme data	Range
Wheat	untreated	13	34.6 – 48.7	
Wheat	NH_3 4 %, pipe	7	44.9 – 52.7	
	NH_3 2 %, injection	1	53.1	
	NH_3 2 %, oven	1	52.9	
	Uea 6 %, watering	1	43.5	
	Urea 8 % + urease, incorporation	2	50.0 – 52.9	
Barley	Untreated	2	40.5 – 40.6	
Rye	Untreated	1	48.3	
Subtotal 1	Untreated	16	34.6 – 48.7	14.1
Subtotal 2	Treated	12	43.5 – 53.1	9.6
TOTAL	Untreated + treated	28	34.6 – 53.1	18.5

Table 2 : REGRESSION EQUATIONS, CORRELATION COEFFICIENTS (R) AND RESIDUAL STANDARD DEVIATION (RSD) BETWEEN ORGANIC MATTER DIGESTIBILITY (y) AND VARIOUS PREDICTORS (x)

METHODS (1)		UNTREATED (n = 16) Equation	RSD	R	TREATED (n = 12) Equation	RSD	R	TOTAL (n = 28) Equation	RSD	R
Reflux EDTA/W41	OD 280	y = 0.026 x + 25.5 ± 3.39		0.60*	y = 0.017 x + 33.9 ± 2.18		0.75**	y = 0.022 x + 28.5 ± 2.90		0.84***
	OD 320	y = 0.032 x + 28.6 ± 3.44		0.59*	y = 0.021 x + 36.7 ± 2.53		0.71**	y = 0.032 x + 29.05 ± 3.05		0.82***
Ambient 20 h										
P -Buffer/ W 41	OD 280	y = 0.030 x + 31.7 ± 3.42		0.59*	y = 0.032 x + 31.3 ± 2.00		0.80**	y = 0.033 x + 30.7 ± 2.81		0.85***
	OD 315	y = 0.043 x + 31.2 ± 3.44		0.58*	y = 0.040 x + 34.4 ± 2.27		0.73**	y = 0.050 x + 29.6 ± 2.97		0.83***
	OD 350	y = 0.072 x + 30.4 ± 3.21		0.66**	y = 0.076 x + 32.4 ± 2.56		0.64*	y = 0.094 x + 27.2 ± 3.01		0.82***
	OD 400	y = 0.159 x + 32.1 ± 3.33		0.62**	y = 0.091 x + 41.3 ± 3.01		0.42 NS	y = 0.190 x + 30.8 ± 3.35		0.78***
P -Buffer/UF	OD 280	y = 0.040 x + 32.7 ± 3.42		0.59*	y = 0.041 x + 33.2 ± 1.75		0.85***	y = 0.044 x + 31.8 ± 2.75		0.86***
	OD 315	y = 0.062 x + 31.5 ± 3.28		0.63**	y = 0.066 x + 31.0 ± 1.90		0.82**	y = 0.067 x + 30.6 ± 2.69		0.86***
	OD 350	y = 0.100 x + 32.6 ± 3.14		0.67**	y = 0.126 x + 31.4 ± 1.61		0.87***	y = 0.131 x + 30.0 ± 2.66		0.87***
Ammonia/W 41	OD 280	y = 0.027 x + 27.3 ± 3.35		0.61*						
(0.025 N)	OD 315	y = 0.035 x + 28.3 ± 3.29		0.63**						
	OD 350	y = 0.047 x + 27.3 ± 3.08		0.69**						
Cellulase	COMS	y = 0.63 x + 24.9 ± 2.61		0.79***	y = 0.48 x + 33.5 ± 2.78		0.55☆	y = 0.78 x + 21.7 ± 2.96		0.83***
	P0.1N-COMS	y = 0.456 x + 29.3 ± 3.30		0.63**	y = 0.69 x + 28.0 ± 2.71		0.58*	y = 0.66 x + 25.4 ± 4.24		0.60***
	P1N-COMS	y = 0.36 x + 29.3 ± 3.50		0.57*	y = 0.86 x + 19.3 ± 3.21		0.57☆	y = 0.27 x + 35.2 ± 4.91		0.29☆
IVOMD		y = 0.28 x + 34.5 ± 3.71		0.49☆	y = 0.15 x + 43.8 ± 2.64		0.61*	y = 0.31 x + 35.0 ± 3.92		0.67***
Crude cellulose		y = -0.060 x + 45.5 ± 4.24		-0.04 NS	y = 1.31 x - 5.5 ± 2.44		0.68*	y = - 0.01 x + 46.6 ± 5.32		- 0.005NS
Lignocellulose		y = - 0.42 x + 65.6 ± 3.48		- 0.57*	y = 0.14 x - 42.3 ± 3.31		- 0.09NS	y = - 0.005 x + 45.8 ± 5.31		- 0.004NS
Undemineralised lignin		y = - 0.87 x + 52.6 ± 3.34		- 0.62**	y = - 045x + 55.2 ± 3.14		- 0.33NS	y = - 0.79 x + 54.9 ± 4.87		- 0.40*
Demineralised lignin		y = - 1.79 x + 54.5 ± 3.72		- 0.48☆	y = - 1.06x + 57.1 ± 3.03		- 0.41NS	y = - 1.48x + 55.6 ± 5.03		- 0.32☆

(1) EDTA = phosphate - EDTA buffer (12) ; P - buffer = phosphate buffer ; W 41 = Whatman 41 filtration ; UF = ultra-filtration ; COMS = organic matter solubility in cellulase ; P0.1N-COMS = COMS after pepsin in HCl 0.1 N treatment ; P1N-COMS = COMS after pepsine in HCl N treatment ; IVOMD = in vitro organic matter digestibility ; *** P<0.001 ; ** P<0.01 ; * P<0.05 ;☆ P<0.10 ; NS = not significative.

BIOLOGICAL IN VITRO AND IN SACCO METHODS
BY J.L. TISSERAND

Laboratoire de Recherches de la Chaire de Zootechnie
de l'E.N.S.S.A.A.-I.N.R.A
26 Boulevard Docteur Petitjean - 21000 DIJON - France

SUMMARY

The in vitro and in sacco methods are often utilized for determining the digestion of treated by-product, especially straw.
Those techniques are, in fact, rapid, cheap and require only
small quantities of forage.
However the results obtained in vitro and in sacco are not always well correlated with in vivo measurements, since the latter depend closely on experimental conditions, in particular,
forage respiration and rationing of animals.
Consequently it seems advisable to recommend :
- the use of one or two standard forage in each experiment,
- the choice of reference method,
- checking the results obtained with in vivo observation.

1 - Introduction

The in vitro and in sacco methods of digestion are very often
utilized in order to evaluate the effect produced by treatments of
lignified by-products and in particular straw.

These techniques actually give an answer quickly in a cheap way
and, what is more important, the quantities of forages utilized are
very small. As a consequence, they are interesting in particular to
test the conditions in which some treatments are made (rate, length
of time,...). Yet, the reliability of the results must be confirmed.

Considering these advantages we must note the fact that the
study concerns only a part of the digestive phenomena. Moreover these are intermittent methods which do not take into account the long-
term effects of treatment on the rumen microbial activity. Finally,
the results obtained strictly depend on the conditions in which the
technique is applied.

We are going to deal successively with the problems raised by
the different types of methods used mainly with lignified forages to
which chemical products are sometimes added, the main results which
were obtained, how they could be reproduced and a comparison with in
vivo measurements.

2 - The main methods
They can be divided into 3 groups : in vitro, in sacco and rusi-tec.

The in vitro methods : A forage is put for incubation in glass containers in conditions as near as possible as those of the rumen in presence of an inoculum preleved in the rumen. This technique can be used in order to evaluate the disappearance of dry matter over a given period of time (1) or to study the products resulting from degradation (AGV production in particular) (2). These experiments can only by conducted over a limited period of time owing to the difficulty to avoid modifications in the microbial population present at the start. In the case of straws, particularly when they have been chemically treated, the main problem consists in the determination of the most convenient complementation : fermentescible, glucides, nitrogen and minerals, trace elements in particular.
In some cases the presence of substances resulting from chemical treatment can modify the microbial population in an important proportion. The ratio between the quantities of forage and inoculum as well as the conditions in which this inoculum was obtained (how it was taken, filtrated through gauze, and how the solid residue was soaked) must always mentioned. The time elapsed between the taking and the meals of the donor must not be neglected.The utilization of an inoculum taken from several animals seems better.

The in sacco methods : The introduction of a nylon bag containing the forage to be studied into the rumen of a fistulated sheep allows us to evaluate the degree of degradation.
With this technique, it is possible to determine the degradation level of the cell walls but also of the nitrogen fraction. It is also possible to evaluate the variations in the cellulolytic activity of a microbial biomass depending on the treatment of the straw which is part of the animal's diet.
The results which are obtained can however vary with many factors such as the quality of nylon used, the size of the bag (ration between the quantity of forage and the bag surface), its position inside the animal's rumen, the way it is washed after removal of the rumen. This technique does not always show the long-term effects of the treatment on the microbial population (NaOH treated straw).
At least there are some variations between the animals (3) (Table 1) which make it necessary to use several subjects.

The Rusitec method : Is in some ways an in sacco method experimented in vitro. The conditions in which it is realized play a predominant part in the results which are obtained. This technique is however used in order to obtain some information at the same time on the intensity of degradation and the nature of the products formed.
As I do not use this technique myself, I will leave it to the specialists to deal with it during the discussion period.

3 - The main problems

But the two problems which seem dominating to me in all cases are : the conditioning of the forages and, what is more important the diets of the animals which give rumen juice or receive bags.

The thinness of the crushing of the forages and perhaps how they are dried have quite an important influence on the results obtained as much in vitro as in sacco. The diet given to the animals plays an important part in the results which are obtained, in particular there are some differences between the values obtained when the animals receive a standardized diet (alfalfa hay and concentrate) and when they are on a straw-based diet (4) (Table 2 and figure 1).

4 - RESULTS

The in vitro techniques of the Tilley and Terry type is largely used in order to study the effects of the conditions in which straw and by-products are treated. When experiment conditions are strictly reproduced, they really show quite clearly the most efficent conditions (temperature, amount of treating product, humidity, length of time). Many equations have been proposed to link the in vitro and in vivo digestibilities. Yet, the values which are obtained generally turn out to be higher than those observed in vivo. The difference between the in vivo and in vitro results can even vary with some factors. This is true in particular of the ration of the NaOH used to treat straws.

The action on microbial activity of the NaOH or NH$_3$ ingested with straw which appears mainly in vivo could explain this phenomenon (5) (Figure 2).

The in sacco method gives results which largely depend on the time spent in the rumens of the animals (Figure 3). The degradation period which gives the best account of what we can measure in vivo must be found. Short periods of time, if not kinetic ones, are related to the voluntary ingestion level, whereas a period of about 72 hours gives a better account of the digestibility of organic matter and of the several categories of cell-wall contents. In this case too, in conditions which may be reproduced, it is possible to obtain reliable information on the efficiency of this or that part of the treatment.

But the choice of a diet for the receiving subjects plays a determining part in the prediction of in vivo digestibility. This technique used with standard forages in sacco (straw or hay) may make it possible to evaluate the effects of a treatment on the rumen microbial population.

Thus in sheep fed with straw in comparison with sheep to which hay is given the introduction of a bag containing non treated straw gives better results. The opposite can be observed with treated straw, which may there too be explained by the effect of the treatment on the rumen microbial population (6) (Table 3).

Many studies compare results obtained in vitro or in sacco with in vivo measurement (7,8,9,10) (Tables 4, 5, 6 and figures 4, 5). All those results demonstrate the importance of the conditions in which the measures are made for their reliability. It seems that the in vitro and in sacco techniques must be authenticated by in vivo measurements. These techniques give us a choice among the conditions of treatment which are many but it seems advisable to verify conclusions with in vivo measures.

According to Demeyer (3) the main conclusions are the following :

A. Comparison in vitro VS in sacco
- % in sacco degradation is reproductible between laboratories,
- potential in sacco degradation cannot be predicted from in vitro potention VFA production. This is not due to accumulation of end products but possibly to a lack of renewal of the flora and fauna in vitro.
- initial rate of in sacco degradation is confounded by the washable fraction that cannot be identified with "easily degradable".-
potential in sacco degradation can be predicted from in vitro rate of VFA production.

B. Between animal variability of in sacco straw degradation
- in sacco straw D.M. degradation (16hrs and 24hrs) may vary between animals (heifers) fet the same diet (based on beet pulp and hay). It is positively correlated with soya D.M. degradability and negatively with rumen VFA concentration.

C. Out of a series of 12 antibiotics and 4 other additives tested, 7 inhibited VFA production in vitro (24hrs) from NDF-hay, including ionophores. It would seem that no additives exist that stimulate NDF fermentation.

5 - CONCLUSION
In view of the variability of the results obtained "in vitro" and "in sacco" (Table 7) which depend for a large part on the conditions in which the tests are conducted, it seems advisable to recommend :
- the use in each experiment of one or two standard forages which could be the same for all laboratories,
- the choice and recommendation of reference methods,
- the checking of the results obtained with in vivo observations.

REFERENCES

(1)   TILLEY J.M.A., TERRY R.A., 1983 - A two stage technique for the in vitro digestion of forage crops.J. Br. grass. Soc., 18, 104-111.
(2)   TISSERAND J.L., ZELTER Z., 1965 - Essai de normalisation d'une technique de mesure de la digestion des fourrages in vi-

tro. Ann.Biol.Boch. Biophy., 5, 101-110.

(3)   DEMEYER D. et DENDOOVEN R., 1987 - Results related to in vi-
       tro and in sacco. Evaluation of lignocellulose digestion in
       ruminant. Proceeding of the EEC seminar. The methods of straw
       evaluation in ruminant feeding. Clermont-Ferrand.

(4)   CHENOST M. et al, 1987 - Communication personnelle.

(5)   THOMSEN K.V., KRISTENSEN V.T., REXEN F., 1973 - Improvment of
       digestibility of cereal straw by NaOH treatment, cité par Gau-
       din, 1977.

(6)   MESCHY F., 1984 - Contribution à l'étude de la valorisation
       des pailles de céréales. Effets du traitement par la soude et
       par l'ammoniac. Rôle de la complémentation énergétique et azo-
       tée de la paille d'orge traitée ou non par la soude.
       Thèse de Docteur-Ingénieur, ENSSAA Dijon, 98 p.

(7)   BUTRUILLE M., 1983 - Etude de l'amélioration de la valeur nu-
       tritive de la paille par le traitement à l'ammoniac en meule.
       Mémoire de fin d'études d'Ingénieur des techniques agricoles.
       ENSSAA Dijon, 59 p.

(8)   GIRARD J.C., LAROCHE J.P., 1983 - Essai de détermination de
       la valeur alimentaire de la paille traitée à l'ammoniac. Ef-
       fet de traitement en four ou en meule. Mémoire de fin d'étu-
       des d'Ingénieur des techniques agricoles, ENSSAA Dijon, 97 p.

(9)   WANAPAT M., SUNDSTOL F., HALL J.M.R., 1986 - A comparison of
       alkali treatment methods used to improvethe nutritive value
       of straw.II - in sacco and in vitro degradation relation to
       in vivo digestibility. Anim. Feed Sci. and technol., (14),
       215-220.

(10)   SUNDSTOL F., KOSSILA W., THEANDER O., THONSEN KV., 1978 -Eva-
       luation of the feeding value of straw. A comparison of labora-
       tory methods in the nordic countries. Acta Agric. Scand. (28),
       10-16.

149

Figure 1: Effect of diet on D.M. degradability in "sacco" of a standard
untreated straw   (CHENOST et al, 1987)
(in sacco)

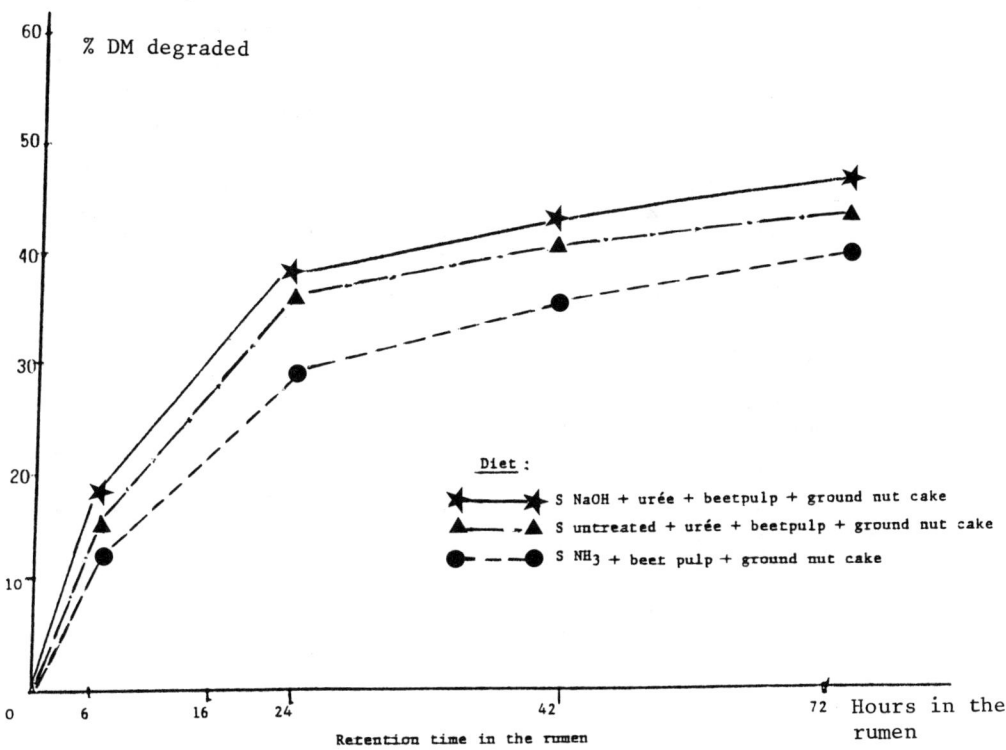

Figure 2: Effect of level of NaOH on the O.M.D. barley straw (50 samples)
(THOMSEN, KRISTENSEN and REXEN, 1987)

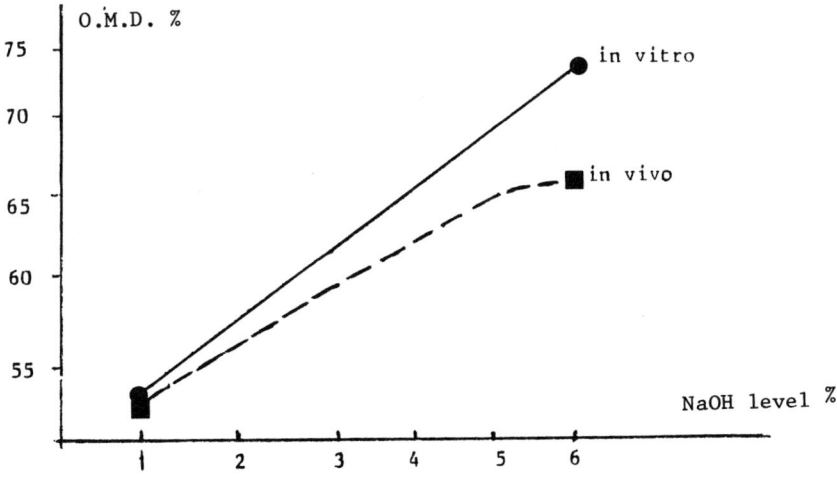

Figure 3: Effect of retention time of DM degradability in the rumen
(CHENOST et al., 1987)

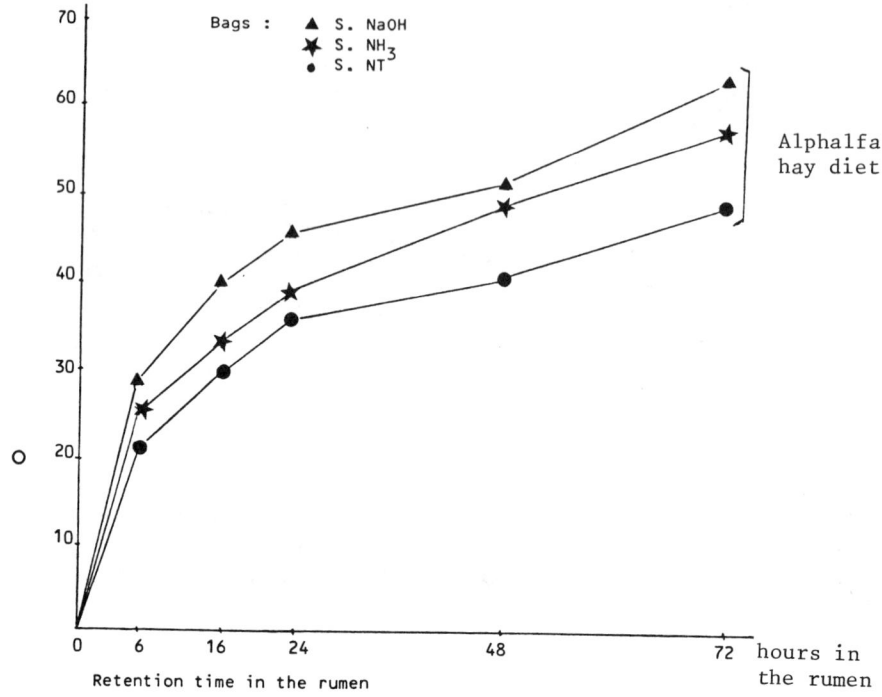

Figure 4: Relationship between in vitro organic matter digestibility
(IVOMD) and in vivo digestible organic matter (in vivo DOM).
Line 2. Possible trend without samples. (F. SUNDSTØL et al, 1987)
(F. SUNDSTØL et al, 1987)

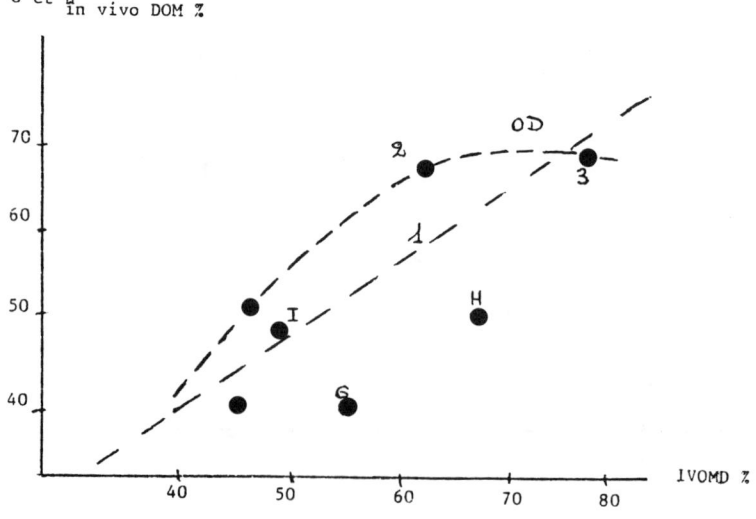

Figure 5: Relationships between digestible dry matter intakes of straw
within various diets (1) by sheep and <u>in sacco</u> values potential
straw dry matter degradability (DDM)   (CHENOST et al)

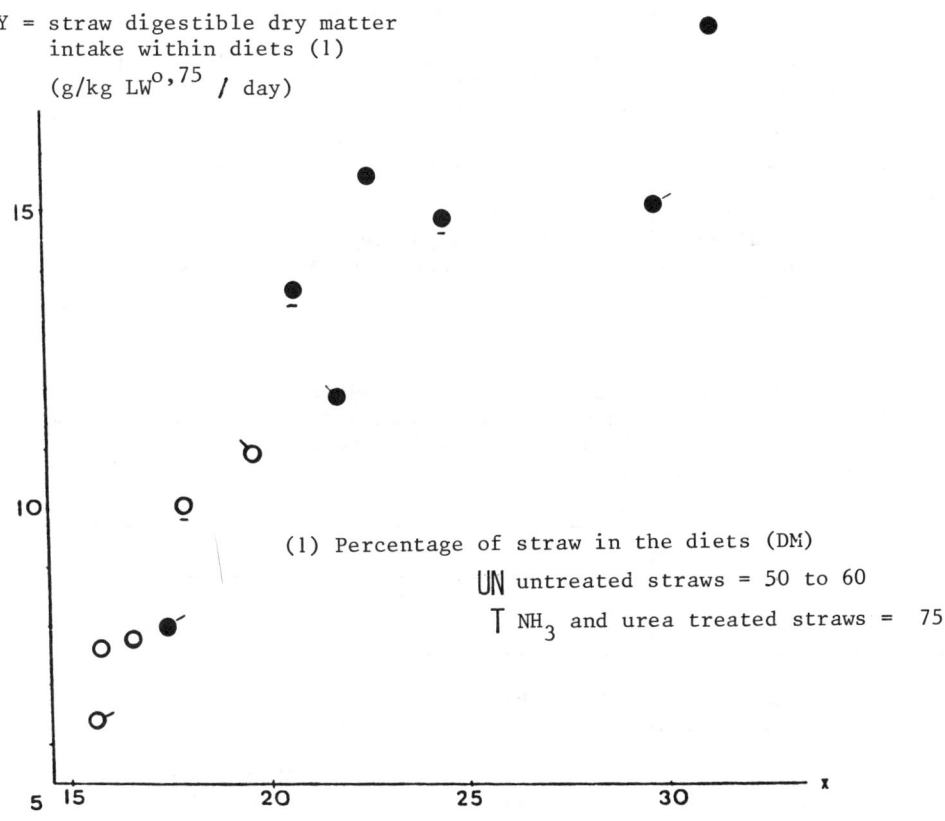

Y = straw digestible dry matter
    intake within diets (1)

    (g/kg LW^{o,75} / day)

(1) Percentage of straw in the diets (DM)

UN untreated straws = 50 to 60

T NH$_3$ and urea treated straws =   75

X = Product (p.100 DDM at 24 h.) x (p.100 DDM at 72 hours)

Where the <u>fistulates'diet</u> is a <u>good lucerne hay</u>[2] and <u>substrates</u> (nylon bags)
the <u>UN or T straws</u> (4 untreated straws 0, ơ, 0, ᕞ and their various NH$_3$ or
urea/NH$_3$ treatment).

<u>Progression equation</u>

Y = DDM intake = 27.22 + 2.896X - 0.476 X^2 ± 1.23 , R = 0.950 , n = 11

Table 1: Between animal variability of "in sacco" lignocellulose degradation
(D. DEMEYER, R. DENDOOVEN, 1987)

Animal no	Degradation (% of washed D.M. in bags) (2)			
	soya		straw	
	7 hrs	24 hrs	16 hrs	40 hrs
103 (75.1)(1)	35.2	86.8 a	15.2 a	29.9 a
104 (100.6)	32.1	70.5	9.8	27.0
105 (92.7)	32.2	75.3	10.2	27.9
107 (89.0)	31.5	70.6	12.1 b	27.8

(1) ( ) = VFA mmol/l rumen liquor
(2) mean values of 12 observations per cel
a.b: Mean values with different superscript are significantly
     different (P 0.05)

Table 2: Effect of treatment and nitrogen complementation on in "sacco"
degradability (DM%) on wheat straw intreated (PNT) or NH_3 treated
(PAA) or with urea (PAU) after 24 and 48 hours in the rumen
(CHENOST et al, 1987)

Diet		In sacco degradability					
		24 hrs			48 hrs		
Straw Complementation		PNT	PAA	PAU	PNT	PAA	PAU
PNT (+ urea)	0	34,5	41,5	–	42,9	57,2	–
	Ground nut cake	36,2	45,0	–	43,0	58,7	–
	Fish meal	36,3	47,1	–	42,8	60,6	–
	(Syx)	(1,50)	(1,21)	–	(1,73)	(1,46)	–
PAA	0	31,5	41,3	–	41,0	58,0	–
	Ground nut cake	32,7	41,9	–	39,7	61,4	–
	Fish meal	40,2	54,6	–	46,7	68,4	–
	(Syx)	(1,18)	(1,79)	–	(0,84)	(1,06)	–
PAU	0	37,0	–	40,3	44,6	–	52,7
	Ground nut cake	35,7	–	42,1	45,0	–	54,1
	Fish meal	41,8	–	44,0	51,8	–	58,6
	(Syx)	(1,24)	–	(1,24)	(1,45)	–	(0,84)

Table 3: Effect of diet on the in sacco degradability

Diet	Hay		Straw	
Degradability in sacco	ADF	Cellulose	ADF	Cellulose
Untreated straw	40,9	48,1	44,5	51,5
NH$_3$ treated straw	55,2	62,6	54,4	62,0
NaOH treated straw	65,7	73,6	40,4	46,3

Table 4: Comparison between in vivo digestibility in vitro and in sacco degradability (M. BUTRUILLE)

	in sacco degradability (48 hrs)		in vitro degradability TISSERAND-ZELTER methods		in vivo digestibility	
	ADF	Cellulose	ADF	Cellulose	ADF	Cellulose
Untreated straw	33,2 + 1,7	45,5 + 1,2	18,5 + 1,4	21,2 + 1,3	39,5 + 5,5	54,2 + 6,1
Ammonia treated straw	45,1 + 2,7	58,1 + 1,7	24,8 + 1,5	26 + 1,9	62,6 + 5,1	66,1 + 5,2
Average gain	+ 36%	+ 25%	+ 34%	+ 23%	+ 21%	+ 29%

Table 5: Comparison between in vivo DM digestibility and in sacco degradability with NH$_3$ treated straw (GIRARD and LAROCHE)

	Untreated Straw	NH$_3$ treated straw oven	NH$_3$ treated straw stack
DM apparente digestibility	46,9 + 2,7	53,6 + 1,9	53,5 + 1,3
DM in sacco degradability	46,1 + 4,6	55,6 + 4,7	59,2 + 3,2

Table 6: A comparison of alkali treatment methods used to improve the
nutritive value of straw. II. In sacco and in vitro degradation
relative to in vivo digestibility (M. WANAPAT, F. SUNDSTØL and
J.M.R. HALL)

	In vitro (48 hrs) IVDMD	In sacco (48 hrs) ISDMD	In vivo IVVDMD
Untreated straw	42,2	41,4	50,8
Urea/urine -treated straw	53,2	52,3	56,3
NH₃ -treated straw	56,8	58,9	63,7
Wet (NaOH) -treated straw	69,2	82,0	73,7
Dry (NaOH) -treated straw	65,7	67,3	66,0

Table 7: Comparison of laboratory methods in the nordic for evaluation of the
feeding value of straw. (F. SUNDSTØL et al, 1987)

	in vitro OM degradability %				OMD in vivo
	DR	SF	N	S	
Untreated barley straw	52	47	48	60	50
NH₃ treated straw	63	59	63	74	65
70 % straw + 30 % C	67	65	63	74	56
70 % NaOH + straw + 30 % C	70	68	68	77	63
straw + molasse pellets	55	49	46	58	42
NaOH straw + molasse pellets	65	61	64	72	52
Barley straw	45	50	49	68	48
NaOH barley straw	75	72	76	83	68

PREDICTION OF INTAKE OF STRAW AND PERFORMANCE BY CATTLE FROM CHEMICAL ANALYSIS, BIOLOGICAL MEASUREMENTS AND DEGRADATION CHARACTERISTICS

E. R. ØRSKOV, M. KAY and G. W. Reid

The Rowett Research Institute, Bucksburn, Aberdeen AB2 9SB

Summary

Five different straws consisting of 2 varieties of winter barley, 2 varieties of spring barley and 1 variety of winter wheat were chosen due to differences in degradation characteristics determined by using nylon bags incubated in the rumen of cattle and describing the straw using the equation: $p = a+b(1-e^{ct})$. In order to increase variations in degradability batches of the same straws were also treated with anhydrous ammonia in sealed stacks.

In addition to description of degradation characteristics several chemical analyses including crude fibre, neutral and acid detergent fibre and lignin and biological analyses including *in vitro* digestibility and near infrared (NIR) analysis were carried out.

The straws were subsequently fed *ad libitum* to groups of steers given a daily supplement of 1.5 kg concentrate and untreated straws were supplemented with urea. The daily dry matter intake of the straws varied from 3.4 to 5.7 kg/d, the digestible dry matter intake from 1.4 to 3.5 kg/d and growth rate from 106 to 608 g/d.

The chemical analyses correlated poorly with intake and growth rate of the steers. However, biological measurements were far superior. *In vitro* digestibility and NIR gave better prediction of intake than *in vivo* digestibility in sheep and ME concentration. Cellulase digestibility was the best laboratory measurement.

By using multiple regression of a, b, c from the exponential equations characterising degradability of the straw, the correlation coefficients with dry matter intake, digestible dry matter intake and growth rate were 0.88, 0.96 and 0.95 respectively.

INTRODUCTION

Many attempts to predict the voluntary intake and nutritive value of roughages by ruminant animals have been made over the last century. In fact one of the greatest weaknesses in almost all systems of feed evaluation developed in Europe is the lack of information on intake. They attempt to predict the responses to nutrients in animals after they have consumed a certain amount of food. The systems give little information about how much the animals will eat. While this is of little consequence for very high quality diets which do not impose physical restrictions to intake, lack of knowledge of potential consumption makes feed formulation and feeding strategies extremely difficult when poorer quality roughages form a large part of the diet.

While it has been generally observed that voluntary intake and digestibility were positively correlated it has not accounted for a very large proportion of the variation. Chenost *et al.*(1) noted a correlation of 0.76 between *in vivo* digestibility and voluntary intake of 83 forages; digestibility therefore accounts for only 58% of the variation in digestibility. Many aspects of digestion kinetics have been discussed recently (3,4). Chenost *et al.* (1) first noted that the degradability of roughages incubated in nylon bags in the rumen gave better predictions of voluntary intake (r 0.82) than *in vivo* digestibility (r=0.79). (2) also noted that the potential degradability derived from the exponential equation of (5) was better correlated with intake of hay than *in vivo* digestibility. The equation $p = a+b(1-e^{-ct})$, where p is DM loss from the bag, a, b and c are constants and t is the time of incubation, was fitted to data obtained from sequential removal of nylon bags from the rumens of sheep so that a range in incubation times was obtained. The potential degradability is given by the asymptotic value (a+b). The relationship is also illustrated in Fig. 1 where it can be seen that (a) gives some indication of solubility, (b) the insoluble but potentially degradable fraction and (c) the degradation rate.

RESULTS AND DISCUSSION

In a recent trial (6,7) five different straws comprising two varieties of winter barley, two varieties of spring barley and one variety of wheat were shown to vary in degradation characteristics of a, b and c. The same straws were also ammonia treated to increase variability. The straws were subsequently given *ad libitum* to steers which in addition each received 1.5 kg of concentrate/d. In order to compare the ability of different measurements to predict intake and growth rate a range of different analysis were made including crude fibre, neutral and acid detergent fibre, *in vitro* digestibility, cellulase digestion of neutral detergent fibre, *in vivo* digestibility with sheep fed at maintenance and also metabolizable energy (ME) concentration.

The chemical analyses of the five straws are given in Table I. In Table II the biological measurements are given including the *in vitro* digestibility, cellulase digestion, 48 h degradability, *in vivo* digestibility and ME concentration. It can be seen that a wide variation was established in the measurements. In Table III the values for the constants a, b and c from the exponential equation of Ørskov & McDonald (5) are given together with the residual standard deviation (RSD). The low RSD indicate that the data fitted well to the exponential equation. In Table IV the range of intake and growth rates of the steers given the 10 straws together with the range in *in vivo* digestibility determined in sheep fed at maintenance. In Table V the correlation of chemical and biological measurements with voluntary intake, growth rate and *in vivo* digestibility are given. Here it can be seen that on the whole chemical measurements excepting near infrared absorbance were poor predictors of intake and growth. On the contrary all of the biological measurements including the cellulase digestibility predicted intake with a high accuracy. The degradability measured with nylon bags gave much better estimates of animal performance than measurements of digestibility and even metabolizability. In Table VI from Ørskov *et al.* (1987) an attempt to predict performance dry matter intake, digestible dry matter intake and growth rate from multiple regressions of either potential degradability (a+b) or of (a+b)+c or a+b+c. The results show quite clearly that addition of the rate constant c significantly increases the accuracy of prediction of all parameters. These observations strongly suggest that a completely new method of assessing the feeding value of roughages may now be devised using the factors in the exponential equation describing rate and potential extent of degradation or an index value derived from the contribution of the factors to predict intake and performance. Assessment of feed values of this kind has great relevance to feed evaluation systems both in Europe and in many tropical countries where low quality roughages are the main feed available to ruminants and when level of consumption by the animals is often more important than metabolizability. A further advantage is that it is much cheaper, quicker and easier to measure degradability of feeds in nylon bags incubated in the rumen than to conduct the feeding trials required for measurement of *in vivo* digestibility and growth rate. *In vivo* digestibility of roughages appear to be of interest only when in particular experiments it is desired to gain information of the exact energy intake of the animals.

REFERENCES

(1) CHENOST, M., GENET, E., DEMARQUILLY, C. and JARRIGE, R. (1970). Proceedings of the 11th International Grassland Congress, p.697-701, University of Queensland, St. Lucia, Australia.
(2) HOVELL, F.D.DeB., NGAMBI, J.W.W., BARKER, W.P. and KYLE, D. J. (1986). Animal Production 431, 111-118.
(3) VAN SOEST, P.J. (1982). Nutritional Ecology of the Ruminant. O.B. Books Corvalles, 374 pp.
(4) ELLIS, W.C. and WYLIE, M.J. (1987). In: Feed Science. E.R. Ørskov, Ed. World Animal Series Subseries B, Chapter 8.
(5) ØRSKOV, E.R. and McDONALD, I. (1979). Journal of Agricultural Science, Cambridge 92, 499-503.
(6) ØRSKOV, E.R., KAY, M. and REID, G.W. (1987). Animal Production. In press.
(7) REID, G.W., ØRSKOV, E.R. and KAY, M. (1987). Animal Production. In Press.

Description of degradability of fibrous residues.

$$p = a + b(1 - e^{-ct})$$

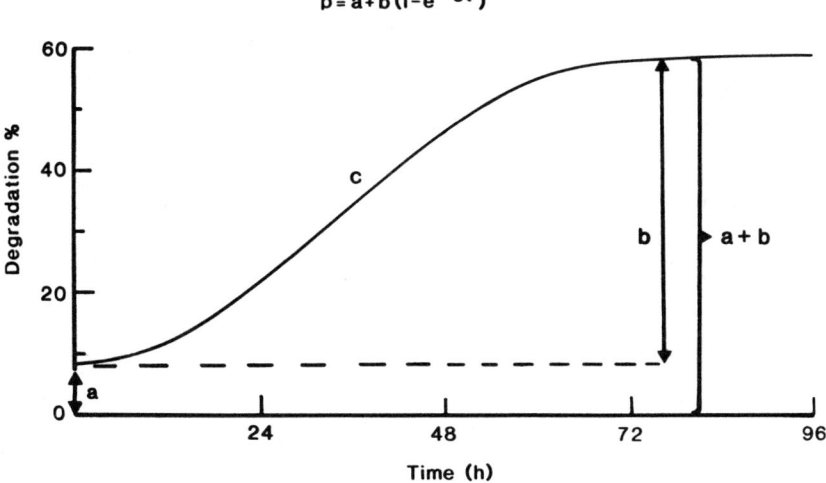

Figure 1. Degradation of fibrous residues as a function of time.

Table I

Chemical composition and metabolizable energy (ME) concentration of different straws offered to sheep either untreated (U) or treated with ammonia (A)

Type	Variety	Treatment	N g/100 g	Ash g/100 g	Crude fibre g/100 g	Neutral detergent fibre g/100 g	Acid detergent fibre g/100 g	Acid detergent lignin g/100 g	% ME concentration MJ/kg
Winter barley	Gerbel	U	0.79	3.7	45.8	87.5	57.9	9.0	7.23
	"	A	1.58	4.6	44.2	84.0	55.5	8.3	8.53
	Igri	U	0.76	3.7	45.4	86.4	55.4	7.7	7.16
	"	A	1.48	3.5	45.0	84.1	55.4	8.0	7.90
Spring barley	Corgi	U	0.67	4.3	42.7	84.0	51.2	6.3	7.82
	"	A	1.60	4.1	41.8	81.0	50.0	6.1	9.50
	Golden Promise	U	0.84	4.8	44.5	85.0	55.5	7.3	7.35
		A	1.54	4.8	42.6	79.9	52.3	6.9	8.40
Wheat	Norman	U	1.18	6.1	39.4	80.7	52.0	8.0	5.98
	"	A	2.11	5.3	37.7	75.5	48.8	7.0	8.37

Table II

Biological measurements of feed quality in 10 different straws either untreated (U) or treated with ammonia (A)

Type of straw	Variety	Treatment	In vitro digestion g/100 g	Cellulase digestion g/100 g	Degradation 48 h g/100 g	ME concentration MJ/kg
Winter barley	Gerbel	U	27.6	24.7	34.4	7.23
	"	A	37.8	35.2	46.5	8.53
Winter barley	Igri	U	29.5	29.3	37.4	7.16
	"	A	37.5	34.0	44.8	7.90
Spring barley	Corgi	U	39.0	34.4	47.3	7.82
	"	A	54.1	47.3	60.0	9.50
Spring barley	Golden Promise	U	36.4	33.5	44.3	7.35
	"	A	45.6	44.5	52.8	8.40
Wheat	Norman	U	31.7	31.5	40.8	5.98
	"	A	44.8	42.9	55.9	8.37

Table III

The effect of type and variety and ammonia treatment on degradation characteristics at different times of incubation of nylon bags in the rumen expressed as the constants in the exponential equation $p = a+b(1-e^{-ct})$. Untreated (U) and ammonia treated (A)

Type of straw	Variety	Treatment	a	b	c	RSD
Winter barley	Gerbel	U	6.0	32.9	0.0337	0.25
	"	A	7.9	54.4	0.0258	1.21
Winter barley	Igri	U	5.1	38.2	0.0391	0.97
	"	A	7.9	45.2	0.0351	0.63
Spring barley	Corgi	U	3.4	48.7	0.0483	0.66
	"	A	6.4	60.4	0.0457	2.04
Spring barley	Golden Promise	U	7.5	48.0	0.0303	1.09
	"	A	9.3	52.1	0.0376	0.34
Wheat	Norman	U	7.7	40-.9	0.0345	1.76
	"	A	9.0	51.9	0.0364	0.81

161

Table IV

Mean and range of intakes of straws and growth by steers

	Mean	Minimum	Maximum
Dry matter intake kg/d	4.73	3.42	5.89
Growth rate g/d	352	106	608
In vivo digestibility % in sheep	46.3	34.3	59.6

Table V

Correlations between chemical and biological measurement and straw intake and growth rate by steers and *in vivo* digestibility by sheep

	Dry matter intake	Growth rate	*In vivo* digestibility
Crude fibre	0.70	-0.57	0.09
Neutral detergent fibre	0.79	-0.77	-0.31
Acid detergent fibre	0.86	-0.79	-0.45
Lignin	0.75	-0.72	-0.69
Neutral detergent cellulase	0.88	-0.95	-0.81
Dry matter degradability			
7 h	0.90	0.95	0.78
24 h	0.91	0.95	0.85
48 h	0.92	0.95	0.87
72 h	0.90	0.92	0.84
Constants in equation			
(a)	0.28	0.37	0.06
(b)	0.85	0.85	0.86
(c)	0.38	0.40	0.40
(a+b)	0.85	0.86	0.80
Digestibility in sheep	0.70	0.77	-
ME concentration	0.74	0.78	-
Near infrared (NIR)	0.86	0.87	0.77
In vitro digestibility	0.89	0.93	0.90

Table VI

Prediction of intake of dry matter (DM), digestible DM and growth rate in cattle from degradation characteristics generated from the equation $p = a+b(1-e^{-ct})$ (Ørskov & McDonald, 1979).

Y variable	Formulae	Multiple Correlation	RSD
DM intake (kg.d)	$0.572 + .0766 (a+b)$	.83	.452
"	$-0.822 + 0.0748 (a+b) + 40.7 c$	.89	.375
"	$-1.56 + 0.159 a + 0.0658 b + 56.4 c$	.88	.383
Digestible DM intake (kg/d)	$1.258 + 0.0642 (a+b)$	.86	.33
"	$-2.595 + 0.06244 (a+b) + 39.0 c$	.96	.195
"	$-2.576 + 0.0554 a + 0.0640 b + 37.7 c$	.95	.204
Growth rate (g/d)	$-0.595 + 0.0175 (a+b)$	.84	99
"	$-0.922 + 0.0170 (a+b) + 0.55 c$	.91	77
"	$-1.267 + 0.0571 a + 0.0126 b + 17.02 c$	.95	54

ANALYSIS OF LIGNIN IN STRAW BY HPLC WITH ELECTROCHEMICAL DETECTOR

GUIDO C. GALLETTI and ROBERTA PICCAGLIA
Centro di Studio per la Conservazione dei Foraggi - C.N.R.
Istituto di Agronomia Generale e Coltivazioni Erbacee
Università di Bologna - Via F. Re, 8 - 40126 Bologna (Italy)
and
GIUSEPPE CHIAVARI and VITTORIO CONCIALINI
Dipartimento di Chimica "G. Ciamician" - Università di Bologna
Via Selmi, 2 - 40126 Bologna (Italy)

Summary

A method for the analysis of phenolics by HPLC with electrochemical detector (ElCD) is reported.
Free phenols, alkali labile - and alkali resistant lignin were analysed in wheat straw, untreated and treated with NaOH, by HPLC with ElCD and UV detector. Lignin monomeric units were obtained by nitrobenzene oxidative hydrolysis. The electrochemical detection simplifies the analytical procedure, permitting the direct injection of the extracts. Extraction losses are avoided, as well as the interference from nitrobenzene. Aniline formed by reduction of nitrobenzene is also detectable and may be used as an oxidatability index.

1. INTRODUCTION

A considerable research effort is currently aimed at finding economic resources such as agricultural by-products, for ruminant feeding. Cereal straw represents an abundant and inexpensive crop residue.

The utilization of cereal straw as an animal feedstuff has been seriously limited thus far due to its high lignin content and, therefore, low digestibility (1,2).

Lignin is a complex three-dimensional macromolecule made up of phenyl-propane units (3). Its association with cell wall polysaccharides negatively affects the utilization of lignocellulosic residues (4).

Straw digestibility can be improved by chemical, physical and microbial pre-treatments (5), which render the lignin-polisaccharide complexes more easily accessible by rumen enzymes (4).

Alkaline pre-treatments are well established (6). They act on some of the ether linkages between lignin monomers with simultaneous formation of free phenolic groups (5), and on the alkali-labile bonds between lignin and cell wall carbohydrates (7).

Such pre-treatments do not sensibly alter the content of lignin and other cell wall components (8), but produce a rearrangement of phenolic compounds (9). As with lignin, free phenols inhibit microbial growth with detrimental effects on nutrients digestion (11).

Crude lignin content is therefore inadequate to evaluate the effects of the pre-treatments and to predict straw digestibility (2), which is better correlated with phenolic fractions composition (2,9), generally subdivided into free phenols, alkali labile and alkali resistant lignin (10). Chesson and Murison have extensively discussed the problems related to straw lignin (11). Since both free phenols and lignin are strongly interrelated and play an important role in straw digestibility, the research on techniques to up-grade straw as an animal feeding needs accurate methods for the analysis of these compounds.

Phenolic monomers have been quantitatively evaluated by HPLC, usually with UV detection (12). The electrochemical detection (ElCD) can be a useful alternative to the UV detection considering the better selectivity of such detection system (13).

The development of an HPLC/ElCD method for the detection of plant phenolics and the results of a preliminary voltammetric study are reported elsewhere (14).

The goal of this work was the evaluation of HPLC/ElCD as a rapid and accurate method for the routine analysis of phenolic fractions from wheat straw (treated with NaOH and untreated), avoiding time consuming and unreliable solvent extraction used in the classical analysis of lignin hydrolyzate.

The electrochemical detector was compared with the more commonly used UV detector and several chromatograms relevant the phenolics found in neutral detergent extracts, alkali and nitrobenzene hydrolyzates are shown.

2. MATERIALS AND METHODS

2.1. Samples. Wheat straw, treated with NaOH (3% of dry matter) (T) and untreated (control (C)), were ground to pass through a 0,2 mm screen.

2.2. Reagents. Phenolic standards were purchased from Sigma (St. Louis, MO, USA). Perchloric acid, hydrochloric acid, nitrobenzene , sodium hydroxide and methanol (HPLC grade) were obtained from Carlo Erba (Milan, Italy). Doubly distilled, deionized water was used for preparing the chromatographic eluent mixture. Reagents to prepare pH 7 buffer according to Van Soest et al. (8) were purchased from Carlo Erba (Milan, Italy).

2.3. Apparatus.

The liquid chromatograph system (Waters Ass., Milford, MA_3 U.S.A.) M 45 consisted of a Rheodyne 7010 injector (20 mm loop) and a 440 UV detector for the ultraviolet detection. A Metrohm, Herisan, Switzerland, equipped with a three electrode detection cell (mod. EA 1096/2) was used for the electrochemical detection and was completed with a VA 641 potentiostat; the glassy carbon working electrod was polished daily using alumina powder (0,3 μm). UV and ElCD detectors were connected in series. A reversed-phase column (120 x 4,6 mm) Viosfer C6, 5 μm (Violet, Rome, Italy) was employed for all separations. The eluting solvent was normally methanol / 0,1% perchloric acid in water 15/85, v/v.

The flow rate was 1.00 cm^3/min, and all experiments were carried out at ambient temperature.

Thick glass tubes with screw Schott caps were used for all extractions under magnetic stirring. 0.45μm cartridge filters (Millipore USA) were used to clarify solutions prior to HPLC analyses.

2.4. Phenolic analysis

2.4.1. Free phenols. Straw (100 mg) was extracted with pH 7 buffer (5 cm^3) for 1 hour at 120° C. After centrifugation at 5000 rpm, the supernatant was decanted, the residue was washed with water and recentrifuged three times. The combined pH 7 buffer extract and washing waters were acidified with 20 mm of 37% HCl, diluted to 25 cm and injected into HPLC.

2.4.2. Alkali labile lignin. 0.1 M NaOH (5 cm^3) were added to the residue from the previous extraction (2.4.1.) and the mixture was heated at 110°C for 10 min. After centrifugation at 5000 rpm, the supernatant was decanted and the residue was washed with water and recentrifuged three times. The combined alkali extract and washing waters were acidified with 20 mm of 37% HCl, diluted to 25 cm^3 and injected into HPLC.

2.4.3. Alkali resistant lignin. 2M NaOH (5cm^3) and nitrobenzene (100 mm^3) were added to the residue from the previous extraction (2.4.2.) and the mixture was heated at 160 °C for 2 h. After cooling, the mixture was diluted to 25 cm^3 with water and filtered.

Direct analysis. 2 cm^3 of the filtrate were acidified with 2 cm^3 of 1 M HCl, diluted to 50 cm^3 and injected into HPLC.

Classical analysis. 2 cm^3 of the filtrate were extracted in a tube with CH$_2$Cl$_2$ (3x2 cm^3) discarding the organic phase. The aqueous residue was acidified with 1 cm^3 of 1M HCl and re-extracted with CH$_2$Cl$_2$ (4x2 cm^3). The combined organic phases were dried over anhydrous Na$_2$SO$_4$ and CH$_2$Cl$_2$ evaporated in rotary evaporator under vacuum. The residue was dissolved in 5 cm^3 of MeOH, diluted to 25 cm^3 with water and injected into HPLC.

3. RESULTS AND DISCUSSION

Figure 1 shows the HPLC profile of a standard phenolic mixture with ElCD detection.

Table 1 collects the HPLC capacity factors of several standards. Nitrobenzene K' is close to the p-coumaric acid and siryngaldehyde values. This is a source of error when alkali resistant lignin is analyzed by HPLC with UV detector after nitrobenzene oxidative hydrolysis (Scheme 1). This problem may be overcome by using ElCD, because nitrobenzene is inactive with this detector.

Figure 2 reports chromatograms of the oxidation reaction products obtained without (a and b) and with (c and d) dichloromethane extraction. As nitrobenzene has no response to ElCD, the peak in figure 2a at the same K' is due to p-coumaric acid. However, a new peak (K'= 2.08), identified as aniline produced by the nitrobenzene reduction, appears in the chromatogram. This peak can be shifted in situations of chromatographic interferences with other phenolic compounds (not the case of the reported chromatogram) by changing HClO$_4$ concentration in the eluent (0.1% HClO$_4$, K'= 2.08; 0.01% HClO$_4$, K'= 7.80; 0.001% HClO$_4$, K'= 19.60). With 0.001% HClO$_4$ the K' value of the aniline peak is shifted beyond the other phenolics. We are currently studying the use of the aniline peak as a rapid oxidatability index of lignin or other natural structures.

The comparison between figures 2a and 2c shows a lower concentration of p-coumaric acid after the classical procedure. This may be attributable to losses of extraction. Also the other compounds are affected by the extraction, although to a lesser extent.

UV detection of the oxidation products obtained without extraction is not feasible because of the large interference from the nitrobenzene peak; the p-coumaric acid peak in d is relatively higher than in c as a consequence of coelution of residual nitrobenzene.

Typical chromatograms of straw phenolic extracts are shown in Figure 3.

Free phenol extracts from untreated and treated straw resulted in the profiles reported in figure 3a and 3b respectively. It is evident that NaOH treatment of straw leads to an overall increase of free phenols, particularly of vanillin, p-coumaric acid and ferulic acid. This observation is consistent with the expected release of phenolic monomers by alkali hydrolysis of esterified phenols. As a consequence of such hydrolysis due to the straw pre-treatment, the alkali labile lignin fraction from treated straw (fig. 3d) was lower than the corresponding fraction from the untreated one (fig. 3c) for all compounds detectable, remarkably for p-coumaric acid and ferulic acid.

Figures 3e and 3f show the HPLC profiles of phenolic monomers produced by nitrobenzene oxidative hydrolysis of alkali resistant lignin. Alkali pre-treatment appears to have no effect on this fraction, which shows negligible differences between treated and untreated straw. This could be easily expected since alkali resistant lignin is a polymeric structure with a high chemical stability.

The alkali resistant lignin fraction is characterized by the presence of syringaldehyde, which was absent in the other two fraction and by a larger amount of vanillin. These two compounds can be explained as nitrobenzene oxidative products of syringyl and guaiacyl units, known to be typical lignin precursors(3).

4. CONCLUSION

Electrochemical Detection is a valid tool in HPLC analysis of phenols. The high selectivity of such detector is of great advantage in eliminating interferences from non-phenolic compounds.

This feature has been exploited in order to improve the analytical procedure for straw phenolics, allowing the direct injection of extracts without nitrobenzene interference and avoiding time consuming extraction and possible losses during such steps.

The differences in phenolic composition originating from alkali pre-treatment of straw are well evidenced by HPLC with Electrochemical Detector.

REFERENCES
(1) FAULKNER, D.B., LLAMAS, G.L., WARD, J.K. and KLOPFENSTEIN, T.J. (1984/85). Improving the intake and nutritive value of wheat straw for beef cows. Anim. Feed Sci. Technol. 12, 125-132.
(2) REEVES, J.B.III (1985). Lignin composition of chemically treated feeds as determined by nitrobenzene oxidation and its relationship to digestibility. J. Dairy Sci. 68, 1976-1983.
(3) THEANDER, O. and ÅMAN, P. (1984). Anatomical and chemical

characteristics. In: Straw and other fibrous by-products as feed. Sundstøl, F. and Owen, E. Eds. Elsevier, Amsterdam. p. 45-78.

(4) BARL, B., BILIADERIS, C.G. and MURRAY, E.D. (1986). Effect of chemical pretreatments on the thermal degradation of corn husk lignocellulosics. J. Agric. Food Chem. 34, 1019-1024.

(5) LINDBERG, J.E., TERNRUD, I.E. and THEANDER, O. (1984). Degradation rate and chemical composition of different types of alkali-treated straw during rumen digestion. J. Sci. Food. Agric. 35, 500-506.

(6) BOLSEN, K.K., TETLOW, R.M. and WILSON, R.F. (1983). The effect of calcium and sodium hydroxides and of sodium acrylate on the fermentation and digestibility in vitro of ensiled whole-crop wheat and barley harvested at different stages of maturity. Anim. Feed Sci. Technol. 9, 37-47.

(7) KLOPFENSTEIN, T. (1978). Chemical treatment of crop residues. J. Anim. Sci. 46, 841-848.

(8) VAN SOEST, P.J., MASCAREHNAS FERREIRA, A. and HARTLEY, R.D. (1983/84). Chemical properties of fibre in relation to nutritive quality of ammonia-treated forages. Anim. Feed Sci. Technol. 10, 155-164.

(9) VAN SOEST, P.J. and Mc BURNEY, M.I. (1985). Problems evaluating the nutritive values of treated straws. Proc. Feeding Systems of Animals in Temperate Areas. Korea Feed Information Center. Seoul, Korea pp. 310-318.

(10) JUNG, H.G., FAHEY, G.C. Jr. and GARST, J.E. (1983). Simple phenol monomers and effects of in vitro fermentation on cell wall phenolics. J. Anim. Sci. 57, 1294-1305.

(11) CHESSON, A. and MURISON, S.D. (1987) Biochemical evaluation of straw as a feedstuff for ruminants. See p. of this book.

(12) JUNG, H.G. and FAHEY, G.C.Jr. (1983). Nutritional implications of phenolic monomers and lignin: a review. J. Anim. Sci. 57, 206-219.

(13) CHIAVARI, G., VITALI, P. and GALLETTI, G.C. (1987). Electrochemical detection in the high-performance liquid chromatography of polyphenols (vegetable tannins). J. Chromatogr. 392, 426-434.

(14) CHIAVARI, G., CONCIALINI, V. and GALLETTI, G.C. (in press). Electrochemical detection in the HPLC analysis of plant phenolics. The Analyst.

169

Table 1: HPLC capacity factors (K') of standard phenolic compounds.
Chromatographic conditions as in experimental section.

compound	K'
1. gallic acid	0.75
2. p-hydroxyphenyl lactic acid	1.70
3. p-hydroxyphenyl acetic acid	2.60
4. m-hydroxyphenyl acetic acid	3.00
5. o-hydroxyphenyl acetic acid	3.50
6. p-hydroxybenzoic acid	3.50
7. p-hydroxybenzaldehyde	4.05
8. vanillic acid	4.80
9. vanillin	5.85
10. syringic acid	6.45
11. syringaldehyde	8.15
12. p-coumaric acid	9.05
13. ferulic acid	12.20
- nitrobenzene	9.15

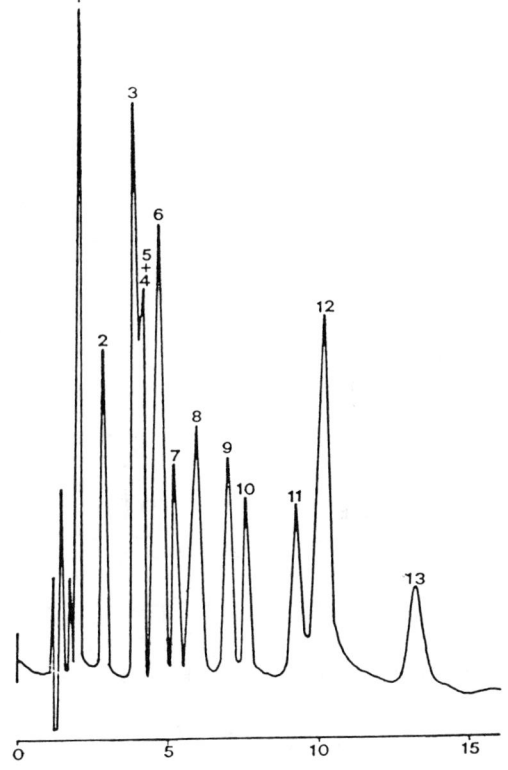

Figure 1: HPLC separation of standard phenols. For peak numbering
see Table 1.

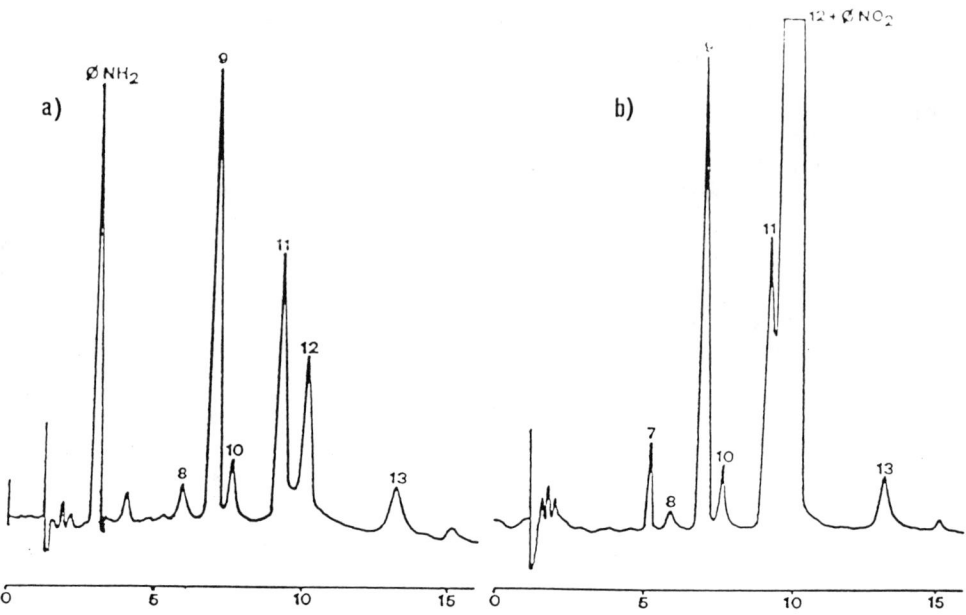

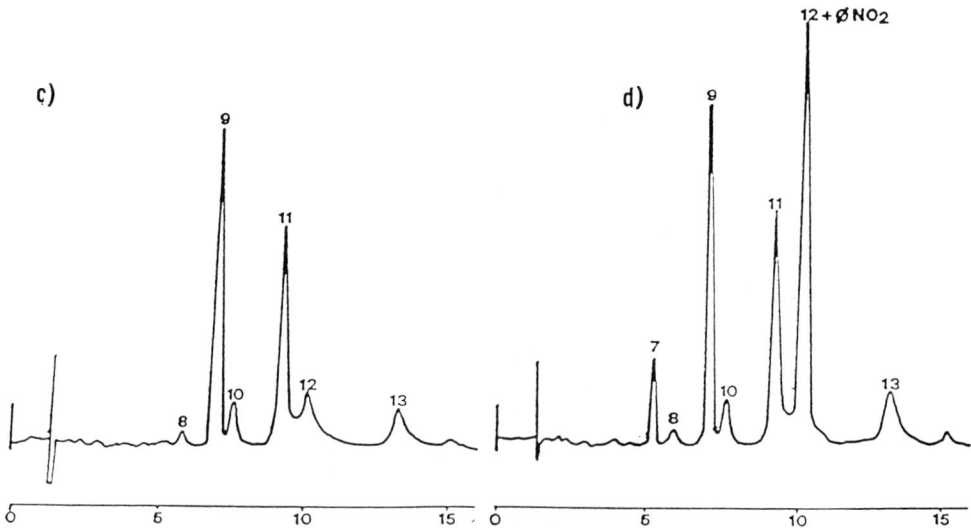

Figure 2: HPLC separation of phenols produced by nitrobenzene oxidative
hydrolysis of straw lignin
a) ELCD (+1.1 V) before CH$_2$CL$_2$ extractions
b) UV (280 nm) CH$_2$CL$_2$ extractions
c) ELCD (+ 1.1 V) after extractions
d) UV (280 nm) after extractions
For peak indentification refer to Table 2.

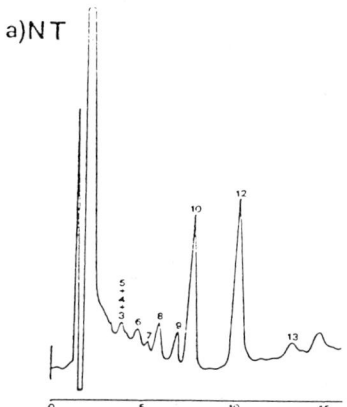

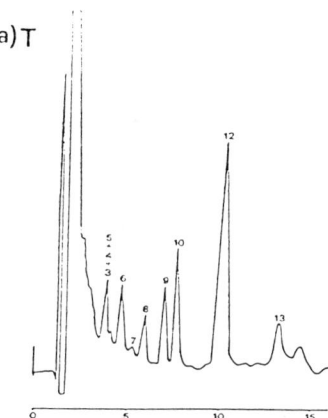

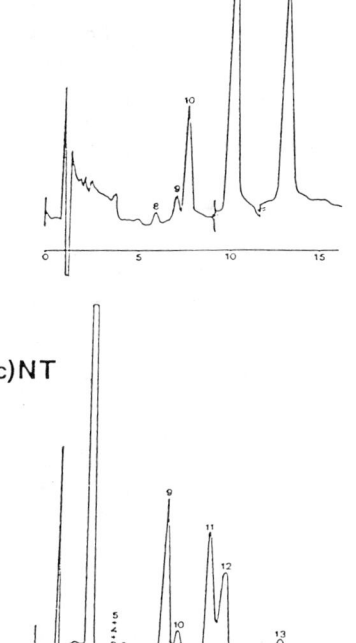

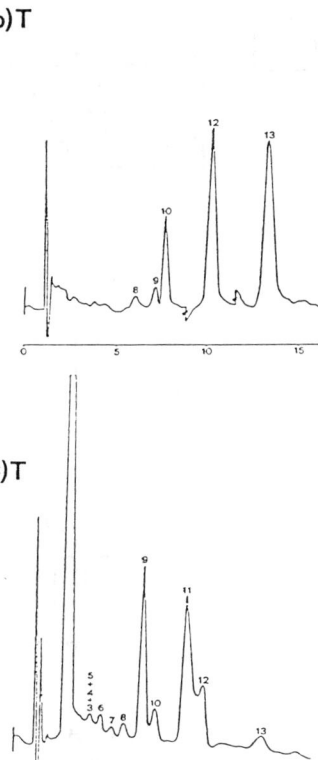

Figure 3: HPLC/ELCD profiles of straw phenolic extracts.
a) free phenols   NT) not treated straw
b) alkali labile lignin T) NaOH treated straw
c) alkali resistant lignin

SCHEME 1

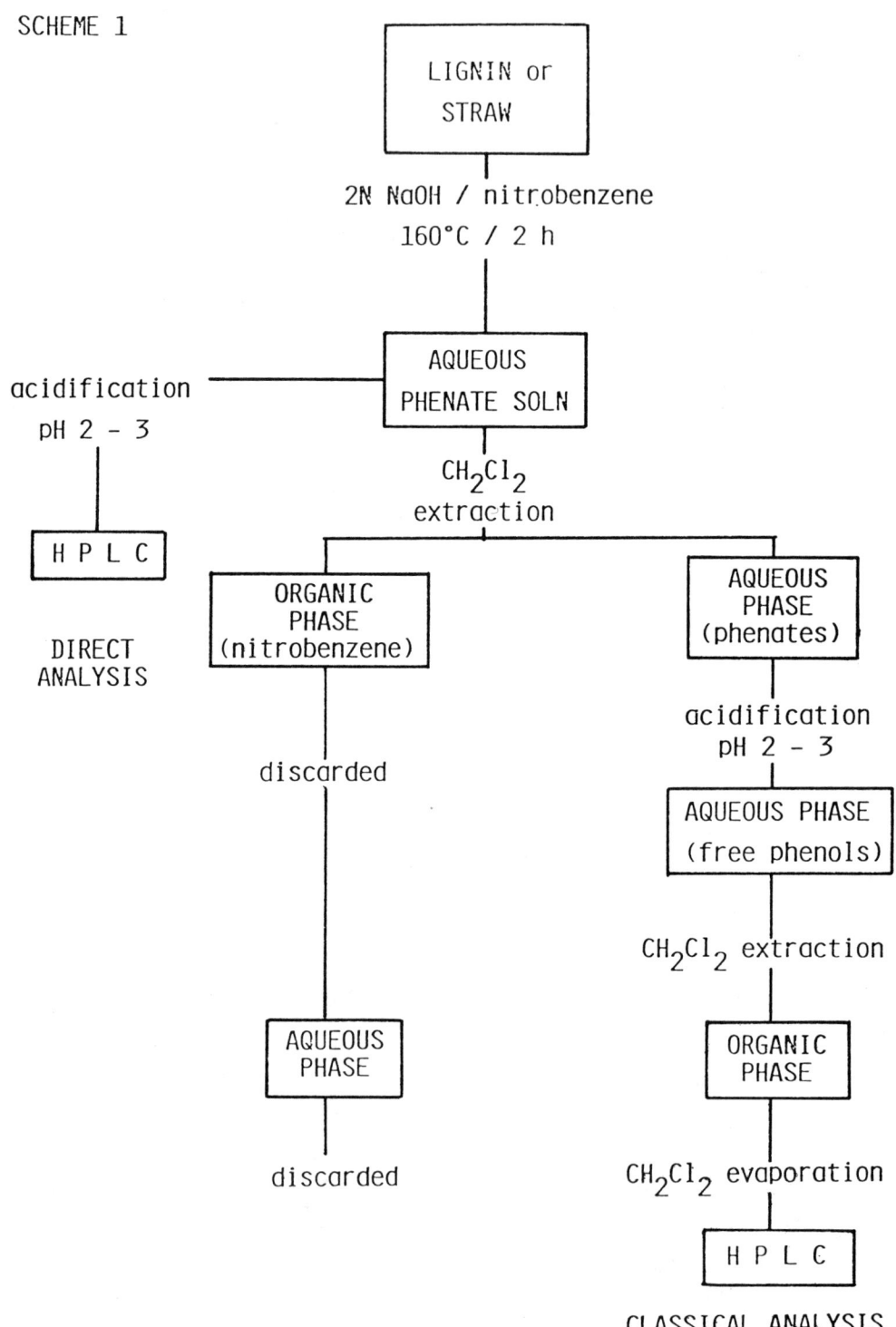

DISCUSSION

New techniques based on physical and physico-chemical properties of straw (Rapporteur: J.M. VAN DER MEER. Chairman: J. DELORT-LAVAL)

As stated in Dr. VAN DER MEER's paper, this group of techniques aims at characterizing the various non-chemical properties of plant fibres related to straw intake and digestibility. These properties classified as mechanical, morphological and physical in table 1 of VAN DER MEER's contribution involve several methods which are complementary to the various methods of chemical analysis. They provide information on the structure or "architecture" of the cell-walls (e.g. distribution of their constituents) and their subsequent properties. The physical and physico-chemical techniques, in combination with chemical analysis, finally, allow a better understanding of the phenomenae that occur in the rumen during the degradation processes of the plant material.

In this respect, E. GRENET gave a short account of the possibilities offered by light microscopy and scanning and transmission electron microscopy. Thanks to the histochemical studies of the anatomy of forages, the actions of bacteria and, moreover, of protozoa and rumen fungi on the various parts of the cell-wall tissues can now be better described.

Since these new techniques are research tools rather than routine techniques and as they involve the use of costly equipment, they will be utilized essentially in research laboratories.

From the discussion that evolved during this session one can hope that routine methods of prediction will appear after the completion of a sufficient and thorough research effort.

In this respect it was well recognized that an exchange of information and of methods was necessary and should be encouraged. The expensive equipment and the sophisticated techniques employed in this new field of prediction methods make this simultaneous development in several laboratories prohibitive.

Therefore a network incorporating various already equipped laboratories, would contribute efficiently to this sharing of information. Each laboratory would thus be complementary to another. Such a network would then facilitate the integration of data through a multiple dimension approach which is necessary with such type of information.

The field of physical properties of straw implies very complex and long term research work, but it is likely to be the one from which most advances in both the understanding of straw degradation processes and the prediction of straw feeding value can be expected.

Important advances are to be expected from N.M.R. (Nuclear Magnetic Resonance) or other physical techniques such as possibilities for tridimensional "scanning" and identifying the key lignin-polysaccharides bonds.

Biochemical and enzymatic methods (Rapporteur: A. CHESSON. Chairman: J. DELORT-LAVAL)

In order to be reliable in evaluating the feed value of a forage, a method of prediction should mimic rumen digestion processes.

As discussed earlier, this is not the case for chemical methods as they merely analyse the contents of cell-walls constituents but not the interactions formed between lignin and polysaccharides of these cell-walls. Yet the latter are a significant factor in cell-wall degradation by rumen microorganisms.

CHESSON's paper highlighted the limitations of biochemical methods in evaluating the feed value of straws and focused on the interest of the physico-chemical and enzymatic methods.

Physico-chemical methods better indicate how lignin accumulates at the cell-wall surface following the removal of polysaccharides by microorganisms from the outermost layer of the cell-wall. The methods can be utilized for the analysis of that surface layer.

Within the chemical techniques available, optical density (OD) of lignin and other compounds solubilised by treatments, and saponification values, may be considered as useful, but still limited, techniques. Their limitations essentially lie in the fact that none of them provide a means of predicting the effect of any treatment without first treating the straw. As it is known that the poorer the initial quality of the straw, the greater its response to alkali treatment, one could speculate on the possibility of adapting prediction equations for untreated material from the measurement of OD or saponification after treatment. For the time being, available evaluation techniques should be adhered to in order to discriminate between treated and untreated material, while OD is better utilized for treated material. It seems, from recent observations, that the use of multiple absorbancies might improve the precision of OMD prediction by discriminating between phenolic compounds and other material (released by treatment) absorbed on the same wavelength.

Enzymatic methods, which are more comparable to biological ones in reflecting the cell-wall degradation processes, are being increasingly used on a routine basis as a means for predicting forage and straw-feeding value. However, one should be aware of the fact that commercial enzyme preparations show considerable variation between producers and batches from the same producer. From the discussion that evolved around this problem, it was recommended that standards should be established which indicated the minimum levels such preparations should contain.

From the presentation of BESLE et al. it appears that OD is a better estimate than cellulase for treated straw and obversely, cellulase is a better estimate for untreated straw.

As far as methods other than enzymatic and biological are concerned, untreated and treated straw should be absolutely considered separately.

No method is entirely satisfactory. This is due to the nature of straw which is merely a highly lignified forage from which all other constituents except cell-walls, have practically been removed.

Biological methods (Rapporteur: J.L. TISSERAND. Chairman: J. AERTS)

This group of methods is based on the use of rumen liquor itself as the reactive medium for measuring either the rate and the extent of the degradability, or the fermentation characteristics (pH, VFA, gas production) of a given straw.

The in vitro methods are a replica of the rumen fermentation processes. Rumen liquor (inoculum) extracted from a fistulated donor animal is incubated on a straw sample (substrate) either in a batch system (in vitro digestibility technique) or in a continuous fermenting system (artificial rumen or RUSITEC). In sacco methods, where straw samples are introduced into the rumen by means of nylon bags are, by definition, the more direct techniques.

Both groups of techniques allow the measurement of rate (kinetics) and extent of the substrate degradability. In addition, in vitro techniques, more particularly RUSITEC, allow the measurement of fermentation products under conditions which vary according to the objectives sought.

The use of these techniques for measuring the extent (and rate) of straw degradation was primarily discussed. The discussion envisaged the various conditions in which a given sample of straw should be tested e.g. fistulated animal diet which should optimize cellulolysis, characteristics of the bags (size, mesh, weight of straw introduced, optimum number and place of the bags within the rumen).

As shown by ORSKOV and CHENOST these techniques allow a very accurate prediction of both OMD and even DOM intake through prediction of DM intake. In general, it is possible to modelize a degradation curve which is of the type:

Dry Matter Disappeared (DMD, in % initial DM) = $a + b \, (1-e^{-kt})$, where, $\underline{a}$ is the initial solubility, $\underline{b}$ the insoluble but potentially degradable fraction, $\underline{k}$ the degradation rate and $\underline{t}$ the time of incubation. This leads to a rather precise prediction of DDM, of DM intake and of DOM intake.

The results of CHENOST showed that for straw, similar to classical forages, the product (DDM % at 24 h) x (DDM % at 72 h) was very closely related to DOM intake, since each factor of the above product represents, respectively, intake and potential digestibility predictors.

The use of in sacco methods in evaluating feed value of straw can therefore be considered as the most reliable, and the most simple technique presently available.

In addition, such a direct biological technique allows the simultaneous prediction of feed values of both untreated and treated material. This technique may eventually replace the classical intake plus digestibility in vivo measurement trials with sheep. It can identify the feeding value a straw will have after treatment and can therefore help in deciding whether to treat or not.

Such a technique can be used to classify species and varieties of straw according to their feed value within a set of "unknown" straw samples before embarking, with more precise measurements, on interesting selected samples. It can also serve to study, within a given sample, the respective value of its various morphological constituents e.g. internodes, nodes, leaves and sheaves, in order to decide,on the fractionation of the plant material from a technological or commercial point of view.

It had been stressed in the discussion on Topic A that, in order to be satisfactory, a prediction technique should be based on correct and reproducible measurements of OMD. The in sacco method fulfills these requirements when an adequate number and types of standards are used from batch to batch.

While *in vitro* methods might be hampered by the influence of the "closed system" on the inoculum population (DEMEYER), their interest lies in the correlation between *in vitro* and *in sacco* degradation rates (DEMEYER) and in the possibility for additional measurements, e.g. rate, quantity and nature of the gas produced during incubation, which are closely related to the degradation ability (VAN DER MEER).

The amount of soluble constituents of a substrate should be taken into account when expressing, after a given length of incubation, degradation ability as a percentage of initial DM.

Throughout the workshop, attention was mainly given to techniques for evaluating cereal straw. It should be borne in mind that the application of these techniques to straws from other plants should require additional research since their cell-wall architecture and, in turn, their degradation processes, might be different.

RECOMMENDATIONS

General

Most participants considered that it would be of considerable value if a restricted number of samples of treated and untreated straw could be held at a single location, available for use as standard or reference material for other laboratories. Straw samples should be of one or two types, e.g. spring barley/winter wheat and should show a wide range of degradability. Sufficient material should be held to provide samples both in a ground and long form for several years (5years). The latter would allow individuals to fractionate straw material as required.

Straw can be used for purposes other than animal feeding. Fractionation of straw into leaf/leaf sheath of relatively high digestibility and stem material of lower values as a feedstuff is practical. Stem material may be better used as a source of cellulose fibre or incorporated into hardboard (strawboard). It would be useful to involve representatives of the pulp and paper industry in future meetings for further consideration. This collaboration has already occurred within the OECD cellulose programme. Similarly there should be an exchange of information between nutritionists and plant breeders who could select for plant varieties with different leaf: stem ratio or which produce straw of high degradation ability without sacrificing grain production.

In vitro methods

It was generally agreed that gross chemical analyses were of little value and their continued use should not be encouraged. Biological methods, based on cell-free enzymes, laboratory cultures of rumen micro-organisms or in sacco methods, were all thought to be more informative and to provide a better evaluation of both treated and untreated straw. However, it was agreed that the methods used should be more rigorously specified. In particular in sacco measurements should be made under optimal conditions for cellulolysis. Similarly, if the "cellulase assay" is to be more widely used, minimum levels of specific activities should be defined and "quality control" should be applied to enzyme batches. The production of an enzyme preparation designed specifically for feed evaluation should be encouraged.

In the long term, instrumental methods of evaluation may replace or supplement existing biological measures. Every encouragement should be given to the collaboration and exchange of information between individuals using these methods. Such methods are likely to be able to measure aspects of cell-wall architecture and the anatomy of plant tissues influencing microbial degradation, reduction of particle size, etc.... which are not presently measured by conventional chemical methods of evaluation.

In vivo methods

While there was general agreement that in vivo measurements of digestibility of feeds in animals fed at maintenance would, in the future, be replaced by other in vitro or in sacco methods, some feed evaluation laboratories would still be using this method over the next few years. When in vivo measurements of digestibility of sheep at maintenance form the basis for feed evaluation, it was recommended that in order to ensure that the maximal digestibility is expressed, the following minimum should be met:

degradable N	18 - 20	g/kg DOM
phosphorus	3 - 4	g/kg DOM
available S	1.5 - 2.0	g/kg DOM.

It was recognized that the actual or effective digestibility of straw in practice will often be less than that determined in sheep fed at maintenance due to higher feeding levels, amount and type of concentrate, frequency of feeding, physiological stage of the animals, etc., but the extent to which it deviated from that would have to be determined in each region or for each feeding system.

For determination of digestibility it was recommended that a minimum of 4 animals should be used with a minimum adaptation time of 14 days and a minimum faecal collection period of 10 days.

It was recommended that determination of digestibility in vivo should be followed or preceded by measurements of voluntary intake, in which case it should be well defined how much uneaten food is accepted. This is particularly important in small ruminants, e.g. sheep and goats, which will select the most nutritive botanical fractions.

Straw in animal feeding trials

It was recommended that when straw was used in animal feeding trials it should be accurately described, e.g. rate and extent of degradation, N, S and P content. Information on these aspects reduces the information required on a variety of straw and climatic conditions of growth. It was considered that evaluation of untreated straw should always precede that of treated straw in order to decide on treatment and to define conditions which are likely to lead to toxicity problems (e.g. sugar content of straw destined for ammonia treatment).

It was considered that the knowledge of principles of ammonia, NaOH treatment and urea/ammonia treatment was now sufficiently advanced, but in some instances, local adaptation may be further studied. New methods for upgrading straw such as those involving biological or oxydative methods also require further study.

LIST OF PARTICIPANTS

ADAMSON, A.H.
Ministry of Agriculture,
Fisheries and Food
Brughill Road
Westbury-on-Trim
UK - BRISTOL BS10 6NS

AERTS, J.
Technical College for Chemistry
Textile on Agriculture
VOSKENSLAAN 270
B - 9000 GENT

ALIBES, X.
Departemento de Agricultura
Ganaderia y Montes
Apartado 727, Montañana 176
E - 50016 ZARAGOZA

ANDERSEN, P.E.
National Institute of Animal
Science, Forsøgsanlaeg Fouloum
Post Box 39
DK - 8833 ØRUM - Sdrl

ANTONGIOVANNI, M.
Departamento di Scienze Zootecniche
Via delle Cascine, 5
I - 50127 FIRENZE

BOER, H.
The Agricultural University
of Wageningen
Animal Nutrition Department
Haagsteeg 4,
NL - 6708 PM WAGENINGEN

CHENOST, M.
Laboratoire des Aliments
INRA - CRZV de Theix
F - 63122 CEYRAT

CHESSON, A.
Rowett Research Institute
Bucksburn
UK - Aberdeen AB2 9 SB

CONSIDINE, P.J.
IIRS Biochemical Units
University College
IRL - GALWAY

COTTYN, G.G.
National Institute of
Animal Science
Scheldeweg 68
B - 9231 MELLE GONTRODE

DELORT-LAVAL, J.
Laboratoire de Technologie
des Aliments des Animaux
INRA - Chemin de la Géraudière
F - 44072 NANTES

DIAS DA SILVA, A.
Instituto Universitario de Tras
os Montes E Alto Duro (UTAD)
P - 5000 VILA REAL

DURAND, Michelle
Station de Recherches de
Nutrition, INRA
Domaine de Vilvert
F - 78350 JOUY-EN-JOSAS

GALLETTI, G.
Centro Studio Conservazione
Foraggi - C.N.R.
Via Filipo Re, 8
I - 40126 BOLOGNA

GIVENS, D.I.
ADAS, Feed Evaluation Unit
Alcester Road
Stratford-Upon-Avon
DK - WARWICKSHIRE CV37 9RQ

GOMEZ CABRERA, A.
Universidad de Cordoba
Escuela Tecnica Ingenieros
Agronomos, Avda Mendez Pidal 5/n
Apartado de Correos 3048
SP - 14080 CORDOBA

GUESSOUS, F.
Institute Agronomique
Hassan II,
BP 704
M - RABAT INSTITUT

HVELPLUND, T.
National Institute of Animal
Science - Forsøgsanlaeg Fouloum
Postbox 39
DK - 8833 ØRUM

MUÑOZ, F.
Departemento de Agricultura
Ganaderia y Montes
Apartado 727
SP - 50016 ZARAGOZA

ØRSKOV, E.R.
Rowett Research Institute
Greenburn Road, Bucksburn
UK - ABERDEEN AB2 9SB

OWEN, E.
University of Reading
Department of Agriculture
Early Gate
P.O. Box 236
UK - READING RG6 2AT

PFEFFER, E.
Institut für Tierernährung
der Universität Bonn
Endenicher Allee 15
D - 5300 BONN 1

RAMALHO RIBEIRO, J.M.C.
INIA, Estacao Zootecnica Nacional
Vale de Santarem
P - 2000 SANTAREM

REINIGER, P.
CEE - DG XII
Secrétariat COST 84 bis
Square de Meeus
B - 1049 BRUXELLES

SAUVANT, D.
Chaire de Zootechnie
INA-PG
16, rue Claude Bernard
F - 75231 PARIS Cedex 05

STEG, A.
Institut For Livestock Feeding
and Nutrition Research (IVVO)
Po Box 160
NL - 8200 AD LELYSTAD

SUNDSTØL, F.
Department of Animal Nutrition
Agricultural University of Norway
NLH - 14320 Ås

TISSERAND, J.L.
Chaire de Zootechnie - ENSSAA
26, bd Docteur Petitjean
F - 21000 DIJON

VAN DER MEER, J.M.
Institute for Livestock Feeding
and Nutrition Research (IVVO)
P.O. Box 160
NL - 8200 AD LELYSTAD

ZADRAZIL, F.
Institut für Bodenbiologie
FAL
Bundesallee, 50
D - 3300 BRAUNSCHWEIG